Clinton Cash

ALSO BY PETER SCHWEIZER

Extortion: How Politicians Extract Your Money, Buy Votes, and Line Their Own Pockets

Throw Them All Out: How Politicians and Their Friends Get Rich Off Insider Stock Tips, Land Deals, and Cronyism That Would Send the Rest of Us to Prison

Architects of Ruin: How Big Government Liberals Wrecked the Global Economy—and How They Will Do It Again If No One Stops Them

Landmark Speeches of the Conservative Movement (with Wynton Hall)

The Reagan Presidency: Assessing the Man and His Legacy (with Paul Kengor)

Do as I Say (Not as I Do): Profiles in Liberal Hypocrisy

The Bushes: Portrait of a Dynasty (with Rochelle Schweizer)

Reagan's War: The Epic Story of His Forty-Year Struggle and Final Triumph over Communism

Disney: The Mouse Betrayed (with Rochelle Schweizer)

Victory: The Reagan Administration's Secret Strategy That Hastened the Collapse of the Soviet Union

Clinton Cash

The Untold Story of How and Why
Foreign Governments and Businesses
Helped Make Bill and Hillary Rich

Peter Schweizer

HARPER LUXE

An Imprint of HarperCollins*Publishers*

HarperCollins books may be purchased for educational, business, or sales promotional use. For information, please e-mail the Special Markets Department at SPsales@harpercollins.com.

FIRST HARPERLUXE EDITION

HarperLuxe™ is a trademark of HarperCollins Publishers

Library of Congress Cataloging-in-Publication Data is available upon request.

ISBN: 978-0-06-240779-5

15 ID/RRD 10 9 8 7 6 5 4 3 2 1

FOR RHONDA

Contents

Clinton Cash

Chapter 1
The Lincoln Bedroom Goes Global

A sk Team Clinton about the flow of tens of millions of dollars to the Clinton Foundation (the formal name is the Bill, Hillary, and Chelsea Clinton Foundation, originally called the William J. Clinton Foundation) from foreign governments, corporations, and financiers and you typically get an interesting explanation: it's a sign of love. "As president, he was beloved around the world, so it should come as no surprise that there has been an outpouring of financial support from around the world to sustain his post-presidential work."[1]

Ask Bill about the tens of millions of dollars he has made in speaking fees around the world, paid for by the same cast of characters, and you will get an equally charitable explanation: it's evidence of his desire to help people. By giving these highly paid speeches, Clinton says, "I try to help people think about what's going on and organize their lives accordingly."[2]

Millions of dollars as a sign of pure affection; millions more for helping people think about their lives. By this logic, politicians who raise millions of dollars a year must be the most beloved people in America—and the most charitable.

The reality is that most of what happens in American politics is transactional. People look for ways to influence those in power by throwing money in their direction. Politicians are all too happy to vacuum up contributions from supporters and people who want access or something in return. After politicians leave office, they often trade on their relationships and previous positions to enrich themselves and their families.

The law dictates how much politicians can collect in campaign contributions, limits their ability to make money on the side, and requires the disclosure of those contributors. Hopefully, politicians are also limited to some extent by their conscience. A sense of decency and good judgment ought to prevent politicians on both sides of the aisle from engaging in certain transactions—even if they think they can get away with it.

But while there is ample debate about which transactions should be limited and how, there is near-universal agreement that the game, however muddy, should be exclusively played by Americans. For this reason, it has long been illegal for foreigners to contribute to US political campaigns. In 2012 two foreign nationals challenged the constitutionality of that law. The US Supreme Court decided 9–0 declaring the law not only constitutional, but eminently reasonable.[3]

The Clintons, however, often take money from foreign entities. And that money, donated to the Clinton Foundation or paid in speaking fees, comes in amounts much larger than any campaign contribution. Indeed, the scope and extent of these payments are without precedent in American politics. As a result, the Clintons have become exceedingly wealthy.

The big question is whether taking such money constitutes a transaction. The Clintons would undoubtedly argue that it does not. The evidence presented in this book suggests otherwise.

Any serious journalist or investigator will tell you that proving corruption by a political figure is extremely difficult. Short of someone involved coming forward to give sworn testimony, we don't know what might or might not have been said in private conversations, the exact nature of a transaction, or why people in power make the decisions they do. This is why the Federal Bureau of Investigation (FBI) sets up sting operations: to catch suspected malefactors in the act.

That is also why investigators look primarily at patterns of behavior. Imagine, for example, that you are exploring whether a politician is doing favors for a major campaign contributor in a manner that might be illegal. If investigators were to find that the *timing* of major campaign contributions occurred immediately before the politician made a highly favorable decision for the donor, and that this pattern could be well established, such timing would certainly warrant further investigation.

This was precisely the approach I took in my 2011 book, *Throw Them All Out,* concerning stock trades and members of Congress. Were members of Congress engaged in insider trading in the stock market? I looked at both their stock trades and their official activities, such as voting on certain bills. I discovered that politicians from both parties had curious patterns in their stock picks, often buying and selling at opportune times. During the 2008 financial crisis, for example, some politicians sold stocks or shorted the market (bet that it would go lower) shortly after receiving secret economic briefings from senior government officials.

Was this proof that insider trading had taken place? No. As I pointed out in the book, we could not know precisely *why* the politicians were making these particular trades at those particular times. But the patterns were highly suspicious. Shortly after the release of the book and a *60 Minutes* segment on my findings, politicians from both parties cooperated in passing the STOCK Act, which was designed to outlaw congressional insider trading. President Barack Obama condemned the practice during his 2012 State of the Union Address and later signed the STOCK Act into law. (The law was subsequently gutted by Congress and the White House, but that's another story.) I can proudly say that my findings were attacked by both Republicans and Democrats.

In a *legal sense* I could not *prove* that insider trading had taken place. I didn't know precisely the motivations at work when stocks were being traded. But the pattern and timing of those trades raised questions so troubling that even members of Congress could not ignore it.

In 2013 I published a follow-up called *Extortion*, which argued that members of Congress from both parties were in the habit of "extorting" campaign contributions and other favors from businesses and outside groups. Money flowing into politics was not just about outside interests trying to "bribe" politicians; politicians were knowingly putting outside interests in a position where they had to buy "protection" from them. I also released to the public for the first time the "party dues" lists whereby politicians were required to pay a certain amount of money to their party in order to obtain seats on certain congressional committees. The more important the committee, the more you were expected to pay. I further explained how politicians from both parties were using leadership PACs to feather their own nests, tapping those funds to pay for things that enhanced their own lifestyles.

Was I able to prove intent or know why politicians were doing what they were doing? Of course not. But as before, the timing of these transactions was highly suspicious. Once again, *60 Minutes* ran a segment about my findings which led to legislation being introduced that would restrict how leadership PAC funds were used. And once again, my findings were attacked by both Republicans and Democrats.

Given my previous focus on bipartisan self-dealing and corruption, why am I now focused on one couple? Do I simply have it in for Bill and Hillary? Am I somehow trying to derail her prospects of being elected president in 2016?

The answer is pretty straightforward: the global dealings of this political couple deserve bipartisan citizen attention as much as congressional insider trading or campaign contribution extortion did. No one has even come close in recent years to enriching themselves on the scale of the Clintons while they or a spouse continued to serve in public office. The ability of any other ex-politician, whether a former president, senator, or congressman, Republican or Democrat, to accumulate such large amounts of money in such a short period of time is unmatched. It's not even close.

To put an even finer point on it: I am focusing specifically on financial transactions involving *foreign* businesses, investors, and governments. Foreign interests can't donate to political campaigns. But they can pay money for speeches. And they can donate to the Clinton Foundation. Are they doing so to buy influence? Does the timing of the payments coincide with key decisions made by US government officials? Are they successful in obtaining favorable outcomes?

Using publicly available sources, including financial records, tax records, government documents, and more, my research team and I have uncovered a repeated pattern of financial transactions coinciding with official actions favorable to Clinton contributors that is troubling enough to warrant (in my opinion) further investigation by law enforcement officers. Just as I couldn't prove that members of Congress were guilty of trading on inside information, I cannot say exactly why these financial transactions are taking place. But as we will see, their unprecedented scale, the often shady nature of the characters involved, their timing, and their frequently favorable outcomes are all, or ought to be, extremely troubling.

As Hillary famously noted, the Clintons were "dead broke" when they left the White House in 2001. This statement was immediately challenged as a gross exaggeration.[4,5] Still, their means were modest compared to those of other politicians, such as George W. Bush, whose net worth is $20 million, or John Kerry, whose net worth is well over $100 million.

Because the Clintons' financial public disclosures are given in ranges, it's impossible to know their precise net worth. The Clintons' confirmed income between 2001 and 2012 was at least $136.5 million, according to the *Washington Post*. *USA Today* estimates Bill Clinton's personal net worth to be $55 million. That's a very big jump from "dead broke" in a very short time. It is important to consider the fact that payments made to Bill Clinton for speeches or consulting fees benefit wife Hillary and their married net worth.

Some of this income comes from book deals. The Clintons have been paid handsomely to write their public memoirs. But the greater part of it by far comes from Bill's speechmaking. According to financial disclosures, since leaving the White House, Bill has been paid an annual average of over $8 million for giving speeches around the world. The fees he collects are enormous and unprecedented, sometimes as much as $500,000 or even $750,000 per speech. It's hard to imagine that Clinton's pearls of wisdom are worth that much to even the most worshipful audience.

But as this book will try to show, Bill's speechmaking does not happen in a vacuum. It is part of a larger pattern of activity that has never before been exposed to public scrutiny.

During Hillary's years of public service, the Clintons have conducted or facilitated hundreds of large transactions (either as private citizens or government officials) with foreign governments, corporations, and private financiers. Some of these transactions have put millions in their own pockets thanks to Bill's lucrative lecture career. Others were part of US foreign policy. Others put millions into their legacy project, the Clinton Foundation. As we will see, the sums involved are nothing short of staggering.

What's more, many of these exchanges have taken place at a time when these outside interests had matters of importance sitting on Hillary's desk, whether in the Senate office building or on the third floor of the State Department. The issues seemingly connected to these large transfers are arresting in their sweep and seriousness: the Russian government's acquisition of

American uranium assets; access to vital US nuclear technology; matters related to Middle East policy; the approval of controversial energy projects; the overseas allocation of billions in taxpayer funds; and US human rights policy, to name a few.

Of even greater concern is that the foreign players giving money to the Clintons include foreign governments (and controversial politicians) in countries like Russia, India, and the United Arab Emirates, where there are major foreign policy issues at stake. In other cases, foreign businessmen appear to have benefited shortly before or after private meetings with foreign officials involving one or both Clintons. There is nothing clearly illegal about these payments. But their source, size, and timing raise serious questions deserving of deeper investigation. While some particular facts or instances have been reported on sporadically elsewhere, the convoluted methods, shady characters, and cumulative pattern of behavior will be described in this book for the first time.

Also described for the first time is the role of the Clinton Foundation at the center of an elaborate system for generating large donations and fees.

In June 1999, as his second term was winding down, Bill sat down with his chief fundraiser and forty business leaders at La Grenouille in midtown Manhattan to outline his future vision for a nonprofit organization.[6] The Clinton Foundation would become the centerpiece of his post-presidential work. And both the Clintons were engaged. Hillary played "an important role in shaping both the foundation's organization and the scope of its work," in the words of the *New York Times*. As the foundation's first chief of staff, Karen Tramontano, put it, "She and I would speak frequently. She had a lot of ideas. All the papers that went to him went to her." She even attended foundation planning sessions while she served in the US Senate.[7]

The foundation's mission appeared as much as anything to protect President Clinton's legacy as well as to bolster his philanthropic work around the world. Its method of operation would be to raise money from donations and regrant the funds or use them to finance its own philanthropic programs, including initiatives involving health care, the environment, and development in the third world.

Yet even before Clinton left office, the foundation found itself mired in controversy. The timing of certain contributions raised questions as to whether they were tied to official favors. On October 6, 1999, Anheuser-Busch Companies gave the first of five payments totaling $1 million for the William J. Clinton Presidential Library and Museum (or Clinton Library for short), which was funded in part by donations given through the Clinton Foundation. As the *New York Times* reported, less than a month earlier "the Clinton administration's Federal Trade Commission dropped a bid to regulate beer, wine, and liquor advertising" allegedly aimed at underage drinkers.[8]

In May 1999 a bankruptcy attorney from Chicago named William A. Brandt Jr. also pledged $1 million. At the time the Clinton Justice Department was investigating Brandt's testimony to Congress to determine whether he had lied under oath concerning a Clinton fundraiser and the lobbying of federal officials. Three months later, in August, the Department of Justice dropped the investigation and determined that "prosecution is not warranted."[9]

In 1999 Dr. Richard Machado Gonzalez and his lawyer, Miguel Lausell, were lobbying President Clinton to boost Puerto Rican hospital Medicare reimbursements. This would benefit, among others, Machado, who owned one of the eligible hospitals. Eight months prior to Clinton proposing increased Medicare payments, Lausell gave the Clinton Library a $1 million gift. Machado gave the foundation $100,000 six months after that.

The controversies reached a fever pitch during Clinton's final days in office, when he pardoned billionaire fugitive Marc Rich, an oil trader and financier who had been indicted on numerous charges by US prosecutors and had fled the country. Rich's business ties included a "who's who" of unsavory despots, including Fidel Castro, Muammar Qaddafi, and the Ayatollah Khomeini. (Rich had traded oil with the ayatollah in violation of US law while Iran held American hostages.) He owed $48 million in back taxes that he unlawfully tried to avoid and faced the possibility of 325 years in prison. As a result, he was on the FBI's Most Wanted List. On his last day in office, President Clinton infamously pardoned Rich, sending shockwaves through Washington. The pardon came after his ex-wife, Denise Rich, donated $100,000 to Hillary's 2000 Senate campaign, $450,000 to the Clinton Library, and $1 million to the Democratic Party.

Condemnation of the whole affair was immediate and nearly universal. Maureen Dowd labeled the Clintons as "grifters" and the *New York Times* bemoaned President Clinton's "outrageous abuse of the pardoning power."[10] Former president Jimmy Carter called it "disgraceful."[11] Even longtime Clinton supporters, like James Carville and Terry McAuliffe, were critical.[12] The *Washington Post* wondered if the "defining characteristic" of Bill and Hillary Clinton was that "they have no capacity for embarrassment."

This last comment expresses a view of the Clintons frequently voiced by journalists and establishment figures over the years. Indeed, speculating on their motives has become something of a Washington parlor game. In this view, either the Clintons are utterly shameless, cynically assuming they will survive whatever scandal comes their way, or they are so convinced of their own virtue and benevolence that they are able to excuse whatever they have to do in the pursuit of their noble ends, no matter how low or unethical. We may never know the answer to this fascinating riddle.

Either way, the Clintons were just getting started. Once liberated from the White House, Bill hit the lecture circuit, collecting $105.5 million from 2001 through 2012 and raising hundreds of millions of dollars for the Clinton Foundation. Significantly, his biggest payments came not from sources in the United States but from foreign investors, businesses, and governments eager to please the former president—and probably hungry for access to the corridors of American power. Meanwhile, Hillary was quickly rising in the ranks of the US Senate, gaining influence and power, especially on matters concerning national security and foreign policy. When she ran for the Democratic presidential nomination in 2008, her power prospects rocketed. While Barack Obama's unexpected victory in the Democratic primaries apparently derailed this inexorable ascent, she still ended up in an even more powerful position than before.

When President-elect Obama first floated Hillary Clinton's name for secretary of state in late 2008, serious questions arose about the sources of funds donated to various Clinton interests. Many were troubled by the fact that so much of the Clintons' newfound wealth was tied to foreign contributors. During her tenure as a senator, two-thirds of Bill's enormous speaking fees had come from foreign sources. (As we will see, after she became secretary of state, Bill's speaking fees and income from foreign speechmaking ballooned.) There was also the fact that tens of millions of dollars had flowed to the Clinton Foundation from the foreign governments of Saudi Arabia, Kuwait, and the United Arab Emirates, as well as from dozens of foreign financiers.

Would Hillary feel indebted to these foreign donors? Would these relationships influence her decisions on matters affecting US interests?

Some foreign newspapers raised concerns about her "impartiality" because of the money funneled to her foundation from certain countries.[13] Some foreign observers viewed these donations not as acts of disinterested charity but as efforts to buy goodwill and influence from the incoming secretary of state. Donations from Indian billionaires and industrialists, wrote the *Indian Express*, were about "jockeying for access and influence. What else explains why [donors are] so keen to donate to the Clinton Foundation, when discharging its own commitments in India has been, at best, very reluctant?"[14] The late Christopher Hitchens, writing in 2009, wondered the same: why didn't these third world oligarchs "just donate the money directly [to charities in their own country] rather than distributing it through the offices of an outfit run by a seasoned ex-presidential influence-peddler"?[15]

The Clintons dismissed such concerns. During Hillary's confirmation hearings before the Senate Foreign Relations Committee, members from both parties openly worried about global influence peddling. Then senator Richard Lugar said it was a serious problem. Lugar is no bomb thrower but as *Time* magazine put it, "a paragon of bipartisan collegiality."[16] He also happened to be a friend of the Clintons.

Lugar's words were direct:

The core of the problem is that foreign governments and entities may perceive the Clinton Foundation as a means to gain favor with the Secretary of State. Although neither Senator Clinton, nor President Clinton has a personal financial stake in the Foundation, obviously its work benefits their legacy and their public service priorities.[17]

Lugar went on:

But the Clinton Foundation exists as a temptation for any foreign entity or government that believes it could curry favor through a donation. It also sets up potential perception problems with any action taken by the Secretary of State in relation to foreign givers or their countries.[18]

Hillary's job was all-encompassing and touched on many vital issues with life-and-death outcomes. As Lugar warned,

The nature of the Secretary of State post makes recusal from specific policy decisions almost impossible, since even localized U.S. foreign policy activities can ripple across countries and continents. Every new foreign donation that is accepted by the Foundation comes with the risk it will be connected in the global media to a proximate State Department policy or decision.[19]

Lugar's colleagues across the aisle shared his concerns. Senator John Kerry, chairman of the Senate Foreign Relations Committee, echoed the general view. "I think it's fair to say that Senator Lugar is not speaking from a partisan's perspective, but I think he is really expressing a view of the Committee as a whole."

Politicians weren't the only ones nervous about the Clintons' flow of foreign funds. Mainstream media outlets like *Time* warned of "the danger that [foreign funds] might taint Hillary Clinton's role as Secretary of State."[20]

Hillary herself rejected the notion that a foreign government giving millions of dollars to her husband while she served as maestra of American foreign policy might present a problem. "Ultimately, there is no conflict between the foreign policy of the United States and the efforts of the Clinton Foundation seeking to reduce human suffering and increase opportunity for people in need," she told the senators.[21]

But the Clintons' attempts to downplay or dismiss the issue failed to quell concerns.

Incoming president Obama and his transition team were nervous about the influence of foreign funds as well. Before announcing Hillary as his choice for secretary of state, Obama directed his aides to conduct detailed and extensive negotiations with the Clinton camp over the issue. Doug Band, a Clinton confidant and top aide at the foundation, negotiated at length with Cheryl Mills, a former Clinton White House attorney who represented the Obama team. (Mills simultaneously served on the Clinton Foundation board, and would shortly be appointed Hillary's chief of staff at the State Department. Like other key Clinton retainers, she will appear several times in these pages.)

The two sides finally hammered out a memorandum of understanding (MOU). Bruce Lindsey, a longtime Clinton friend who ran the foundation, inked the deal between the Clinton Foundation and the incoming administration so Hillary's nomination could go forward. Valerie Jarrett, Obama's hard-nosed confidante, signed for the incoming president.

The MOU required the Clinton Foundation to submit to several conditions designed to address widespread concerns about possible foreign influence coming through donations and speaking fees. For one thing, the Clintons agreed to submit all future paid speeches to the State Department ethics office for review. They also committed to publicly disclose on an annual basis the names of any major donors to the Clinton Foundation and its initiatives. Finally, the Clintons said they would seek preapproval from the Obama administration on direct contributions to the Clinton Foundation from foreign governments or government-owned businesses.

Both Bill and Hillary were unequivocal in stating that they would be transparent about the flow of foreign money. In her written answers to the Senate Foreign Relations Committee, Hillary promised that "the Foundation will publish annually the names of all contributors for that year."[22] Bill went on CNN and said, "If she is going to be secretary of state, and I operate globally and I have people who contribute to these efforts globally, I think that it's important to make it totally transparent." Obama administration National Security Council spokesman Tommy Vietor agreed: "Going forward, all donors will be disclosed on an annual basis, and new donations from foreign governments will be scrutinized by government ethics officers."[23]

Some Clinton loyalists found these requirements heavy handed; they believed Bill and Hillary were "forced to go above and beyond the bar that would have been set for anyone else."[24] But who else in American politics would be so audacious as to have one spouse accept money from foreign governments and businesses while the other charted American foreign policy? Or would permit one spouse to conduct sensitive negotiations with foreign entities while in some instances the other collected large speaking fees from some of those same entities?

For that very reason, the agreement was widely criticized for not going far enough. Senator Lugar was direct: "The only certain way to eliminate this risk going forward is for the Clinton Foundation to foreswear new foreign contributions when Senator Clinton becomes Secretary of State." The *Washington Post*'s editorial page agreed, pointing out that "even if Ms. Clinton is not influenced by gifts to her husband's charity, the appearance of conflict is unavoidable."[25] The *Post* warned, "The new administration is buying itself a heap of potential trouble with this agreement."[26]

Still, the agreement did the trick. The commitment to disclose and seek preapproval for government-tied funds left the Senate, the press, and the public with the widespread impression that these issues had been fully addressed. Hillary was confirmed as secretary of state by a 94–2 margin.

But the claimed commitment to transparency was fleeting. The Clintons violated it almost immediately. As we will see, the Clinton Foundation failed to disclose gifts amounting to millions of dollars from foreign entities and businessmen who needed Hillary's help as secretary of state to approve a transaction with serious national security implications. The Clinton Foundation also collected money from foreign government-owned businesses without getting prior Obama administration approval. And the pattern of taking money from businesses or individuals that owned entities that had matters before Hillary would continue unabated.

Some might say it is unfair to connect Hillary's public career as a US senator and secretary of state with her husband's private commercial activities. After all, they both led active public lives and spent significant amounts of time apart. She seems to prefer their home in Northwest Washington, DC, while Bill spends much of his time in Chappaqua, New York.

But by their own account, the two often work in tandem and are in regular communication. Hillary says, "[W]e have an endless conversation. We never get bored. We get deeply involved in all the work that we do, and we talk about it constantly."[27] Journalists who have traveled with the Clintons confirm this. When Andrew Jack of the *Financial Times* traveled with Bill in Africa for seven days, he noted "his frequent calls with Hillary during the trip."[28]

Spouses have long been seen as avenues for cronyism, corruption, and influence. That is why federal government ethics laws require politicians to disclose not just their own financial assets, holdings, and income, but those of their spouses as well. Enriching a politician's spouse or family is one of the most common methods of political corruption. As secretary of state, Hillary pushed for international anticorruption standards that addressed this very concern.

Others might argue that this is simply a "Bill problem." They would like to divide the Clintons into "good Clinton" and "bad Clinton." Hillary is the "good" one, the devoted and tough-minded public servant. Bill is the "bad" one, ethically challenged, pursuing money and personal desires. One magazine headline explained it this way: "Hillary's big ethical problem: Bill."[29]

But as we will see, this is a crude caricature of their complex relationship. In a way, all that has really happened is that the Clintons have reversed roles. When Hillary entered the Senate, and then the State Department, she became the one who had real power, rather than Bill.

How did the Clintons amass so much wealth in such a short period of time? The answer makes for fascinating reading.

For one thing, the Clintons have operated at the fringes of the developed world, often appearing to assist in facilitating huge resource-extraction deals that are worth hundreds of millions of dollars. The era of globalization has opened up a Wild West bonanza where profits can be made on a scale not seen since the height of nineteenth-century colonialism. The Clintons' most lucrative transactions originate not in places like Germany or Great Britain, where business and politics are kept separate by stringent ethical rules and procedures, but in despotic areas of the developing world where the rules are very different. Money also comes from foreign businessmen in Europe or Canada who have amassed their wealth in parts of the world where corruption and payoffs are simply a part of doing business.

We will see a pattern of financial transactions involving the Clintons that occurred contemporaneous with favorable US policy decisions benefiting those providing the funds.

Here is how it worked: Bill flew around the world making speeches and burnishing his reputation as a global humanitarian and wise man. Very often on these trips he was accompanied by "close friends" or associates who happened to have business interests pending in these countries. Introductions were made, deals struck, and photo ops arranged before an admiring foreign press. Meanwhile, bureaucratic or legislative obstacles were mysteriously cleared or approvals granted within the purview of his wife, the powerful senator or secretary of state. Huge donations then flowed into the Clinton Foundation while Bill received enormous speaking fees underwritten by the very businessmen who benefited from these apparent interventions.

Of course, it is perfectly possible that in some cases Hillary did nothing at all to ensure these favorable outcomes. Perhaps these foreign interests made large payments to Bill simply in the hope of influencing Hillary. Maybe they were mistaken in thinking that multimillion-dollar payments to Bill and the foundation would have the desired effect. We don't know. Either way, though, the Clintons ended up with the money.

I realize how shocking these allegations may appear. Are these activities illegal? That's not for me to say. I'm not a lawyer. But as someone once said, the most troubling thing about Washington is not what's illegal but what isn't. The Clintons are lawyers themselves and they know very well what legal lines they may not cross. By using their legal finesse, the Clintons have often skirted the boundaries of ethical conduct. They have been frequently censured and criticized for their conduct, but have usually escaped serious legal consequences. In a way, what you are about to read is similar to what they have always done, from Little Rock to the Lincoln Bedroom. They are just doing it now on a truly global scale.

Unsavory foreigners with an interest in climbing higher up the global status chain have clearly seen the Clintons as a path to respectability and influence.

Take the case of Gulnora Karimova, the eldest daughter of the dictator of Uzbekistan. In a country dominated by organized crime, forced labor, and torture, Gulnora is loathed by her country's citizenry. As one US diplomatic cable put it, "Most Uzbeks see Karimova as a greedy, power-hungry individual who uses her father to crush business people or anyone else who stands in her way. . . . She remains the single most hated person in the country."[30] Being the most hated person in Uzbekistan is saying something. Her father, who still runs the country, is widely reported to have boiled his political opponents to death in the 1990s.

Karimova is also glamorous and ambitious, and for a while she sported a fashion and jewelry line she tried to establish in Europe and the United States. According to a "secret/noforn" cable sent from the US embassy in Tashkent, Uzbekistan, to the CIA and other intelligence agencies in July 2009, she was "hoping that a connection with him [Bill] will allow her to establish good relations with the Secretary of State [Hillary]."[31] How to go about it? She started by cosponsoring a Clinton Foundation fundraiser in Monaco. She posed with Bill for a photo at the event and soon NBC's

Today Show reported that Bill Clinton was "among her friends."[32]

Where it all might have led we will never know, because in 2013 Karimova had a falling out with her dictator father. As of this writing, she is thought to be under house arrest in Uzbekistan.

Brash Gulnora Karimova was only expressing what so many foreign oligarchs and interested investors already know. And the Clintons know it, too. Supporters and opponents have called the Clintons many things over the years, but one word you never hear is *naïve*.

Chapter 2
The Transfer

On September 6, 2005, former president Bill Clinton found himself, of all places, in Almaty, Kazakhstan.[1] A country with broad steppes and rugged mountains, Kazakhstan was a place where Genghis Khan once roamed. More recently, the comedy film *Borat* lampooned it as an impoverished country full of incompetents. In truth, however, the country sits atop a vast storehouse of minerals that includes an estimated $5 trillion worth of natural resources.[2] Highly prized are the country's immense uranium deposits—the mineral used to fuel nuclear reactors and build nuclear bombs.

Bill Clinton's Kazakhstan sojourn was ostensibly an effort to help the country's HIV/AIDS patients gain access to lower-priced antiretroviral therapies. Yet according to the World Health Organization (WHO) and the United Nations Program on HIV/AIDS, at the time of Clinton's visit, only an estimated fifteen hundred Kazakhs needed such treatments. In 2005 the prevalence of HIV/AIDS in Kazakhstan accounted for between 0.1 and 0.3 percent of its 15.4 million citizens, low compared with African countries like Botswana (24.1 percent) and South Africa (18.8 percent of adults).[3]

All the more curious was the fact that Clinton had agreed to public and private meetings with the nation's dictator, Nursultan Nazarbayev, who had ruled Kazakhstan as president since 1990. Having risen through the ranks of the Communist Party during the Soviet days, Nazarbayev dropped the working-class rhetoric after the collapse of the Soviet Union and reverted to a classic despot. Indeed, "president" was a selected title. Kazakhstan doesn't have elections as we think of them in the West. Nazarbayev regularly wins reelection with more than 90 percent of the vote. (In the last election, the candidates running against Nazarbayev claimed they voted for him.)[4]

In short, Nazarbayev gets what he wants, one way or another. Despite a long marriage and an airline stewardess for a mistress, he was the father of only three daughters—no sons. Lacking a male heir, he arranged a relationship with the former Miss Kazakhstan Assel

Issabayeva, and impregnated her via test tube. On April 2, 2005, she gave birth to his *Sultanchik*. Problem solved.[5]

According to the *Huffington Post*, "Nazarbayev himself is rumored to be one of the richest men in the world, although no one knows exactly how rich, since he is alleged to have hidden interests in a variety of businesses." Kazakhstan's five billionaires all have close ties to Nazarbayev. Two of them are his relatives.[6]

Nazarbayev craves acceptance from the West. But he has a nasty habit of throwing political opponents and journalists into jail. Torture is common. The list of Kazakh human rights violations, according to the US government, besides torture includes arbitrary detention; restrictions on freedom of speech, press, and assembly; pervasive corruption; and human trafficking.

So why would former president Bill Clinton bestow an air of international respectability on a backwater billionaire dictator with a treacherous human rights record? And why would he do so on the eve of a national election in that country, when Clinton's mere presence could be read as an endorsement of the dictator's "candidacy"?

It helps to look to Clinton's traveling companion, Canadian mining tycoon Frank Giustra. Short, compact, and sporting a gray-haired Caesar haircut,

Giustra is estimated to be worth several hundreds of millions of dollars. Bill flew on board the mining magnate's private jet: a "luxurious MD-87, complete with a bedroom and shower, gold-plated bathroom fixtures, leather upholstered reclining seats, flat-panel TVs and original paintings on the cabin walls. The blankets are emblazoned with 'Giustra Air.'" It features a boardroom and sleeps eighteen comfortably.[7]

"The plane is a business tool. No more, no less," says Giustra bluntly. And one of its useful functions has been doing the Clintons favors. For some years, Giustra has made his jet available to Bill to travel the globe delivering big-money speeches, as well as to travel to campaign events for Hillary's 2008 presidential campaign. As a Canadian citizen, Giustra couldn't donate to Hillary's campaign, but he could certainly offer use of his plane to Bill. He could also steer tens of millions to the Clintons and entities that they control.[8]

Giustra built his empire by cutting deals in some of the most dangerous parts of the world. At the time of his 2005 travels with Clinton, he lived in a palatial 12,000-square-foot home in western Vancouver. "Obsessively private," according to Canadian media, he operated out of a thirty-first-floor corner office on Burrard Street, a sloping boulevard with scenic views of Vancouver's port.

Less a mining executive than a penny-stock specu-
lator, Giustra made his money pumping and dumping
mining stocks in the Canadian stock exchanges.[9] As the
Globe and Mail, Canada's most prestigious newspaper,
put it in a generally sympathetic portrait, Giustra got
rich "through a Byzantine system of shell companies,
furtive share purchases and elaborate compensation
schemes."[10] In Kazakhstan he was looking to close a
large deal.

Giustra had done mining deals in sub-Saharan Africa
and South America. He knew how to do business with
autocrats. For an autocrat, the allure of doing a favor
for an ex-American president, especially a former president with a powerful wife, likely held special value. As
Giustra admitted in 2006 to the *New Yorker* in a rare
moment of candor, "All of my chips, almost, are on Bill
Clinton. He's a brand, a worldwide brand, and he can
do things and ask for things that no one else can."[11]

According to Clinton and Giustra, they first met in
2005.[12] Technically, that might be correct. But their
business ties actually go back decades earlier.

Both men were involved with mining entrepre-
neur Jean-Raymond Boulle, whose company Diamond
Fields invested in an Arkansas diamond mine that
Clinton approved when he was governor.[13] At the time,
Diamond Fields had its eye on an Arkansas state park

known to have diamond deposits. So Boulle went to Little Rock and hooked up with Clinton pal Jim Blair.[14] (Blair made headlines in 1994 as the man who helped Hillary Clinton turn $1,000 into $100,000 in futures.) Blair took Boulle to see Governor Clinton and pitched a diamond mine in the Crater of Diamonds State Park.[15] Boulle claimed the mine could become "one of the world's largest diamond producers."[16] Governor Clinton signed off on the project and helped get the property green-lighted for mining in 1987. Clinton pal Bruce Lindsey (who went on to become a senior White House adviser and now serves as chairman of the board of the Clinton Foundation) provided legal services to the fledgling company. For good measure, Diamond Fields set up its corporate headquarters in Hope, Bill Clinton's hometown.[17]

When Bill was elected president, Boulle was an invited guest at the inauguration in Washington, DC. That night, as the Clintons celebrated their victory at several inaugural balls around town, Hillary wore a 3.5-carat diamond ring that came from one of Boulle's mines.

Giustra, through a variety of domestic and offshore holding companies, had more than sixty thousand shares of stock in Diamond Fields in the early 1990s.[18] But by 2005 the public face of the Clinton-Giustra relationship was all about philanthropy. The two would establish something called the Clinton Giustra Sustainable Growth Initiative (CGSGI) as a project of the Clinton Foundation. CGSGI is supposed to foster economic growth in the developing world. Its activities are often sited near "natural resource industry" projects such as mines or oilfields in which Giustra is invested.

Access to Kazakh mining concessions is highly competitive. Large mining companies from Australia to Russia vie for them. Giustra's company, UrAsia Energy, was a new player with no background in the uranium business and was therefore far from the logical choice for Kazatomprom, the Kazakh atomic energy agency. Other companies with decades of experience in the field should have been first in line for this lucrative deal. "Everyone was asking Kazatomprom to the dance," said Fadi Shadid, a senior uranium industry stock analyst. "A second-tier junior player like UrAsia—you'd need all the help you could get."[19] UrAsia Energy was a mere shell company. But with Nazarbayev's approval, that was about to change.

Giustra had his eye on three mines several hundred miles from Almaty. The deal was obscure from the start: the mining concessions were transferred to mysterious offshore entities including Jeffcott Group Ltd., which was registered in the British Virgin Islands. Giustra and others involved in the venture later claimed they didn't even know who actually owned the mysterious entity. "We dealt with corporations and entities that had title to the assets," said Chris Sattler, executive vice president of corporate development and investor relations of Uranium One (of which UrAsia Energy would soon become part). "In fact, we dealt with their representatives. . . . Therefore, we have no knowledge of the beneficiaries or shareholders behind Jeffcott."[20] On other occasions, Frank Giustra claims to have known precisely whom he was dealing with in the transaction.

Clinton's itinerary included a lavish private feast with the Kazakh dictator, as well as a public press conference.[21] For the former president it was a reunion of sorts. Clinton and Nazarbayev had first met back in 1994, when the Kazakh autocrat came to Washington to meet the new president.[22] The two discussed several topics and signed a Charter on Democratic Partnership, "which recognized Kazakhstan's commitments to the rule of law, respect for human rights, and economic reform."[23] Nazarbayev had a habit of signing documents he had no intention of honoring. Clinton and Nazarbayev met again in December 1999, when they discussed a number of issues, one of which likely included concerns involving two mining and metal companies that were having troubles in Kazakhstan. A Canadian firm, World Wide Minerals, and a London-based firm, Trans-World Metals, had seen property confiscated by the Kazakh government.[24]

The September 2005 visit had been organized in part by Sergei Kurzin, a round-faced Russian nuclear physicist from Siberia who had done business in Kazakhstan before. In addition to arranging the meeting in Almaty, he assisted Giustra in creating UrAsia Energy.[25]

It's unclear if Kurzin and Clinton had met before, but they would have several more meetings in the years that followed. And they had something else in common: fugitive financier Marc Rich. Recall that in January 2001, on his last day in office, Clinton had issued a presidential pardon for Rich. Kurzin had previously worked for Rich traveling around Russia in search of suitable investment opportunities.[26]

Kurzin, in a 2008 interview with *New York Times* reporters Jo Becker and Don Van Natta, said about the visit, "timing was everything."[27] After the *Times* piece ran, Kurzin reported getting an angry phone call from Giustra. The secretive Canadian "yelled like hell at me over the phone after he saw the piece," Kurzin said later. "He was furious that I talked to a journalist."[28]

What transpired at dinner with Clinton, Nazarbayev, and Giustra depends on whom you ask. It was by all accounts a lavish affair, with upward of seventy-five guests.

Bill maintained that the entire visit was about dealing with HIV/AIDS in Kazakhstan. Giustra insisted that the mining deal he wanted to secure did not involve Nazarbayev or the Kazakh government. As he put it, "The mining agreements I reached in Kazakhstan were concluded after lengthy negotiations with private companies—not the Kazakhstan government."[29] Bill has gone even further, claiming that "formal endorsement from the Kazakh government was not required to acquire the assets."[30] He went on to make a technical legal argument: "Kazatomprom was not a signatory to either of the memorandums of understanding signed by Mr. Giustra's company."[31]

But these were, at best, elaborate evasions. Corporate executives for the uranium company later admitted to journalists and US diplomats that Kazakh officials absolutely needed to sign off on the deal. Jean Nortier, CEO of the company that would eventually control the assets, said, "When you do a transaction in Kazakhstan, you need the government's approval. UrAsia got the approval, and when UrAsia merged with Uranium One, that approval was given again."[32]

Leaked State Department cables from the US ambassador in Kazakhstan further refute Bill Clinton's claim. Giustra acquired the assets in Kazakhstan through his shell company UrAsia Energy and then transferred those assets through a merger with a company called Uranium One.[33] According to a 2009 US diplomatic cable revealed by WikiLeaks, Paul Lewis Clarke, senior vice president of Uranium One, claimed that Uranium One's UrAsia acquisitions "were approved by many of the same people still in power," including the then prime minister Danial Akhmetov (who later became minister of defense), and "Kazatomprom president [Vladimir] Shkolnik, then the Minister of Energy and Mineral Resources."[34] Any asset transfer of uranium rights needed to be approved by Kazakh officials.[35]

A key Kazakh official involved in the deal was Mukhtar Dzhakishev, the president of Kazatomprom, the government agency that runs Kazakhstan's uranium and nuclear energy industry. A technocrat with pro-Western sympathies, Dzhakishev was eager to do business with the United States and would later visit Clinton in 2007 at his home in New York. According to Dzhakishev, the uranium deal came up in discussions that night at the banquet.[36] Clinton and Giustra dispute this.

But more than that, suggestions have been made that Dzhakishev and other Kazakh officials had already been under pressure for months to close the deal and grant the lucrative uranium concessions to Giustra.[37] For reasons that remain unclear, approval was being held up on the Kazakh end. Giustra was understandably anxious and may have asked Bill to intervene.

In a 2009 video of a statement to authorities on an unrelated matter, Dzhakishev claimed that then senator Hillary Clinton pressured Kazakh officials to secure the deal for the Canadians. According to Dzhakishev, Kazakh prime minister Karim Massimov "was in America and needed to meet with Hillary Clinton but this meeting was cancelled. And they said that those investors connected with the Clintons who were working in Kazakhstan have problems. Until Kazakhstan solved those problems, there would be no meeting, and all manner of measures would be taken." Massimov returned to his country and called Dzhakishev and told him to work it out.[38] Dzhakishev then claims he was contacted by Tim Phillips, an adviser to Bill. According to Dzhakishev, Phillips told him that there would be no further meetings with Hillary until Kazakh officials approved Giustra's uranium deal.[39]

Dzhakishev was certainly in a position to know. He played a central role in the Giustra uranium deal. He was among the first Giustra met in Kazakhstan to discuss it. Some time later he met with Bill Clinton at his home in Chappaqua, New York, to discuss the broader uranium market in Kazakhstan.[40]

The alleged threat to withhold American aid would not have been perceived as an idle one. The Kazakhs received large sums of money from the US government as part of a post–Cold War nonproliferation program. (In 2011, for example, they received $110 million for "combatting weapons of mass destruction.") At that time, Hillary sat on the powerful Senate Armed Services Committee. More specifically, she sat on the Subcommittee on Emerging Threats and Capabilities. Hillary's subcommittee had responsibility for oversight of nonproliferation programs.[41]

Dzhakishev also claimed that Phillips "began to scream" at him that it was important to get the deal done for "Democrats" involved in it.[42] Dzhakishev says he took Phillips to see Kazakh officials, including assistant to the president Karim Massimov, who later became prime minister. When Phillips was asked by the *Washington Post* about Dzhakishev's account, he didn't respond. He has, however, changed his online résumé and has removed any references to having been a Clinton Foundation fundraiser.[43]

Meanwhile, Bill gave Nazarbayev the international credibility he craved. Standing before the gathered media in front of a large gold-inlaid national seal of Kazakhstan, Bill Clinton took the podium with a grinning Nazarbayev at his side.[44] Bill talked about his global AIDS work before praising Nazarbayev for "opening up the social and political life of your country." Clinton's glowing assessment was not shared by anyone in the human rights community. Indeed, Robert Herman, who worked for the Clinton State Department in the 1990s and later joined the nonprofit Freedom House, called the statement "patently absurd."[45] Certainly the US State Department would not agree with Clinton's fawning praise. For years, it had categorically stated that Kazakhstan had "failed to significantly improve its human rights record."[46]

As the international media recorded his words, Bill also came out publicly in support of Nazarbayev's bid to have his country head the prestigious Organization for Security and Cooperation in Europe (OSCE). "I think it's time for that to happen, it's an important step, and I'm glad you're willing to undertake it," he said. Nazarbayev quickly issued a press release proudly claiming support from Clinton. The ex-president neither refuted nor challenged Nazarbayev's public relations victory lap.

Clinton's endorsement was remarkably audacious. The OSCE was primarily a human rights organization, formed as a result of the 1975 Helsinki Accords. The international body held little power, but it was an honor Nazarbayev sought. Putting Nazarbayev's Kazakhstan at the helm of the OSCE was like putting Iran in charge of the International Atomic Energy Agency. It made no sense. Still, it would be a prestigious appointment for the dictator.

Hillary was at the time a legislative branch commissioner for the Commission on Security and Cooperation in Europe, one of only nine US senators on the panel. In 2004 Hillary had cosigned a letter to the State Department stating that Kazakhstan's bid to head up the OSCE "would not be acceptable" because of widespread corruption and human rights problems. In July 2008 when the commission held hearings titled "Promises to Keep: Kazakhstan's 2010 OSCE Chairmanship," Senator Ben Cardin, Democrat of Maryland and the cochair of the commission, said Kazakhstan's "record on human rights and democratization does indeed raise concerns. The State Department's yearly reports, as well as those by numerous human rights groups inside and outside of Kazakhstan, lay out in detail the problem areas."[47]

According to the official transcript, Hillary didn't show up for the hearings.

Clinton and Giustra left Kazakhstan the day after the banquet. Within forty-eight hours, Giustra's company

UrAsia signed two memoranda of understanding out-lining the transfer of uranium mining assets, which Kazakh authorities later approved: buying a 30 percent stake in the Kharassan uranium project and 70 per-cent in another project—the Betpak-Dala joint ven-ture.[48] The deal stunned longtime mining observers. Choosing UrAsia to buy into those mines was a "mys-tery" said Gene Clark, the chief executive of *Trade Tech*, an industry newsletter. "UrAsia was able to jump-start the whole process somehow," he said. The company was now a "major uranium producer when it didn't even exist before."[49]

In the months that followed, Giustra gave the Clinton Foundation $31.3 million.[50] It was the first of several large donations he would make as he went on to secure other lucrative natural resources deals in developing countries around the world. We will see him again in other chapters.

As mentioned earlier, at the time of Clinton's visit, Kazakhstan was on the verge of a national election. Days after Clinton departed, the opposition party's campaign headquarters were ravaged by fire in an arson attack. On October 12 heavily armed police tem-porarily arrested the opposition party's leader. The OSCE said the election "was marred by an 'atmosphere of intimidation' and 'ballot-box stuffing.' "[51]

In December 2005 Nazarbayev won reelection with more than 90 percent of the vote. Bill sent him a note of congratulations. "Recognizing that your work has received an excellent grade is one of the most important rewards in life," he wrote. "At the start of your new term as president, I would like to express confidence that you will continue to live up to the expectations of your people."[52] The Kazakh dictator promptly released Clinton's congratulatory note to the public.

With the Kazakh concession in hand, UrAsia Energy Ltd. significantly expanded its assets. UrAsia quickly went about directing shares of the company's stock to friends in Canada. Giustra took 3 million shares. He gave half a million more to Robert Cross, a former brokerage colleague, whom he also placed on the board. According to the *Globe and Mail,* his friend and fellow investment dealmaker, Ian Telfer, received 2.2 million shares of his own.[53]

Telfer, like Giustra, had been kicking around in the mining business for decades, involved in several high-profile penny-stock mining deals.[54] "I'm more of an opportunist than a visionary," he admitted.[55] But this deal was special. And he would provide the Clinton Foundation with funds of his own.

With the shares doled out, UrAsia went public and was "among the largest [offerings] on record" to be brokered on Canada's Venture Exchange.[56] Canadian firms BMO Nesbitt Burns Inc., Canaccord Adams, and GMP Securities Ltd. handled the placement of the shares, and became supporters of the Clinton Foundation as well, as we will see.[57]

Then phase two began. In February 2007 UrAsia Energy announced that it would merge with Uranium One, a uranium company based out of South Africa and Canada.[58]

Like all transactions involving uranium in Kazakhstan, the merger required approval by the Kazakh government. That same month, Dzhakishev, the head of Kazatomprom, went to Chappaqua for a private meeting with Bill Clinton.[59] Frank Giustra allegedly arranged the meeting.[60] According to Dzhakishev, they discussed uranium markets and the future of nuclear power. Just as Giustra needed Kazakh government approval, the Kazakhs might need US government approval for their aspirations to purchase a stake in Westinghouse, a major US manufacturer of nuclear power plant components.[61]

Yet pressure was mounting in Washington about Nazarbayev's human rights record and Kazakhstan's fitness to head an international human rights body like the OSCE. Senator Joe Biden, chairman of the Senate Foreign Relations Committee, fired off a letter on March 13, 2007, to President Nazarbayev, making it clear he wanted Kazakhstan to clean up its act or he would not support their bid. "Unless visible progress is attained quickly, I will not be able to support Kazakhstan in its quest to assume chairmanship of the OSCE."[62]

The Clintons, however, took a different tack. Hillary, who had expressed concerns about Kazakhstan heading up the OSCE prior to the deal, now was strangely silent.[63] Bill was emboldened: he invited Nazarbayev to attend the Clinton Global Initiative (CGI) as his guest. The Kazakh dictator was happy to make the trip, and on September 25, 2007, he was a featured attendee at an exclusive CGI meeting in New York.[64]

Two months later Nazarbayev was awarded the OSCE chair, a post he took in 2010.[65]

Meanwhile, in February 2007 shareholders approved the merger between UrAsia and Uranium One.[66] Although Giustra tried to characterize the transaction as a Uranium One takeover of his company, UrAsia Energy Ltd., it was actually a reverse merger. Giustra, his friends, and other shareholders wound up controlling 60 percent of the new company.[67] And in the months that followed, they began acquiring uranium assets in the United States itself.[68] Within the next year, they began negotiations with the Russian State Nuclear Agency, which, in 2009, bought a stake in the company, as described in the next chapter.[69]

Following the lucrative merger, many of the deal's largest shareholders wrote multimillion-dollar checks to the Clinton Foundation and its project, the Clinton Giustra Sustainable Growth Initiative. In addition to his $31.3 million donation, Giustra announced a multiyear commitment to donate $100 million, and half of his future profits, to the Clinton Foundation.[70] Giustra's commitments made the Canadian mining investor one of the largest individual contributors to the Clinton Foundation, rivaling those far wealthier than himself, like Bill Gates, who has given more than $25 million to the Clinton Foundation.[71]

As we will see, Bill Clinton would show up at critical times in other developing countries where Giustra had business. As Canada's *Globe and Mail* put it, "it just so happens that Bill Clinton keeps popping up in places where Giustra is buying resource assets."[72]

The collective commitments and donations from investors who profited from the deal would ultimately exceed $145 million.[73] (The Clinton Foundation only reports ranges, not exact amounts.) These investors include the following business associates of Giustra:

- Frank Holmes, another major shareholder in the deal, wrote a check to the Clinton Foundation for between $250,000 and $500,000.[74] Holmes also lists himself as an adviser to the Clinton Foundation.

- Neil Woodyer, Giustra's colleague who founded Endeavour Financial, pledged $500,000 and committed to providing "ongoing financial support."[75]

- Robert Disbrow, a broker at Haywood Securities, which provided $58 million in capital to float shares of UrAsia's private placement, sent between $1 million and $5 million to the Clinton Foundation a few months later.[76]

- Paul Reynolds, an executive at Canaccord Capital, Inc., donated in the same range, between $1 million and $5 million.[77] The UrAsia deal was the largest in Canaccord's history.

- GMP Securities Ltd., another large shareholder in UrAsia Energy, committed to donating a portion of its profits to the CGSGI. GMP made great money on the private placement of shares and as an underwriter on UrAsia Energy deals.[78]

- Robert Cross, who was a major shareholder and serves as director of UrAsia Energy, committed a portion of his future income to the Clinton Foundation.[79]

- Egizio Bianchini, the Capital Markets vice chair and Global cohead of BMO's Global Metals and Mining group, had also been an underwriter on the mining deals.[80] BMO paid $600,000 for two tables at the CGSGI's March 2008 benefit.[81]

- Sergei Kurzin, a Russian dealmaker involved in the Kazakhstan uranium deal and a shareholder in UrAsia Energy, also made the CGSGI a $1 million pledge.[82]

- Ian Telfer, the chairman of UrAsia Energy, who would become the new chairman of Uranium One, committed $3 million.[83]

Bill Clinton hailed the windfall as a selfless philanthropic gesture that would support economic growth and health care in the developing world. "I'm proud of the coalition in the natural resources industry that has come together," he said.[84] A group of Canadian mining investors just happened to become conspicuously large contributors in the Clinton Foundation over a very short period of time.

Giustra went even further in bringing in funds for the foundation. In 2006, he hosted a birthday party/ fundraiser for Bill Clinton at the Fairmont Royal York Hotel in Toronto that featured an impressive guest list.

The event was headlined by Kevin Spacey and included Billy Crystal and Bon Jovi.[85] In March 2008 there was another superstar fundraising gala including Tom Cruise and Robin Williams in Toronto.[86] In Vancouver on October 17, 2008, Giustra and Clinton addressed the British Columbia Business Council on corporate social responsibility.[87]

Any actions the Clintons may have taken to support Canadian Giustra in the uranium deals could not be justified on the grounds that they were creating jobs for Americans or helping American companies be more competitive overseas, the explanation politicians often give to justify doing favors for companies or donors.

But the international scope of the deals would expand beyond Kazakhstan, Canada, Washington, and Chappaqua to include some of the most powerful government officials in Russia. The flow of money would only increase.

Chapter 3
Hillary's Reset

THE RUSSIAN URANIUM DEAL

Perhaps Hillary Clinton and Vladimir Putin had gotten off to a rough start. When she was running for the Democratic presidential nomination in 2008, Hillary had talked tough about the Russian president. Contradicting President George W. Bush's oft-quoted statement that he "was able to get a sense of [Putin's] soul," Hillary had pointedly countered that Putin "doesn't have a soul." When asked about the comment, Putin shot back, "At a minimum, a head of state should have a head."

But when Hillary was confirmed as secretary of state in January 2009, dealing with Vladimir Putin would become a major part of her job. And the uranium deal in Kazakhstan, whose shareholders were sending in tens of millions of dollars to the Clinton Foundation and were also providing speechmaking opportunities for Bill, would set the stage to bring Putin into the cast of characters.

The uranium deal that was sealed in 2005 during Bill Clinton's visit to Kazakhstan and then fortified by the 2007 Kazakh-approved merger would soon morph into a third transaction intersecting with some of Hillary's most consequential and difficult national security decisions as secretary of state. And as we will see, there is no evidence that she disclosed to US government ethics officials, the White House, or her cabinet colleagues the apparent conflicts of interest at play as she steered US nuclear policy.

In the final years of the Bush administration, relations with Moscow had cooled. The Russian incursion into neighboring Georgia, Bush's plans to erect a missile-defense shield, and Russian pressures on Ukraine had heightened tensions between the two nuclear powers.[1] What President Barack Obama and Hillary Clinton had in mind was a "reset." At Foggy Bottom, Hillary offered the Kremlin a chance to clean the slate and begin anew.[2]

Moscow was all in favor of a reset and viewed it as an opportunity to develop more trade and investment opportunities with the West.[3] And in spite of her pointed comments about Putin's soul, Hillary's appointment as secretary of state was generally praised in Moscow. Authorities saw her as offering a "balanced view of US relations with the Russian Federation."[4] She was "by far not the worst" outcome for Moscow, said one official, noting that there were advisers around Obama who were "very critical of our country."[5] Not a ringing endorsement perhaps, but Hillary was someone the Russians believed they could work with.

At the heart of the reset was what *Newsweek* called "a bevy of potential business deals."[6] These included deals involving oil and natural gas, which are the backbone of the Russian economy.[7] But not far behind were Kremlin ambitions to expand its share of the world nuclear market. Uranium, civilian nuclear power plants, and the technical services that supported them were considered a huge growth industry for Moscow.[8] In 2006 the Kremlin had approved plans "to spend $10 billion to increase Russia's annual uranium production by 600 percent."[9] Putin considered the nuclear energy sector "a priority branch for the country, which makes Russia a great power."[10] Russia not only wanted to build nuclear plants around the world, it also wanted to control a large chunk of the global uranium market.[11]

But an important side note to the Russian reset was how it involved a collection of foreign investors who had poured vast sums of money into the Clinton Foundation and who continued to sponsor lucrative speeches for Bill. Those investors stood to gain enormously from the decisions Hillary made as secretary of state.

The Russian State Atomic Nuclear Agency (Rosatom) handles all things nuclear in Russia. Unlike the US Department of Energy or the Nuclear Regulatory Commission, Rosatom is not just deeply imbedded with civilian nuclear power but actually controls the Russian nuclear arsenal.[12]

Longtime Rosatom head Sergei Kiriyenko is a tall, lanky technocrat who served in the Komsomol, the Soviet Youth League, during the Soviet era. He went on to become energy minister and then prime minister of Russia while Bill Clinton was president of the United States. (Indeed, when Russian president Boris Yeltsin made Kiriyenko prime minister in 1998, it brought "instant endorsements" from the Clinton administration.)[13] He and his agency operate in a special way in Russia, without any independent supervision from the Russian parliament. Rosatom "is subject only to the decision-making of the Kremlin," as one nuclear scholar at UC Berkeley puts it. "Unlike the oil and gas industries, the nuclear sector is under the direct supervision of the state."[14]

Rosatom not only built the controversial Bushehr nuclear reactors in Iran, it also supplies them with uranium.[15] Rosatom also operates in North Korea,

Venezuela, and Myanmar.[16] As the agency makes clear in its annual report, it places a primacy on protecting information "constituting state secrets."

During her tenure as secretary of state, Hillary Clinton and senior aides received numerous diplomatic cables discussing Moscow's nuclear ambitions. In October 2009, for example, she received a cable exposing Rosatom's plan to leverage Ukraine into a long-range supply contract with the Russian state nuclear fuel company, and its efforts to create "zones of pressure" on Eastern European governments.[17]

In December 2009 the US ambassador to Kazakhstan sent a classified cable to Washington laying out Russian efforts to exert control over Kazakh uranium markets.[18] The cable noted that Rosatom sought to control this market as part of a broader initiative to reestablish itself as a world power. The memo also stated that Russian military intelligence, the GRU, was involved in these nuclear ambitions.[19]

Even before that cable was sent, there were signs of Russian moves on the uranium market. In June 2009 Rosatom bought a stake in Uranium One. It was not a controlling stake, only 17 percent, but the Russians were just getting started.[20]

Uranium One was an inviting target. Production was booming, jumping from 2 million pounds of uranium in 2007 to 7.4 million in 2010. But Uranium One was also aggressively buying uranium assets in the United States. By 2010 the Canadian company had "61 ongoing or planned projects on some 293,000 acres in Wyoming."[21] The firm also owned ten thousand acres of uranium claims in Utah, as well as holdings in Texas and South Dakota.[22] In sum, Uranium One was projected to control up to half of US uranium output by 2015.

In December 2009 Rosatom chief Kiriyenko appeared before the Presidium, a selection of Russian government officials. He laid out an aggressive plan to acquire uranium assets outside of Russia. "An opportunity has opened up to buy foreign assets that are profitable and, for now, not very expensive," he said. "With this program of buying uranium deposits, we can guarantee this to any customers of ours." Then prime minister Putin announced at the meeting that the Russian government would allocate the money for the transactions to Rosatom's equity capital.[23]

The Kremlin's move came at a sensitive time. Hillary Clinton was directing negotiations for the 123 Agreement with the Russian government concerning civilian nuclear energy. The 123 Agreement is a nuclear nonproliferation treaty whose name derives from the fact that it falls under Section 123 of the US Atomic Energy Act. It requires that the United States have a

123 Agreement negotiated and in place to make nuclear cooperation possible with foreign countries. In short, as the US State Department put it, the 123 Agreement with Russia would "support commercial interests by allowing U.S. and Russian firms to team up more easily in joint ventures."

The pact had previously been negotiated by the Bush administration, but when Russian forces went into Georgia in 2008, the administration withdrew a request that Congress approve it. The Obama–Clinton reset meant that the agreement was back on and (along with input from the US Department of Energy) that Hillary was in charge. Congress would eventually approve the 123 Agreement in January 2011.

In March 2010 Hillary was in Moscow for a meeting with Putin. Putin had set in motion the purchase of a controlling stake in Uranium One by Rosatom only a few months earlier. During a meeting on March 19, Hillary and Putin discussed a wide variety of issues related to trade. He expressed displeasure with US trade policy, presumably because Russian companies were affected by US sanctions. Whether the Uranium One deal was discussed is not known.

The primary purpose of Hillary's trip was to increase pressure on Iran. Instead, Putin promised Moscow's assistance with the completion of a civil nuclear power station by the summer. Hillary blasted the move, saying it "would be premature to go forward with any project at this time, because we want to send an unequivocal message to the Iranians."[24]

As part of its reset with Moscow, the Obama administration wanted to make progress on the New START nuclear talks and sought commercial opportunities in areas like civilian nuclear power. On that front, Hillary was optimistic. "If we continue to work together, we can move beyond the problems to greater opportunities."

In May 2010 the Obama administration submitted the proposed text of the US-Russian Civilian Nuclear Cooperation Agreement to Congress. Weeks later, Rosatom announced it was seeking to buy majority control (52 percent) of Uranium One. To some observers in the uranium market, it all made sense. "It was no accident that Rosatom's choice fell to Uranium One," wrote one paper, given the uranium assets it held.[25]

Several multimillion-dollar Clinton Foundation donors were at the center of the deal. As we saw in the previous chapter, one of these, Ian Telfer, was chairman of Uranium One. A longtime mining investor and associate of Frank Giustra, Telfer made his fortune as a gold investor and has served as the chairman of the World Gold Council.

The Clinton Foundation also failed to disclose major contributions from entities controlled by those involved in the Uranium One deal. Thus, beginning in 2009, the company's chairman, Telfer, quietly started funneling what would become $2.35 million to the Clinton Foundation through a Canadian entity he controlled called the Fernwood Foundation.[26] According to records released by the Clinton Foundation, Telfer had personally contributed $100,001 to $250,000 to the Clinton Foundation in 2007. But according to Canadian tax records, Telfer's Fernwood Foundation donated more than $2 million to the Clinton Foundation while Hillary was secretary of state. The Clinton Foundation's public disclosures don't list Fernwood as a donor.[27]

In 2009 Fernwood contributed $1 million to the Clinton Giustra Sustainable Growth Initiative (CGSCI).[28] In 2010 its donation was $250,000. In 2011 it gave another $600,000 and in 2012 the amount was $500,000.[29] According to Canadian tax records, nearly all of the funds CGSCI collects are transferred directly to the Clinton Foundation in New York.[30] In other words, it operates as a pass-through.

The fact that these donations are not listed in Clinton Foundation public disclosures violates the Clinton Foundation's memorandum of understanding with the Obama White House described in chapter 1, and contradicts Hillary's correspondence with the Senate Foreign Relations Committee. It also raises questions about what other undisclosed multimillion-dollar donations from foreign entities could have been channeled to the Clinton Foundation.

The Russian uranium deal involved other major Clinton Foundation donors. Two men listed as "financial advisors" for Uranium One and the Russia deal, Robert Disbrow and Paul Reynolds, were also multimillion-dollar contributors.[31] Another important shareholder in Uranium One was US Global Investor Funds, whose CEO was Frank Holmes.[32] Holmes was not only a major contributor to the foundation, he was also the chairman of Giustra's Endeavour Mining Capital Corp. Holmes describes himself as "an advisor to the William J. Clinton Foundation on sustainable development in countries with resource-based economies."[33] The managing director for global affairs at Endeavour Financial during this deal was Eric Nonacs, who simultaneously served as "senior advisor" to the Clinton Foundation. Nonacs, before taking the job, had been a foreign policy adviser to Bill during his post-presidential years.[34]

As part of the merger with Uranium One, key shareholders, including Telfer and Giustra, were required to hold their shares for at least six months.[35] (Dzhakishev believes that Giustra made $300 million in the deal.)[36] Giustra's firm, Endeavour Financial, continued to act as a financial adviser to Uranium One. In July 2008, for example, they arranged credit for the firm as part of a deal involving several Canadian investment banks.[37] In early 2008, according to Rosatom executive Vadim Zhivov, negotiations had already begun between Rosatom and Uranium One to buy a stake in the company.[38]

Was Giustra an investor in Uranium One via US Global Investor Funds? He did not return repeated calls asking for comment. It is unclear whether by 2010 Giustra was still directly involved in the deal, as he often conducts deals through shell companies.[39]

For shareholders of Uranium One, the Russian government acquisition would mean huge payouts. In addition to giving every shareholder a special one-dollar-per-share dividend, Moscow had big plans for Uranium One.[40] According to corporate records, Telfer alone had shares and options amounting to more than 1.6 million shares.[41]

"We would like just to use Uranium One as the global platform for future growth and all the future acquisitions and all M&A activity," said Zhivov, who directed the transaction for Rosatom.[42] Moscow wanted Uranium One Inc. "to be transformed into a global growth platform."[43] This had to sound lucrative to Canadian investors, though Zhivov admitted there was a "hard road ahead" to prove that "a Russian state-owned company can . . . play by the rules of the modern developed world."[44]

Russia wanted the deal for commercial and strategic reasons. The Canadian investors wanted the deal because it stood to make them richer. But politics in the United States would prove critical. Because uranium is a strategic industry, the Russian purchase of a Canadian company holding massive US assets required US government approval. Playing a central role in whether approval was granted was none other than Hillary Clinton.

When the Uranium One deal was announced in June 2010, news of the bid "panicked some shareholders and alarmed industry observers worried that the Vancouver-based company might end up serving the Kremlin's strategic interests," as one Canadian newspaper put it.[45]

The Kremlin went into full public relations mode. It dispatched Russian ambassador to the United States Sergey Kislyak to meet with mining executives in Colorado to soothe concerns about the deal. "Do you mind some investment? It is a normal commercial operation—not something that is operating on any political guidance," he said in an interview. "It doesn't matter whether it is uranium or steel or oil or gas," Kislyak said. "What is important is that the positive ties between our two countries seem to be getting more and more expanded. Politically, that is very important."[46]

Kislyak's distinction between business and politics is highly misleading: the funds for the Uranium One acquisition came from Putin directly and were approved by the Russian Presidium. And of course Russia has a history of using natural gas and energy exports to neighboring countries as a political tool.[47]

Four senior congressmen—Peter King of the Homeland Security Committee, Ileana Ros-Lehtinen of Foreign Affairs, Spencer Bachus of Financial Services, and Howard McKeon of Armed Services—voiced grave concerns about the deal. They were troubled by Rosatom's "activities—and the context within which it operates in Russia—[which] should raise very serious concerns for United States national security interests." The fact that Rosatom had helped Iran in building the Bushehr nuclear power plant "should raise red flags. . . . Although Uranium One USA officials are reportedly skeptical that the transaction would result in the transfer of any mined uranium to Iran, we remain concerned that Iran could receive uranium supplies through direct or secondary proliferation," they wrote. "We believe the take-over of essential US nuclear resources by a government-owned Russian agency . . . would not advance the national security interests of the United States."[48]

Wyoming senator John Barrasso also wrote a letter to the Obama administration raising concerns about Russian control of uranium assets in his state, citing Russia's "disturbing record of supporting nuclear programs in countries that are openly hostile to the United States, specifically Iran and Venezuela."[49]

In short, a bipartisan group of congressmen felt that Russia could not be trusted to allocate US uranium in keeping with US nuclear interests. Then congressman Ed Markey pushed a bill in the House with Congressman Jeff Fortenberry, "expressing disfavor of the Congress regarding the proposed agreement for cooperation between the United States and the Russian Federation."[50] Markey said, "Russia continues to train Iranian nuclear physicists, supply sensitive nuclear technology to Iran. . . . Does Russia want cooperation with the United States, or with Iran and Syria? Because it can't have both."[51]

In light of the obvious national security concerns, Uranium One and Rosatom officials offered concessions. Uranium One, for example, did not have an export license from the Nuclear Regulatory Commission (NRC) allowing it to ship uranium outside of the United States. Supporters of the deal argued, therefore, that no one should fear that American uranium might end up in, say, Iranian reactors.[52] But in correspondence with the NRC, Uranium One executives did not rule out trying to obtain an export license in the future. They could only say that "Uranium One does not intend today (and does not envision in the foreseeable future) any export of U_3O_8 from the United States derived from the Uranium One U.S. Facilities."[53]

Despite the glaring concerns, the Russian majority control purchase of Uranium One was approved by the Committee on Foreign Investment in the United States (CFIUS). CFIUS is a small and somewhat secretive executive branch task force created in 1975 to evaluate any investment transactions that might have a direct effect on American national security. Besides the secretary of state, CFIUS includes cabinet officials such as the secretary of defense, the secretary of homeland security, and the treasury secretary. CFIUS wields enormous power to stop or limit investment deals. Ironically, Uranium One officials, after CFIUS approved the deal, did mention global markets as an important reason why the deal made sense. "Donna Wichers, Uranium One Senior Vice President, said her company is pushing for uranium mines in Wyoming with an eye toward growing markets both in the United States and abroad as countries plan for new nuclear power reactors. 'We've got China—they're looking at opening 500 nuclear power plants in the next 40 years; India—several hundred. . . . So you can see worldwide there is a huge demand for nuclear power.' "[54]

There were all sorts of warning signs about Russia's push into the uranium market. For example, the US International Trade Commission was in the midst of a large investigation into allegations dating as far back as 1991 that Russia was dumping uranium on US markets to damage the American uranium industry.[55] In early 2010 Admiral Dennis Blair, the director of national intelligence, appeared before a congressional committee and warned about the perils of doing business with state-owned entities in Russia, stating that "criminally linked oligarchs will enhance the ability of state or state-allied actors to undermine competition in gas, oil, aluminum and precious metal markets." He didn't name specific Russian entities involved, but referred to the problem as "a growing nexus in Russian and Eurasian states among governments, organized crime, intelligence services and big business figures." He indicated that the United States needed to address the Russian instances of "bribery, fraud, violence and corrupt alliances with state actors to gain the upper hand against legitimate businesses."[56]

In the midst of this complex and controversial transaction, which would require US cabinet–level approval, a small Canadian investment company named Salida Capital became intimately involved with the Clinton Foundation.

According to Canadian tax records, Salida Capital received in 2010 an anonymous donation of $3.3 million into their charitable foundation (Salida Capital Foundation), which allowed the tiny firm to make the dramatic announcement that it would contribute millions to the Clinton Foundation.[57] In 2010 it donated $780,220 to the Clinton Foundation. This amounted to about 90 percent of all Salida's charitable giving that year. It was part of a multimillion-dollar commitment that would send more than $2.6 million to the Clintons between 2010 and 2012.[58]

Salida Capital also cosponsored a speech by Bill Clinton on May 21, 2010, in Calgary, Canada. While the speech was publicly listed by the Clintons as an event for "The Power Within," a Canadian motivational-speaking organization, according to State Department documents filed by Bill Clinton's office, sponsors for the event included Salida Capital.

Salida Capital invests in natural resource companies, including several in the Russian-dominated portions of Ukraine. In 2010, when Salida moved aggressively

into the Ukrainian market, their chief business partner in the country happened to be the personal adviser
to Energy Minister Yuri Boyko, who helped create the
trading company Vladimir Putin used to control the
Ukrainian natural gas trade. Boyko was described in
a confidential State Department cable as being "very
close to Russia" and as the "point of contact for the
Kremlin" on energy dealings in the country.[59]

In 2011 a company named Salida Capital would
be identified in a Rosatom annual report as a wholly
owned subsidiary of the Russian state nuclear agency.[60]
Is it the same firm? There is compelling evidence that
it is, but we cannot say for sure.[61]

I contacted Salida Capital in Toronto on three occasions and provided it with the opportunity to deny that
it is connected to the Salida Capital listed as a subsidiary of Rosatom. It has refused comment.

The timing of events raises questions. If it were the
same firm, an entity owned and controlled by Rosatom
funneled millions of dollars to the Clinton Foundation
at the very time Hillary would have been involved in
deciding whether to approve Rosatom's purchase of
Uranium One.[62]

But the Clintons' fortune didn't end there. In June,
shortly after the Rosatom deal was announced, Bill
was in Moscow for a particularly well-compensated

speech. He was paid $500,000 to deliver remarks at an event organized by a firm called Renaissance Capital (RenCap).[63] Bill had not given a speech in Russia in over five years and then it had been for a British firm, Adam Smith International. His pay for that speech was only $195,000.[64]

RenCap, which is registered in Cyprus, is populated by former Russian intelligence officers with close ties to Putin. In correspondence with the State Department seeking approval for the speech, Clinton's office simply describes the firm as "an investment bank focusing on emerging markets." According to *Businessweek*, when Putin became president of Russia in 2000, RenCap "hired several executives with connections to the Kremlin and Russian intelligence service, now known as the FSB [Russian Domestic Intelligence Service]." Yuri Kobaladze, executive director at the firm, served for thirty-two years as a KGB and SVR (the foreign intelligence arm of the Russian government) officer, retiring with the rank of general.[65] Yuri Sagaidak, the deputy general director at RenCap, was a colonel in the KGB.[66] Vladimir Dzhabarov served *simultaneously* as an officer in the FSB and first vice president at RenCap from 2006 to 2009.[67]

RenCap was also watching the Uranium One deal. Only three weeks before Clinton's speech, on May 27,

RenCap had been pushing Uranium One stock. "We believe the company is well positioned to provide impressive volume growth in the global sector and play the uranium spot price recovery," RenCap wrote in a twenty-eight-page report on the company. It actively encouraged investors to buy the stock.[68]

Clinton's hour-long, half-million-dollar speech on the theme of Russia "going global" was followed by a plenary session that included Renaissance Capital executives and senior Russian government officials.

During his Moscow visit, Bill also met with Putin himself.

Just days earlier the FBI had made a series of arrests, breaking up a Russian spy ring. Ten sleeper agents, using encrypted data transferred through digital images, invisible ink, and a sophisticated system for transferring information by switching bags at a train station in Queens, had been broken up. Among the spy ring's targets: a leading fundraiser for Hillary who also happened to be a Clinton friend. A Russian sleeper agent named "Cynthia Murphy" was instructed "to single out tidbits unknown publicly but revealed in private by sources close to State Department."[69] According to the FBI, intercepted communications showed that the chief assignment of the ring would be "to search and develop ties in policy-making circles in U.S."[70]

When Bill sat down with Putin, it didn't take long for the subject of Russian espionage to come up. "You have come to Moscow at the exact right time," Putin told the former president, according to the *New York Times*. Waving a finger at him, Putin continued, "Your police have gotten carried away, putting people in jail."[71] In response, "Clinton appeared to chuckle."[72]

Clinton and Putin had a close relationship. President Boris Yeltsin first appointed Putin prime minister in 1999, while Bill was still president, and they had remained in contact ever since. In January 2009, while at the World Economic Forum in Davos, Bill had gone to Putin's private party at the Sheraton, where he was greeted by the Russian leader as "our good friend" before cheering him with vodka shots. The pair then headed off to a private room where they "talked deep into the night."[73] In September 2013, as the Ukrainian crisis built, Clinton offered what the Russian news agency RIA Novosti called "Rare U.S. Praise for Putin" on CNN. Clinton described the Russian leader as "very smart" and "brutally blunt." When he was asked by CNN's Piers Morgan if Putin ever reneged on a deal, Clinton responded: "He did not. He kept his word on all the deals we made."[74]

Remember, for the Russian purchase of Uranium One to go through, it required approval by CFIUS, of which Hillary was a member. "We have provided all relevant information requested in the U.S., and elsewhere and we expect approval in due time," said spokesman Dmitry Shulga.[75]

Hillary Clinton had long had a reputation as a CFIUS hawk, opposing the sale of US strategic assets to foreign governments. She had also been a consistent critic of lax reviews by that body in the past. After a Bush administration CFIUS review approved the 2005 purchase of several ports in the United States by the sovereign wealth fund of the United Arab Emirates, then senator Clinton was quick to denounce it. When the Senate Armed Services Committee held hearings on the matter in early 2006, Hillary promptly assumed the role of chief prosecutor. She not only argued that the CFIUS decision was wrong, she condemned administration officials for failing to consider the national security implications of the ports deal. She was particularly concerned because the deal involved not just a foreign company, but a foreign government. "For many of us," she said, "there is a significant difference between a private company and a foreign government entity."[76]

In 2007 Hillary led the charge to pass legislation to significantly strengthen CFIUS. And during her 2008 presidential bid, it was Hillary alone among the major candidates from either party who raised the case for strengthening CFIUS as an important way to protect America's economic sovereignty and national security. Her presidential campaign rightly described her as "an outspoken proponent of strengthening CFIUS."[77]

When she became secretary of state, Hillary Clinton continued to support a robust CFIUS and led efforts by the panel to block Chinese companies from buying a mining business, a fiber-optic company, and even a wind farm in Oregon.[78]

But however hawkish Hillary might have been on other deals, this one sailed through. The Russian purchase of Uranium One was approved by CFIUS on October 22, 2010. Hillary's opposition would have been enough under CFIUS rules to have the decision on the transaction kicked up to the president. That never happened.

The result: Uranium One and half of projected American uranium production were transferred to a private company controlled in turn by the Russian State Nuclear Agency. Strangely enough, when Uranium One requested approval from CFIUS by the federal government, Ian Telfer, a major Clinton Foundation donor, was chairman of the board, a position he continues to hold.

In 2010, in reporting to the US government, Russian officials said they were looking to buy just slightly more than 50 percent of the company and promised "not [to] increase its share in Uranium One, Inc."[79] But by the beginning of 2013, the Russian government moved to buy out the company's other shareholders entirely. Today it owns the company outright.[80]

The Russian purchase of a large share of America's uranium assets raised serious national security concerns for precisely the same reasons Hillary had condemned previous deals. A foreign government would now have direct control over a very valuable commodity; the Russian government would reap hundreds of millions of dollars in revenues every year; and it would allow the Russian government to use Uranium One assets to honor supply contracts with US reactors while freeing up other uranium assets to send to more dangerous regions of the world—where Russia was already known to be involved. Lawmakers in Washington had raised these concerns.

Still, despite a long record of publicly opposing such deals, Hillary didn't object. Why the apparent reversal? Could it be because shareholders involved in the transactions had transferred approximately $145 million to the Clinton Foundation or its initiatives? Or because her husband had profited from lucrative speaking deals arranged by companies associated with those who stood to profit from the deal? Could it be because Bill—and possibly she herself—had quietly helped build the uranium assets for the company to begin with? These questions can only be answered by Hillary herself. What is clear is that based on State Department ethics documents, she never revealed these transactions to her colleagues, the Obama White House, or to Capitol Hill.

For Moscow, the approval was a major victory. Kiriyenko, the head of Rosatom, told Russian president Dmitry Medvedev that the United States would now become "a key market" for Rosatom.[81] Because Uranium One also owned the rights to those large mines in Kazakhstan, uranium flows to Russia increased. As one Uranium One official put it in a corporate presentation, the company's operations "facilitate substantial exports of uranium to Russia."[82]

In 2013 Rosatom announced plans to take 100 percent control of Uranium One. It didn't even bother to ask the Obama administration for approval this time, because the transaction "involved the same parties" and the move did not technically "change the corporate structure of Uranium One."[83]

Pravda hailed the move with an over-the-top headline: "RUSSIAN NUCLEAR ENERGY CONQUERS THE

WORLD." Taking full control of Uranium One would "consolidate control over uranium assets in the former Soviet Union and pave the way for the expansion of access to resources in Australia and South Africa."[84] The Russian takeover of Uranium One yielded shareholders a premium price. Rosatom offered Telfer and other shareholders a 32 percent premium on the share price, yielding them millions.[85]

In the fall of 2013 Rosatom passed operational control of the Bushehr nuclear reactor to Iran, and in September Vladimir Putin and Iranian president Hassan Rouhani announced that "Tehran and Moscow will cooperate in the future construction of a second nuclear power plant at Bushehr," adding that "construction work is to start soon."[86]

Meanwhile, Uranium One made an audacious bid to mine for uranium on state land in Arizona, near the Grand Canyon. Using a shell corporation called Wate Mining, it proposed accessing the site through Navajo Nation lands. The company apparently hoped that the Navajo Nation wouldn't notice who controlled the company, which was obscured on government forms. "The fact that the applicant failed to fully disclose ownership information does not sit well," said the Navajo Nation Department of Justice.[87] Plans for the mine have been suspended in light of protests.[88]

Global deals involving the transfer of funds and nuclear technology were not limited to Russia. Another troubling transaction that occurred during the same period, while Hillary was in the Senate, involved characters representing India whose political interests appear to have been advanced by their friendship with the Clintons—accompanied in turn by large donations and payments.

Chapter 4
Indian Nukes

In May 1998 the government of India shook the world. With a series of five underground nuclear tests, the government set off a corresponding series of political explosions.

Code-named Operation Shakti (the word means "strength" in Sanskrit), the 58th Engineer Regiment of the Indian Army took special measures to ensure that test preparations went undetected by the United States. With its bold act, India, in the words of one of the country's leading commentators, "acquired de facto nuclear weapon status."[1]

For President Bill Clinton, the tests were a surprise slap in the face. Preventing the spread of nuclear weapons and technologies had been a Clinton administration priority. Early in his presidency he had launched "a personal initiative to halt, roll back and eliminate the nuclear [programs] of both India and Pakistan."[2] The tests were an embarrassing public dismissal of these efforts.

Clinton was livid. He erupted in a "volcanic fit" when he heard the news, according to foreign policy adviser and longtime friend Strobe Talbott.[3] Clinton took the tests as a personal affront, as well as a threat to the nuclear nonproliferation and test ban treaties he was pushing. He responded with "an intense effort to threaten international isolation" unless India signed the test ban treaty and "took other steps to reduce nuclear dangers."[4]

The nonproliferation treaty (NPT) entered into force in 1970 and recognized five countries as nuclear powers: the United States, the Soviet Union, Great Britain, France, and China. The NPT was designed to prevent any other country from attaining nuclear weapon status. If a country signed the treaty, it would be given the benefit of access to peaceful nuclear technology.

Clinton chose to denounce India's nuclear tests with Chinese president Jiang Zemin at his side. (This was particularly offensive to India, which considered Beijing a regional rival.) He also lent American support to United Nations Resolution 1172, which called on India to stop testing and required them to become parties to the NPT. But most importantly, Clinton imposed a series of restrictions on the export of US nuclear technologies to India with the express purpose of "keeping the lid on Indian nuclear and ballistic-missile technology."[5]

Clinton's India sanctions were motivated by a strong belief in the importance of the NPT. Bill and Hillary Clinton have vigorously supported enforcing and extending the treaty. Both as first lady and then as a US senator, Hillary shared her husband's fervent support for the NPT and the test ban treaty.[6] In a 2007 article in Foreign Affairs, then senator Clinton declared, "As President, I will support efforts to supplement the Nuclear Nonproliferation Treaty."[7] Throughout the 2008 presidential campaign and during her confirmation as secretary of state, she voiced continued support for staunch nonproliferation efforts. "The Non-Proliferation Treaty is the cornerstone of the nonproliferation regime, and the United States must exercise the leadership needed to shore up the regime," she said during her Senate confirmation hearings. As secretary of state she promised that the administration would "place great importance on strengthening the NPT and the nonproliferation regime in general . . . we must reinvigorate our commitment to the Nuclear

Non-Proliferation Treaty (NPT) in order to prevent the spread of nuclear weapons and the potential for nuclear terrorism."[8]

India had never signed the nonproliferation treaty and was not about to. But as the Clinton administration passed and the Bush administration took office in January 2001, New Delhi began thinking about getting the sanctions lifted. Hoping to make that happen they hired expensive lobbyists and encouraged Indians in the United States to build rapport with both political parties. There were also a series of large payments made at pivotal moments to the Clinton machine. Some of these payments came in the form of lucrative speeches, paid for by Indian entities with a direct interest in having the sanctions lifted. Others came in the form of donations to both Hillary's Senate campaigns and her presidential bid, by those who could legally do so. But mostly, they came as millions in donations to the Clinton Foundation.

Tracing the real source of some of those millions would prove impossible, but their effect on the Clintons' policy toward India seems apparent. In the end, both Bill, who initially imposed the sanctions against the Indian government, and Hillary, who supported that policy, played a vital role in getting them lifted. Shortly after the legislation passed, the Indian government granted one of its most prestigious civilian awards to a close Clinton family friend precisely because, as they saw it, he got Hillary to support the legislation.

Sant Chatwal might not strike one as a consummate political insider. A Sikh from India with piercing brown eyes, Chatwal arrived in the United States in 1975 by way of Ethiopia and Canada. Earlier in his life, Chatwal served in the Indian military as a jet pilot. In the United States he set about building a commercial empire of Indian restaurants and hotels, primarily in New York City. First came the Bombay Palace restaurant chain, followed by the luxurious Hampshire Hotels. Chatwal is a study in contrasts—a globe-trotting businessman with celebrity friends and high-level political connections, yet an earthy Punjabi who still enjoys eating *sarson ka saag*. Even after more than thirty years in the United States, he remained a staunch Indian patriot, and still refers to India as "my motherland."

His deep friendship with the Clintons began with a mutual love for Indian cuisine. Bill first tasted Indian food at a political fundraiser held at Chatwal's New York City restaurant, the Bombay Palace.[9] But, as we will see, some savory financial transfers helped, too.

Chatwal has always been exceedingly blunt about how and why he steered money in an effort to influence events in Washington. "I used to spend money on senators and congressmen," said Chatwal. While in 1988 that "investment" had been in Michael Dukakis, Chatwal "next started betting on various presidents" and "happened to click with Clinton."[10] The former governor of Arkansas was exceedingly thankful. Chatwal says Clinton offered him whatever post he wanted once he was elected president, but Chatwal said he simply wanted closer US-Indian relations. When Hillary ran for the Senate in 2000, Chatwal became one of her largest soft-money donors.[11]

By the time Bill left the Oval Office in 2001, Chatwal was firmly in the Clintons' inner circle. Bill appointed him a trustee of the Clinton Foundation, an appointment reserved only for longtime friends and large financial benefactors. Chatwal had lavished money on the Clintons, including hundreds of thousands in soft-money donations and millions in campaign funds raised, and he continued his largesse once Bill was a private citizen. Chatwal helped arrange for millions of dollars in lucrative speaking fees and steered additional millions to the Clinton Foundation.[12] When Hillary ran for the Democratic presidential nomination in 2007, he was cochair of her presidential exploratory committee. He even received that most prized of gifts in the Clinton universe: an invitation to attend Chelsea's wedding.

Sant Chatwal's son Vikram also became a Clinton benefactor. Widely known for his partying ways, Vikram became Hillary's 2008 campaign bundler.[13] Tooling around New York in an Aston Martin, he was known to run up large bar tabs and date everyone from Lindsay Lohan to various supermodels. Like his father a committed Sikh, he was known around town as the "Turban Cowboy."

Vikram considers the Clintons close friends. According to the *New York Observer*, " 'I know him [Bill Clinton] very well,' he said of the former President. He added that the two men have often sat down and talked about books and Gandhi, as well as, he said, 'women and models I've dated. He, like any man in the world, appreciates beauty.' "[14]

When Vikram got married in India in 2006, Bill Clinton attended the wedding. Guests "were welcomed by dancing eunuchs, elephants painted entirely white and whitewashed men wearing angel wings on white horses."[15] The Clintons also attended Sant Chatwal's other son's wedding, a more calm affair at Tavern on the Green in New York in 2002.

Perhaps not surprisingly, Sant Chatwal has a history of legal trouble involving financial transactions and has declared bankruptcy on at least one occasion. In 1995 he came under a cloud of legal suspicion concerning the bilking of millions from Indian banks. In the United States he was chased by the IRS and the New York State government for $30 million in unpaid taxes.[16] In a visit to India with Clinton in May 2001, Chatwal was arrested and charged with defrauding the New York City branch of the Bank of India out of $9 million he borrowed in 1994. "He posted bail equivalent to $32,000, then fled India, boarding a flight to Vienna, despite an attempt by authorities to detain him" reported the *New York Daily News*.[17]

In 1997 the Federal Deposit Insurance Corporation (FDIC) "sued Chatwal over his role as a director and a guarantor of unpaid loans at the failed First New York Bank for Business," the *Washington Post* reported. Regulators were frustrated that Chatwal claimed he couldn't repay the money (reported to be "in excess of $12 million"), despite the fact that he continued to live in a New York penthouse worth millions of dollars.[18]

Three years later, with no settlement on the horizon, Chatwal entertained guests in his lavish penthouse for Hillary's Senate campaign, raising $500,000.[19] On December 18, 2000, just a few months after the fundraiser (while the Clintons were still in the White House), the FDIC "abruptly settled" the case against Chatwal, according to the *Washington Post*, allowing him to pay a mere $125,000 and walk away.

The Chatwals undoubtedly enjoyed the perks and access that came with contributing and raising money for politicians like the Clintons. But what Sant Chatwal wanted for all that money extended far beyond the ordinary transactions that take place in Washington. He wanted to influence American policy toward India, particularly as it related to the sensitive area of nuclear technology. He openly admitted that he "spent tons of money, time and effort to make sure that the [Indian-US] nuclear deal goes through."[20] Some of that money was spent in India, where, according to a leaked diplomatic cable between the US embassy in Delhi and the US State Department, at least two ministers and several members of parliament were claimed to have been paid off, with reports of "two chests containing cash" ready for use as "pay-offs" to win support for the Indian-US nuke deal. Chatwal was alleged to be involved, but he maintains the allegation is baseless.[21] What we do know is that millions were spent on cultivating the relationship with the Clintons, who not only received money directly through lucrative speaking deals, but also reaped millions in donations to the Clinton Foundation.

On July 18, 2005, President George W. Bush and visiting Indian prime minister Manmohan Singh signed a letter of intent at the White House to allow India access to US nuclear technology. The agreement was part of a Bush administration policy to work closely with India to serve as a counterbalance to China. But the agreement required Congress to amend US law and make a special exception for India.

The plan met immediate criticism on Capitol Hill. Democrats and Republicans both argued it would lead to greater nuclear proliferation by rewarding a country that had violated the NPT. Remarkably silent during this debate was Hillary Clinton, who not only sat on the Senate Armed Services Committee, but was also a senior member of the Subcommittee on Emerging Threats and Capabilities, which dealt specifically with nuclear proliferation issues.

In September 2005 Bill Clinton flew on Frank Giustra's plane from Uzbekistan to Lucknow, India. The capital city of the state of Uttar Pradesh, Lucknow was not Mumbai or any of India's other cosmopolitan cities. Clinton's visit set off an intense flurry of local interest and activity. The road from the airport to his hotel was "freshly tarred" for his arrival and party workers hung banners along the road praising Clinton's visit. Along for the ride were Giustra, Doug Band, fundraiser Tim Phillips, and Sant Chatwal, who had made the arrangements.[22]

Clinton and his companions checked into the Taj, a palatial hotel with graceful pillars on the banks of the Gomti River in the heart of the city's business district. Bill's six-person delegation had two entire floors to themselves and enjoyed a large feast with evening entertainment. Before the festivities began, Clinton joined Chatwal for a private meeting where he was introduced to an obscure member of the Indian parliament named Amar Singh.[23]

Amar Singh has an easy swagger and a broad grin, marking a flamboyant manner and a combative attitude that has suited him well in the sharp-elbowed world of Indian politics. (He once got into a fistfight on the floor of the Indian parliament.) Heavyset, with thick glasses and thinning hair, Singh has another notable quality. His "access to big money is . . . legendary," according to the Indian press.[24]

Singh would be implicated in a number of financial and vote-buying scandals in Indian politics. In 2011 he was indicted on charges that he bought votes in parliament to secure the nuclear deal.[25] A trial was never held.

What Singh discussed with Clinton and Chatwal was never made public. They met for about an hour, but in that short span of time a close collaboration and friendship between the Indian politico and both of the Clintons began.

After the meeting, the three men headed off for a big bash at the state chief minister's bungalow. According to reports, the "bullet proof dining hall" was outfitted with twenty-six air conditioners and the event included 150 members of India's elite—including Bollywood stars, industrialists, and politicians—who dined on delicacies while enjoying live performances.[26] There were dancers and music from jazz fusion to a song titled "Sexy Rocksy Chicago Girl."[27]

Despite having only just met, Clinton and Singh offered immediate and enthusiastic praise for one another. Singh took to the podium to praise Clinton for his "immense love for India" and proposed that he be granted Indian citizenship.[28] Clinton then rose and talked about his love for India and addressed the host as "friend Amar Singh." The former president then publicly extended an invitation for Singh to attend the Clinton Global Initiative (CGI) in New York in a few days as his guest.

Clinton spent fifteen hours in Lucknow and then left. Opposition parties denounced the lavish party and criticized Singh and state officials for, in the words of one Indian newspaper, "hosting a mega bash for former U.S. President Bill Clinton at a time when hundreds were dying in the State due to Japanese encephalitis."[29] Singh was openly triumphant, explaining to the media how Clinton's visit helped his party "score over its rivals."[30]

Clinton's visit was a major coup for Singh. Asked later how he managed to get Clinton to visit his town, Singh said, "I would say he is a charming man and very kind to lesser mortals like me. I don't see any other reason for him to take this trouble."[31]

Following their brief meeting Singh was immediately—and mysteriously—elevated in Clinton World. Singh took Bill Clinton up on his invitation to attend CGI in New York. The massive gabfest was attended by thousands of politicians, entrepreneurs, and so-called deep thinkers. During the Cold War, the Soviet hierarchy was reflected in its arrangement on Lenin's Tomb during the annual May Day parade. In the Clinton universe, the hierarchy was reflected in the seating chart at CGI; it allowed people to figure out who was in and out of the Clinton orbit. In 2005 Singh not only attended the Global Initiative, he was granted a place at the head table. It was a remarkable elevation for a man who was in all other respects a complete unknown. As one Indian-American publication put it when they interviewed him after the Initiative meeting, Singh "could not explain why the Clintons gave him space at the head table." He told them,

If they let me to sit on the head table, the same question was asked to me by the prime minister of

Mauritius—which country are you heading? I said I belong to Uttar Pradesh and am a humble political worker. They were also astonished. . . . So, I don't know what it is. [Bill] Clinton is the best person to answer this question why he gave me that kind of honor.[32]

Following the Clinton confab, Singh had a private dinner with the Clintons at their home in New York. When asked, Singh refused to say who else was at the dinner. During the visit Singh said he cultivated his relationship with Hillary Clinton. "I met Madame Clinton and in spite of her busy schedule, she was kind enough to give me considerable amount of time on one-on-one meeting," said Singh.[33] (Apparently he came bearing gifts; he gave the senator from New York perfume oils in a Taj Mahal presentation case.) Singh's relationship with the Clintons also drew the interest of the Indian media, which was well aware of his antics, and noted that he "seems to dote on the Clintons."[34]

In 2006 a bill was introduced in Congress called the Henry J. Hyde United States–India Peaceful Atomic Energy Cooperation Act of 2006. Its purpose: to finalize an agreement that would gradually lift restrictions on nuclear trade with India. Hillary was both a senior member of the Senate Armed Services Committee and a cochair of the Senate's India Caucus, which a group of senators formed to work together with Indian government officials to improve US-India ties. But she showed no immediate favor for the Hyde Act as it started to make its way through Congress. The *Times of India* noted in 2006 that "India could be looking at the possibility of a Democrat presidency, Hillary Clinton, Obama, or anyone else—friends of India doubtless, but perhaps opponents of the nuclear deal."[35]

Hillary supported a series of amendments that would impose stricter terms on the Indian government. These included three amendments offered by Senators Barbara Boxer, Byron Dorgan, and Russell Feingold. One was a "killer amendment" that would have effectively gutted the bill by capping India's fissile production. But that amendment failed. The initial legislation passed, but there would be additional legislation that would need to be signed, and Hillary's role was central in getting that approved. Hillary was still a reluctant and questionable supporter of the bill, prompting a headline in the Indian American media that the community was "upset" with her stance on the issue.[36] As the *New York Times* reported, it was Hillary "whose support is viewed by Indian-American leaders as crucial to winning broader Democratic backing for the plan."[37]

Up to this point the Clinton Foundation had experienced only limited public success in securing contributions from Indians. But now, those with a keen interest in seeing the nuclear deal approved began steering money to the Clintons.

Indian industrialists and elites, who could not contribute to Hillary's political campaigns, much less vote for her, started making highly publicized appearances at Clinton campaign fundraising events. In June 2007 Chatwal put together a dinner for Clinton featuring Indian billionaires Srichand Hinduja and Lakshmi Mittal. The fundraisers targeted Indians who were now American citizens or who had permanent status. "They [Hinduja and Mittal] can't give money," noted Chatwal. "It's to bring a little attraction." The attraction of course was for Indians in the United States who could donate, and who might want to do business with these industrialists.[38] These introductions are worth a great deal to those in a position to exploit them.

Hinduja and Mittal couldn't donate to Hillary's presidential campaign, but they could and did write large checks to the Clinton Foundation. (Mittal contributed between $1 million and $5 million.) Indeed, India quickly became a rich vein of Clinton Foundation support. In Washington, the Confederation of Indian Industry hired lobbyists to push for a nuclear deal;

at the same time, they sent the Clinton Foundation a check for between $1 million and $5 million.[39] (These donations were revealed only after Hillary's nomination as secretary of state, and while the foundation is no longer required to disclose donors since she left office, once the nuclear deal was sealed such donors appeared to cease their generosity.) The Hindustan Construction chairman and managing partner, Ajit Gulabchand, donated money while in New York in late September 2007.[40] Today Hindustan Construction is involved in several nuclear-power construction projects in India. And there were mysterious donations never really accounted for—as we will see.

By the summer of 2008 Hillary's presidential bid had failed and the United States Nuclear Cooperation Approval Nonproliferation Enhancement Act (H.R. 7081)—a bill finalizing the export of nuclear technologies to India—required action in the US Senate. Hillary had endured a bruising presidential nomination fight against Senate colleague Barack Obama, who would now become the Democratic standard-bearer. But when it came to the nuclear deal, Indian officials still looked to Hillary. According to Professor Vijay Prashad of Trinity College in Connecticut, "Obama's caution about the deal put the fear of failure through elite circles in New Delhi, and so pressure mounted to get Washington to act. Senator Hillary Clinton's nod was considered to be essential."[41]

Notably enough, the most important Clinton advisers on nuclear proliferation matters issued blistering criticisms of the nuclear deal. Strobe Talbott, a long-time friend of both Bill and Hillary who had served in the State Department during Bill's presidency, wrote scathingly that with the terms of the agreement, "the [Bush] administration granted India almost all the privileges of an NPT member, especially with regard to helping India develop its civilian nuclear power industry. . . . In return, the United States (and the world) received nothing in the form of concrete Indian steps toward nuclear restraint in its military programs." The deal was "really a step toward a breakdown in the international nonproliferation regime."[42]

Robert Einhorn, Hillary's adviser on nuclear proliferation during the 2008 presidential bid, was also withering in his criticisms of the deal, which he strongly opposed. Einhorn had also served in the State Department during Bill's presidency, and Hillary would tap him in 2009 to handle proliferation issues during her tenure as secretary of state. Einhorn called the deal "a radical departure from longstanding legal obligations and policies that precluded nuclear cooperation with states not party to the Nonproliferation Treaty."[43]

In short, the agreement severely threatened the NPT that Bill and Hillary themselves had strongly supported. As the *Times of India* put it, "Why is this deal important? Because for the first time, someone has decided to let India have its cake and eat it too. You stay out of the NPT, keep your weapons, refuse full scope safeguards, and yet get to conduct nuclear commerce in a system that is dead against such a formulation. That's the bottom line of this deal."[44]

It was for this reason that additional longtime Clinton friends and allies, like Congresswoman Ellen Tauscher, also opposed the 2008 nuclear deal. In an apocalyptic *New York Times* op-ed piece, Tauscher warned that "the Nuclear Nonproliferation Treaty—for 50 years, the bulwark against the spread of nuclear weapons—would be shredded and India's yearly nuclear weapons production capability would likely increase from 7 bombs to 40 or 50." She continued: "The Indian nuclear deal threatens international security not only by undermining our nuclear rules, but also by expanding India's nuclear weapons program. That's because every pound of uranium that India is allowed to import for its power reactors frees up a pound of uranium for its bomb program."[45]

A few months after her piece, Tauscher was tapped by Hillary to serve as her under secretary of state for arms control and international security at the State Department.[46]

Back in 2008 Bill was paid $150,000 to give a satellite video address to the India Today Group, a media conglomerate whose chairman, Aroon Purie, was strongly in favor of the nuclear deal.[47] According to the Clintons' financial disclosures, required by Senate ethics rules, Bill had not given a paid speech in India for more than five years. But as the Indian nuclear deal vote loomed, he sat down in his Harlem office and made comments about world events to a live audience of Indian corporate and government officials gathered at the Taj Palace Hotel in New Delhi.[48]

Clinton discussed several subjects, including the looming US-Indian nuclear deal, and reassured the audience that while "some Democrats have some questions about the agreement . . . the new government tends to honor agreements of the previous one." In other words, if the deal was approved in Congress in March 2008, the next president, whether Republican or Democrat, would likely honor the agreement.

As the drive to get the Clintons on board mounted, Sant Chatwal helped organize one of Bill's biggest public speaking paydays, arranging for him to receive $450,000 to speak at a London charity event. The speech, noted the *Chicago Tribune*, brought him

$170,000 more than he "charged for ordinary overseas for-profit appearances."[49]

Apparently the father of the hostess was surprised by how much Bill was paid. "If we had been charged less, we could have given a bit more" to charity, he said. Bill's fee accounted for 30 percent of the $1.5 million raised at the event for global relief efforts.[50]

In late September 2008, with the fate of H.R. 7081 still very much in question, Indian prime minister Manmohan Singh arrived in New York and met with a core group to discuss the fate of the nuclear cooperation deal. Huddled together in the Kennedy Rooms at the Palace Hotel, Manmohan Singh plotted strategy with Chatwal, Amar Singh, and others.[51]

Hillary had not been a supporter of the bill; indeed, her closest aides were all publicly opposed to it. But in September 2008, as the bill's fate hung in the balance, Amar Singh sat down for a two-hour dinner in Washington with Hillary. Opposition to the bill had come primarily from Democrats. Hillary had supported the "killer amendment" two years earlier. It was even possible that the Senate might not vote on the bill. Yet in the days following, Singh expressed confidence based on what he heard from Hillary that the deal would go through.[52]

Having grown accustomed to the deal-making and influence-buying ways of the Indian parliament, Singh was open with the Indian media about what transpired in New York. Hillary Clinton probably considered herself fortunate that his comments were not reported in the American media. According to Singh, Hillary reassured him that Democrats would not hinder the passage of the India-US civil nuclear agreement through the US Congress.[53] When Indian journalist Aziz Haniffa asked if Senator Clinton "has promised and pledged to give all the support and try to pass [the deal] through in the Congress," he said yes, adding, "because of the Clintons I am close to the Democrats."[54]

Five Democratic senators opposed to the bill—Robert Byrd, Jeff Bingaman, Daniel Akaka, Russ Feingold, and Tom Harkin—blocked a vote. Amendments like those introduced in 2006, which Hillary had voted for, were reintroduced. This time, however, according to Indian activists who wanted to force a vote, Hillary's office was "working closely" with them.[55]

The vote was called, and the bill was passed. "The passage by the United States Senate was the last step in securing this historic accord," as one of the leaders in the effort to secure the deal put it. He even called it "the greatest moment in Indian-American political history."[56]

In the end, Hillary pushed for the passage of the Indian nuclear deal, despite the public opposition of her closest advisers and the fact that it was a clear reversal of her previous policy positions. As secretary of state, she would talk about her commitment to creating a "21st century version of the NPT," while also insisting that "the NPT will neither be altered nor replaced." But that is precisely what her efforts on behalf of the Indian nuclear deal had done.

Weeks after the vote, Hillary was nominated to be secretary of state by the newly elected Barack Obama. Part of the agreement struck with the Obama transition team was a requirement that the Clinton Foundation reveal the names of those who had donated money to the Foundation in the past and going forward.

One of those listed was Amar Singh, the Indian politician who had risen so quickly in Clinton World. The mention of his name got scant attention in US media, but those in India who tracked politics took immediate notice. The Clinton Foundation revealed that Singh had given between $1 million and $5 million. But there was a slight problem: based on Indian government financial disclosures, Singh's net worth was approximately $5 million. If true, that meant Singh had given between 20 and 100 percent of his entire net worth to the Clinton Foundation!

When the *Times of India* asked Singh about the huge donation, he shrugged it off. "I have nothing to say," he told them. "I won't deny anything." Pressed further, Singh responded cryptically that "the payment could have been made by someone else on his behalf."[57]

The payment or contribution was revealed smack in the middle of a session of the Indian parliament. Members of the opposition parties were up in arms. They mocked Singh's alleged generosity. "He would be a saint or a mahatma to make such a gesture," said political observer Vishwanath Chaturvendi.[58] A core group of senior government ministers, concerned about the appearance of the payment or contribution, called Singh in to explain. Singh apparently told them he had not given the money "and no cheque could be traced to him." When asked why he was listed as a donor, he said "maybe" it was because he had facilitated the payment and therefore it "erroneously" appeared in the records. Singh never explained where the money came from. Government ministers were reportedly concerned that the whole episode might result in a criminal inquiry because of the "insinuation that Amar could have swung the Democrats' support for the Indo-U.S. nuclear deal as a quid pro quo."[59]

Members of Singh's political party denied that the money came from them. "The party has not donated any such money," declared Mohan Singh, a member of parliament (and no relation).[60]

In New York, the Clintons were stone quiet. Hillary was preparing for the confirmation hearings and Bill hadn't said anything. Amar Singh refused to give more interviews about the matter.

One of Singh's colleagues offered an explanation: the politician put wealthy friends in touch with the Clintons and was mistakenly given the credit: "Some of them may have mentioned Singh's name while making contributions which found its way into the records."[61] But this seems highly unlikely. Donations to the foundation would come via wire transfer or check—presumably not in cash. So the foundation likely would have known where the funds came from. Yet the Clinton Foundation has never explained their origin. Nor has it ever been determined who precisely donated the money. While donors connected to the Russian uranium deal such as Ian Telfer's Fernwood Foundation never had their donations revealed, in this case the donation was revealed but didn't appear to be accurate as to the true source of the funds.

What is known is that the Indian government rewarded many of those who helped clinch the deal and got the Clintons to support it. Securing the nuclear deal was a profound victory for elements in India who saw it as an important step forward in becoming a nuclear power. When the bill passed the Senate on October 2, it was Chatwal who made the first call to the Indian prime minister with the "fantastic" news.

For his diligent work in securing passage of the bill, in early 2010 Sant Chatwal was presented by the Indian government with the Padma Bhushan Award, one of the country's most prestigious civilian honors. "He played an important role in getting Hillary Clinton to support the nuclear deal," said Sanjaya Baru, who was a media adviser to the Indian prime minister. "He is close to the Clintons. That is why he got the Padma [Bhushan] award."[62]

Chatwal explained that he had worked hard to secure the deal. In a series of Indian media interviews, Chatwal noted that Hillary had changed her position on the issue and boasted about the role he played. At first, back in 2006, Chatwal said, "Even my close friend Hillary Clinton was not in favor of the deal then."[63] But then he began working with her: "But when I put the whole package together, she also came on board." He continued, "In politics nothing comes free. You have to write cheques in the American political system," Chatwal said. "I know the system. I had to work very hard. So I did as much as I could."[64] In another interview he bluntly explained, "It took me four years and millions of dollars, which I paid out of my own pocket. I am very proud of that because I love my motherland."[65]

No one appears to have asked them about these candid remarks.

In September 2011 Amar Singh was arrested under the Prevention of Corruption Act for bribing three members of parliament during a crucial 2008 vote related to the Indian nuclear deal. In July of that year the Left Party had pulled out of the ruling coalition over the nuclear deal, which it strongly opposed. The ruling coalition, which included Singh's party, needed to prove it had enough votes to govern. On July 22, hours before the trust vote, large rolls of cash had allegedly been doled out by Singh, according to Indian authorities. Singh was later arrested and placed in Tihar Jail, one of the largest prison complexes in the world. While no trial was ever held, he was expelled from his political party and has retired from politics, at least for now.[66]

In April 2013 Vikram Chatwal, the Turban Cowboy, was arrested on heroin and cocaine charges. Security staff at the Fort Lauderdale, Florida, airport reportedly found half a gram of cocaine and six grams of heroin in his underwear.[67]

On April 17, 2014, Sant Chatwal stood in the Federal District Courthouse in Brooklyn and pleaded guilty to having "funneled more than $180,000 in illegal contributions between 2007 and 2011 to three federal candidates," including Hillary Clinton. He also pled guilty to witness tampering.[68] Prosecutors alleged that Chatwal "used his employees, business associates, and contractors who performed work on his hotels . . . to solicit campaign contributions on Chatwal's behalf in support of various candidates for federal office and PACs, collect these contributions, and pay reimbursements for these contributions, in violation of the Election Act."[69]

During the course of the federal investigation, FBI agents recorded Chatwal discussing the flow of money to politicians. He said without the cash, "nobody will even talk to you." He added, "that's the only way to buy them."[70]

Chatwal also pleaded guilty to interfering with a grand jury investigation by telling a witness that "he and his family should not talk to FBI or IRS agents," or if they did to lie about it. "Never, never" admit to reimbursements, he told them. Later, he allegedly told the person, "cash has no proof."[71]

While those who transferred cash in an effort to secure the nuclear deal have all faced legal jeopardy for one reason or another, the recipients of those transfers have moved on. The Clintons have never explained who donated the millions the foundation attributed to Amar Singh. And they have never discussed the role

Sant Chatwal and his flow of money might have played in getting Hillary to change her views on the nuclear deal. Indeed, although Chatwal was a longtime member of the Clinton Foundation board of trustees, since his admission of guilt the foundation has erased any mention of him from the Clinton Foundation website.[72]

Chapter 5
The Clinton Blur (I)

BILL AND HILLARY'S GLOBAL NEXUS OF
PHILANTHROPY, POWER, AND PROFIT

O n a beautiful evening in October 2011 the Clinton Foundation held an elaborate gala at the Hollywood Bowl in Los Angeles called "A Decade of Difference." The night's entertainment featured "socially responsible artists in music, film, and television" brought together to "celebrate the work and impact of President Clinton." A company called Control Room, which modestly bills itself as "the world's leading producer of massive global events," put the events together.[1]

Lady Gaga sang a song. Looking over at Bill, she said "I just love you and your hot wife." She praised the Clintons and promised the crowd, "Tonight, I thought we'd get caught up in a little Bill romance." She then proceeded to belt out her hit "Bad Romance," but made it Clinton specific.[2]

The Clinton Foundation is not your traditional charity. A traditional charity doesn't have a globe-trotting ex-president, an ex–secretary of state, and their daughter running the show. But for all the benefits that derive from such star power, the real problem is delineating where the Clinton political machine and moneymaking ventures end and where their charity begins.

The stated purpose of the Clinton Foundation is to "strengthen the capacity of people throughout the world to meet the challenges of global interdependence." It was founded in 2001 and boasts a staff of 350. Out of the foundation springs a hydra of projects including the Clinton Health Access Initiative, Clinton Climate Initiative, the Clinton Giustra Sustainable Growth Initiative (CGSGI), and Clinton Hunter Initiative.

But while the window-display causes of the Clinton Foundation, such as alleviating AIDS suffering, preventing obesity, and promoting economic growth in the developing world, are commendable, and while the foundation has done some legitimately good work, the moral authority of these works seems to provide a screen and pretext for a storehouse of private profit and promotion.

Some might argue that since the Clinton Foundation is a public charity, the flow of funds—even from questionable foreign sources seeking favors—is not really such a big deal. After all, the funds go to help people and the Clintons don't directly profit from the money that gets raised. But it is a big deal, at least according to federal law. If the donors are giving money to the Clintons to influence them, it should still be considered a bribe. American corporations that steer contributions to politically connected charities overseas in hopes of currying favor are violating the Foreign Corrupt Practices Act (FCPA). American corporations have been dinged for giving money to legitimate charities linked to politicians. In 2002, for example, the pharmaceutical company Schering Plough settled with the SEC over charges that it had violated the FCPA by donating $76,000 to a legitimate charity in Poland called the Chudow Castle Foundation. It's a well-respected charity, but that was besides the point. The SEC said the donation was made to influence a Polish government health official who sat on the charity's board. The company settled the claim with the feds for $500,000.[3]

As secretary of state, Hillary Clinton supported aggressive enforcement of the FCPA. When some business organizations tried to water down the law, she declared she was "unequivocally opposed to weakening" it. Hillary took a "strong stand when it comes to American companies bribing foreign officials."[4]

So the fact that the Clinton Foundation is a charity should not deter us from investigating and exploring the flow of foreign money into its coffers. Indeed, a charity deserves special attention because it is the perfect tool of influence. Foreign governments, corporations, and financiers who can't legally contribute to American political campaigns can write large checks to the Clinton Foundation in addition to paying high fees for speeches.

The Clintons frequently elide the distinction between their philanthropic work, their self-promotional and public relations efforts, and their moneymaking ventures. As *Fortune* puts it in an eyebrow-raising sentence, the Clinton Foundation is "a new turn in philanthropy, in which the lines between not-for-profits, politics, and business tend to blur."[5]

Bill Clinton has said as much himself. In describing the foundation's role, he positions it as a unique go-between for businesses, governments, and non-governmental organizations (NGOs). The result is the creation of what he calls "public-goods markets." He sees this as the wave of the future: "This is the kind of thing I believe will be a critical component of all philanthropic activity for the foreseeable future," he told one reporter. "I believe that in the years ahead, the organization and expansion of public-goods markets will become one of the most important areas of philanthropy, and will be an area where philanthropy sometimes blurs into strict private enterprise."[6]

In short, what the Clintons have attempted to do is create a crossroads for government, business, and NGOs, with the Clinton Foundation squarely in the middle. The Clinton Foundation calls this Bill's "convening power," his ability to bring together elites from business, politics, and the nonprofit world.[7]

There is nothing intrinsically wrong with this approach, which, if pursued in a scrupulous way, has the capacity to do a lot of good. The Clintons' ability to convene various public and private interests around a common cause or project does create leverage for getting things done in the global arena. But the blur also creates opportunity for moving a lot of money around with very little accountability. Being a convening power has another useful benefit: it means that the organization doesn't actually need to get its hands dirty. While there are plenty of photos of Bill, Hillary, or Chelsea holding sick children in Africa, the foundation that bears their name actually does very little hands-on humanitarian work. "When President Clinton's foundation was formed, the first thought was to run its own projects," says Harvard professor Rosabeth Moss Kanter. But then they came up with the convening-power model.

"What's brilliant is that President Clinton provides the platform and enlightening speakers, but other people do the actual work of change."[8]

This causes confusion about who is actually doing what. As relief work and humanitarian veteran Miles Wortman explains, "The Clinton Foundation 'partners' with other foundations in the provision of services. When the Gates Foundation, for example, provides revenue to the Clinton Foundation, and it in turn partners with the Gates Foundation in the provision of say, antiretroviral drugs, is this double accounting of activity?"

This approach positions the Clinton Foundation in a way a politician could especially love: with little direct responsibility, it is able to take credit for good results and avoid blame for bad ones.

Another important function of the Clinton Foundation appears to be employing longtime Clinton associates. Like any political machine, jobs must be provided to those who served the Clintons when in power and who may serve them again in the future. This may help to explain why the foundation's senior ranks are populated with so many former political aides and associates, as opposed to those with extensive experience in charitable work.

Ira Magaziner, who served the Clintons when Bill was in the White House—among other things, he was the author of Hillary's famously convoluted health care reform proposal—has played a central role in the foundation.[9] As he put it in 2009, "The biggest part of the Foundation includes four operating initiatives, accounting for about 90 percent of the Clinton Foundation budget, all of which I started and run."[10] These include the Clinton Health Access Initiative, which deals with matters related to HIV/AIDS around the world; the Alliance for a Healthier Generation, a domestic program focused on nutrition and health; the Clinton Hunter Initiative, which focuses on agriculture in Africa; and the Clinton Climate Initiative, which focuses on issues related to climate change. Even with structural changes in 2011 that diminished Magaziner's administrative control, he still plays a key role.

These Clinton Foundation initiatives are part and parcel of the Clinton Foundation apparatus. The CGSGI, for example, despite being ostensibly based in Canada, has an executive director based in New York City. An examination of CGSGI's financial records indicates that the bulk of the money it collects gets transferred to the Clinton Foundation itself. It largely functions as a pass through. Senior positions in the foundation have been filled by Clinton insiders like Bruce Lindsey, Bill's longtime friend and political adviser; John Podesta, who was Bill's chief of staff at the White House; Valerie Alexander, a senior communications adviser for Hillary's 2008 campaign; Amitabh Desai, former legislative aide to then senator Clinton; and Laura Graham, a deputy assistant in Bill's administration from 1995 to 2001.[11]

The chief development officer at the Clinton Foundation is Dennis Cheng, who previously served as national finance director and New York finance director for Hillary's run for the Democratic presidential nomination in 2007–2008. When Hillary became secretary of state, Cheng joined her at Foggy Bottom, where he served as the deputy chief of protocol of the United States. That gave him the ability to ensure that Clinton financial supporters were well represented in the pecking order when foreign heads of state made their official visits to Washington.[12]

The Clinton Foundation also hands out honorary titles such as "adviser" to businessmen and investors who are ostensibly involved in the activities of the foundation (and who are contributors). As we have already seen, investors operating in the developing world regularly use the title of "adviser to the Clinton Foundation" on their résumés. They travel with Bill when they visit developing countries in which the Clinton Foundation has activities and where the investors have or are seeking investments.

The Clinton Foundation board of directors (or board of trustees as it has sometimes been called) is largely made up of the Clintons and their closest political aides and advisers. The tightness of the board has raised alarm bells at places like the Better Business Bureau (BBB). In 2013 the BBB conducted a charity review of the Clinton Foundation and found that it failed to meet minimum standards of accountability and transparency. It dinged the organization on its management and financial controls and pointed out that, despite having a staff of 319, the board of directors at the time had only three board members, who did not actually review the performance of the CEO. The BBB also said that board members did not receive information about financial arrangements with outside fundraising firms and consultants.[13]

Similarly, Charity Navigator, which evaluates and ranks philanthropic groups, will not rank or grade the Clinton Foundation. The explanation? The foundation's "atypical business model" makes it difficult, if not impossible, to evaluate.[14]

The Clinton Foundation has added corporate executives or business investors to its board of trustees from time to time, especially if they are major contributors. One can only wonder how tight the screening process is, given that at least four Clinton Foundation trustees have either been charged or convicted of financial crimes including bribery and fraud.

Vinod Gupta, the founder and chairman of the database firm InfoUSA, was a major Clinton financial supporter who served as a foundation trustee. In 2008 he was charged with fraud by the Securities and Exchange Commission (SEC) for using company funds to support his luxurious lifestyle. He was alleged to have used more than $9.5 million in corporate funds to pay for personal jet travel, millions for his yacht, personal credit card expenses, and the cost of twenty cars. He settled with the SEC for $4 million.[15]

Company shareholders also filed suit against him for misuse of corporate funds, including paying Bill a $3 million consulting fee, and using corporate assets to fly the Clintons around. Gupta defended his relationship with the Clintons, saying that those payments and his relationship with the Clintons earned huge dividends for Infogroup. The company settled with shareholders to the tune of $13 million.[16]

Sant Chatwal, whom we met in the previous chapter, was another foundation trustee who has been in legal trouble over the years, including his conviction for illegal campaign financing, obstruction of justice, and other charges.[17]

Victor Dahdaleh, another trustee, was charged by the Serious Fraud Office (SFO) in Great Britain with paying more than 35 million pounds in bribes to executives in Bahrain to win contracts of more than 2 billion pounds. He has worked for the American aluminum company Alcoa as a "super-agent."[18] (The billionaire had his bail revoked in the case because he contacted prosecution witnesses.)[19] Dahdaleh was found not guilty after the SFO offered no evidence against Dahdaleh because a key witness, Bruce Hall, pleaded guilty to conspiracy to corrupt but refused to testify.[20] Alcoa ended up pleading guilty in the US case arising out of the transaction and settled with the US Justice Department for $384 million. Dahdaleh was not charged in the United States individually.[21]

Current Clinton Foundation board member and trustee Rolando Gonzalez Bunster has been named in a fraud case in the Dominican Republic involving his company InterEnergy. The charges were filed by the Dominican government's Anti-Corruption Alliance (ADOCCO).[22] In 2013 Bunster was charged along with officials of a government agency concerning alleged "ballooned" fees charged to the government. The company dismisses the charges as "baseless allegations."[23]

The flow of funds into the Clinton Foundation comes from a variety of sources. While the foundation boasts that it has hundreds of thousands of contributors, it relies heavily on a group of high-dollar donors to fund its operations. Since it reports contributions in ranges, not exact amounts, it is difficult to know precisely how dependent it is on those donors. But approximately 75 percent of its money has come from contributions of $1 million or more. And as we will see, many of these contributions came from foreign nationals who decided to give large gifts or make large pledges at times when they had business before the US government.

As we have seen, the Clinton Foundation failed to report multimillion-dollar contributions from foreign entities like Ian Telfer's Fernwood Foundation. Another Canadian mining investor whose contributions were never disclosed by the Clinton Foundation is Stephen Dattels. This mines-to-metals tycoon has donated millions of shares of stock to the foundation.

On June 8, 2009, Dattels donated two million shares of stock in his company Polo Resources—worth about $40,000 at the time. Eight weeks later, on July 29, according to WikiLeaks, the US ambassador in Bangladesh urged the prime minister and energy minister to reauthorize the Phulbari Mines for the use of "open pit" coal mining. Dattels's Polo Resources is an investor in the mine.[24]

By donating shares in small mining companies, Dattels is creating a powerful incentive for the Clintons to help his companies succeed. If the stock price rises, the value of the foundation's shares will rise. In the case of Dattels, this potentially creates a significant conflict of interest for Hillary Clinton.

This was not the first contribution Dattels made to the Clinton Foundation. Back in 2007 he had committed extensive financial support to CGSGI over a five-year period. He committed to do the same in 2012. The Dattels Family Foundation's private website mentions the Clinton Foundation as a recipient of its support. But the name Dattels appears nowhere on Clinton donor disclosures nor does that of his company, Polo Resources. Again, the Clinton Foundation has failed to report a foreign contribution. How many more undisclosed foreign donors might there be? It is impossible to know. But this was a basic and simple requirement that demands further investigation. And we will meet more undisclosed donors later in this book.

The flow of funds into the Clinton Foundation, which was supposed to be transparent, is far from it. As we saw in the previous chapter, even when contributions are disclosed, as in the case of an obscure Indian politician, he was apparently not really the source of those funds. Is this happening on other occasions?

Perhaps the most important function of the foundation is to bolster Bill and Hillary's reputations as global humanitarians by bringing relief and care to people all over the world. This reputation not only flatters the ex-president's ego and benefits Hillary's political career, but it also has real value both in terms of global influence and financial reward. But how much good has the Clinton Foundation actually done?

At the Hollywood Bowl event, the publicity material included some sweeping claims about the Clinton Foundation's accomplishments. "Over the past ten years," it reads, "President Clinton's vision and leadership have resulted in nearly 4 million people benefiting from lifesaving HIV/AIDS treatments."[25] This is perhaps the most popular and oft-repeated success of the foundation, and it stems from Bill's efforts to negotiate and help create an international system whereby the cost of treatment drugs for HIV/AIDS victims would be radically reduced. "We set out to organize a drug market to shift it from a high-margin, low-volume, uncertain payment process . . . we were able to lower the price to just under $140 a person a year."[26]

The claim is repeated when he is introduced for speeches around the country and when he is interviewed in the media. But what exactly does "we were able to lower" mean?

The Clinton Foundation did sign some compacts, but prices were already dropping quickly because generic versions of treatment drugs were coming on the market.[27] According to public health experts, the foundation piggybacked on the efforts of other organizations. "He may take a little more credit than is due," admits Princeton Lyman, who served in the State Department under Hillary and dealt with issues related to HIV/AIDS in Africa.[28]

Here's how the Center for Global Development explains how HIV/AIDS drugs prices were lowered: "Essentially, policy entrepreneurs like Peter Piot of UNAIDS—along with activists based within organizations as Doctors without Borders, Partners in Health *and later the Clinton Foundation* [emphasis added]— brought together the pharmaceutical manufacturers with developing world governments by negotiating the lower prices."[29]

Another claim often advanced by Bill himself is that the Clinton Foundation is on the frontlines of the HIV/AIDS crisis in the developing world. As Magaziner puts it, "The Clinton Foundation is now involved in treating over two-thirds of the world's children who are on treatment for AIDS."[30]

But what exactly does "involved" mean?

You might get the impression, if you look at the impressive photo displays on the Clinton Foundation website, that they are actually administering drugs to sick people. But the foundation doesn't actually get involved in directly treating people. While organizations such as Doctors Without Borders, the Red Cross, or Samaritan's Purse establish their own health care infrastructures—Doctors Without Borders had more than 300,000 HIV patients directly under their care in 2012—the Clinton Foundation effectively has none.[31]

Instead it serves as a middleman. "They've gone around in a very deliberate process of finding what they call 'care partners,'" says Jim Yong Kim, who cofounded Partners in Health, which works with the Clinton Foundation. "That's what Partners in Health is—our specialty has been working in rural areas."[32]

The world needs its middlemen, of course. But what this really means is that in practice, the foundation's work is heavily geared toward managing relief agency funds provided by foreign governments, such as Ireland, and dealing with health ministry bureaucrats in the developing world. In the relief world the Clinton Foundation works like a management consulting firm, such as McKinsey. But unlike McKinsey or another management firm, specific metrics on specific work by the foundation itself is hard to come by.

Clinton's motivation for taking on AIDS as a philanthropic cause has raised serious debate. Many who have been working in the field say he did a lousy job as president regarding the AIDS issue, largely ignoring it. As

Greg Behrman, the author of a definitive book on the global AIDS crisis put it to the *New York Times*, "As president, though, the record is clear. Clinton was not a leader on global AIDS and the consequences have been devastating."[33] Andrew Jack of the *Financial Times*, who traveled with Clinton to see his work on AIDS, asks whether, in light of his poor record as president, he is seeking some kind of "atonement."[34]

According to Bill, his interest in working on AIDS issues stems primarily from a conversation he had with Nelson Mandela shortly after leaving the White House. Clinton says Mandela asked him to work on these issues to help Africa.

Does Clinton's motivation matter? It does if his ultimate purpose is to make himself look good. If that is the case, he will focus on appearances rather than actual results. And making the Clintons look good is clearly central to the foundation's purpose. Its website is replete with pictures of Bill, and increasingly of Hillary and Chelsea, on humanitarian missions in remote locales in Africa or Asia. The press office also churns out media releases announcing foundation news or the activities of the Clinton family.

The Clinton Foundation's media machine focuses heavily on the family's activities. One of its projects involved helping to pay for the refurbishment of a pediatric clinic in the African country of Lesotho. When Bill showed up in July 2006, he was greeted at the Maseru airport with a red carpet and a receiving line of government officials. For good measure, "cultural groups performed dances and songs," according to US diplomatic cables. The king of Lesotho gave Bill a knighthood.

Following the "celebratory reception," Bill headed to the pediatric clinic his foundation had helped equip where he was serenaded by "choirs and children."[35] Ignored in foundation releases and related press reports was the fact that months earlier, in December 2005, the Baylor College of Medicine and Bristol-Myers Squibb had opened a pediatric clinic in the same town. But there was no parade or celebration. "No one has star power like Clinton," noted Dr. Mark Kline, president of the Baylor International Pediatric AIDS Initiative. "But the casual observer might be led to believe that no one else is doing anything, and that may draw resources away from others."[36]

But beyond good publicity, the foundation serves other purposes as well. As we have already seen, Clinton's visits to foreign locales frequently mix business with charitable work. When Bill flies into a country with an entourage, which may include businessmen with matters before the local government, he is there ostensibly to do (or simply talk about) his philanthropic work. But these visits often involve making useful introductions that coincide with major business deals in which Clinton Foundation donors are involved.

The Clinton Foundation also provides opportunities for foreign leaders and foreign investors to burnish their (sometimes shaky) reputations and images by association with its praiseworthy activities.

Dictators like Nursultan Nazarbayev in Kazakhstan, Meles Zenawi from Ethiopia (whom we will meet in chapter 7), and Paul Kagame of Rwanda might have terrible reputations when it comes to human rights, but they are invited guests at Clinton Foundation events where they are praised for their leadership. Kagame, for example, was a "Clinton Global Citizen of the Year" in 2009. He was praised by the foundation as a "brilliant military commander" and given the award for "leadership in public service." What you won't read in his bio is the fact that Kagame arrests his political opponents and censors journalists. Nor is there mention of the fact that the United Nations accuses Kagame's militias of raping and slaying thousands of Hutu. It is widely believed that Kagame is largely responsible for fueling the civil war going on in the neighboring Democratic Republic of Congo.[37]

Whenever Kagame speaks before the Clinton Foundation or meets with Bill, he is quick to publicize it. He clearly recognizes that partnering with an ex-president grants him added legitimacy.[38]

The Clintons point out that neither Bill, Hillary, nor Chelsea take a salary from the Clinton Foundation. This is true—the hundreds of millions that pour into the foundation do not benefit the Clintons directly. But they profit from the foundation in a way that is both indirect and far more lucrative: by taking enormous speaking fees for talking about their charitable work.

In his early post-presidential years Bill's speeches were largely about his views of the world or his experiences in office. But in more recent years many of his speeches involve talking about the work of the foundation.

In October 2006, for example, Bill was paid $150,000 for a speech to the Mortgage Bankers Association for "discussing world events and his work on behalf of the William J. Clinton Foundation."[39] In September 2006 he was paid $450,000 to speak at the Fortune Forum, which is a charitable fundraising event in London. These are just a few examples among many instances. Clinton's go-to speech, entitled "Our Common Humanity," is largely about the work of the foundation.

The Clintons' charitable work puts money in their pockets in other ways, too. In 2007 Bill released a book called *Giving* that highlighted the charitable work of the Clinton Foundation and those who work with it. He made $6.3 million from sales.[40] The book was widely criticized. Peter Baker, now of the *New York Times*, called it an "extended public service announcement masquerading as a book."[41]

Blurring their charitable, political, and financial interests has served the Clintons well. When Hillary became secretary of state, the practice continued. Indeed, it reached a whole new level.

Chapter 6
The Clinton Blur (II)

In 2009 Hillary Clinton was in Russia, where she pushed Russian officials to sign a multibillion-dollar airplane agreement with Boeing. The $3.7 billion purchase was a big deal for the aerospace company. Two months after Boeing won the contract, the company pledged $900,000 to the Clinton Foundation. The *Washington Post* called it "an indicator of a mutually beneficial relationship between one of the world's major corporations and a potential future president. Clinton functioned as a powerful ally for Boeing's business interests at home and abroad, while Boeing has invested resources in causes beneficial to Clinton's public and political image."[1]

When Hillary became secretary of state she announced a new commitment to what she called "commercial diplomacy" or "economic statecraft." The idea was simple: she would use her diplomatic leverage to help American companies be more competitive overseas. If they needed help in a foreign country, Hillary would be there as a supportive partner.

This was no idle commitment. As *Businessweek* put it in a retrospective look at her tenure, "There's no doubt Clinton has had success using her personal clout to help a handful of companies close a handful of deals."[2]

Hillary's commitment to commercial diplomacy was laudable to the extent that she was committed to helping American firms be competitive in the global marketplace. But in practice it would prove difficult to distinguish the personal and political aspects of this kind of activity.

In State Department parlance Hillary's commercial diplomacy was executed as part of what it called "public private partnerships." And the public-private partnerships came in many forms. The goals of these partnerships were often praiseworthy. But they often benefited friends of the Clintons.

Power Africa, for example, like all such partnerships, has a noble goal: to help African countries develop large energy projects.[3] But as *Forbes* magazine points out, initiatives like Power Africa tend to favor politically connected firms. Winners include firms like Symbion Power, which counts former ambassador Joe Wilson as a member of its board. (Wilson, who we will meet again in chapter 8, is a Clinton friend and political ally.)[4] Another firm involved with Power Africa is Hecate Energy. Its founder David Wilhelm has no background in the field. For most of his professional life he served as a lobbyist and partner in Wilhelm and Conlon Public Strategies. Before that, he was the manager for Bill Clinton's 1992 presidential campaign.[5]

The pursuit of commercial diplomacy required a new infrastructure within the State Department. Shortly after her confirmation as secretary of state, Hillary created the Office of Global Partnerships. The director of this office would serve as the "chief liaison between corporate America, the State Department, and governments around the world."

To run this sensitive office, she turned not to a diplomat, a former corporate executive, or even someone with NGO experience overseas but to longtime political operative Kris Balderston.[6]

Balderston had served for eight years on Hillary's Senate staff and also did a stint in Bill Clinton's White House. His most famous role in Clinton World involved keeping the infamous List, which rated people as friends or enemies on a point system.[7] In a December

8, 2008, memo Balderston had suggested the idea for a State Department "corporate office" to create a series of public-private partnerships matching private capital with public governmental power. Hillary loved the idea and adopted it immediately, putting Balderston in charge, despite his having no background in the area of international business.[8]

Other senior positions were given to political aides who had more experience in the world of Washington than in global affairs. Indeed, during her tenure both the State Department and the United States Agency for International Development (USAID), which fell under Hillary's control, saw a substantial rise in staff. Staffing at the State Department increased 17 percent from 2008 to 2012, and USAID staffing was up 30 percent.[9]

One can hardly blame Bill and Hillary for seeking to place friends and supporters in jobs under their control. Like other prominent political figures, the Clintons need to keep a large constellation of aides, advisers, and friends gainfully employed. Some of this employment, as indicated above, is handled by way of the Clinton Foundation. But the State Department was a convenient place for rewarding supporters as well. To enhance her scope of patronage, Hillary made extensive use of what is called the special government employee (SGE) rule. This special category of staff allowed the

Clintons to have their aides simultaneously involved with the Clinton Foundation, State Department, and various outside commercial interests.

The SGE rule was originally designed to ensure that experts like scientists and engineers could be tapped for their expertise by the federal government without giving up their regular jobs at a research lab or university. The assignment was also supposed to be temporary—totaling no more than 130 days out of 365.

But Hillary used the SGE status not for scientists or academics but for political aides, some of whom simultaneously held jobs at Clinton-affiliated firms. Take Huma Abedin, who served as Hillary's deputy chief of staff at State. As an SGE, Abedin was able to remain on the payroll of the Clinton Foundation, as well as on that of a corporate consulting firm called Teneo, which was started in 2009 by Bill's longtime aide Doug Band.

Teneo, where Bill was a paid adviser, represented firms who had often either paid for Bill's speeches or donated to the Clinton Foundation. Also involved in Teneo was Declan Kelly. An SGE at State for a while, Kelly joined Teneo in 2011. Teneo's clients included Fortune 500 companies, governments, and high-net-worth individuals. The companies it represented included Coca-Cola, UBS, and Standard Chartered.

The arrangement worked seamlessly until March 2012, when Bill ceased to be a Teneo adviser. One of Teneo's clients was MF Global, the commodities brokerage run by Clinton friend John Corzine.[10] MF Global collapsed after a series of highly leveraged trades. Some customers accused the firm of raiding their private accounts to shore up its finances after risky bets went sour. When news broke that MF Global was a client, Bill apparently felt it best to sever his ties.

SGE Abedin played a central role in everything Hillary did. She assured a Senate committee that there was no cross-pollination between her job at the State Department and her other work at Clinton-connected entities. She explained that she provided "strategic advice and consulting services" to Teneo's management team but did not provide "insights about the department, my work with the secretary or any government information to which I may have had access." But public concerns were not so easily allayed. As the *New York Times* put it, "the lines were blurred between Ms. Abedin's work in the high echelons of one of the government's most sensitive executive departments and her role as a Clinton family insider."[11]

SGE Caitlin Klevorick, who worked as a consultant to Bill Clinton and the Clinton Foundation, joined the State Department in 2009 as a special assistant to

Cheryl Mills. In that capacity she "provided expert knowledge and advice to the counselor and the chief of staff and other department officials on a variety of important foreign policy issues," according to the State Department. SGE status allowed her to keep her firm CBK Strategies, where she simultaneously worked for corporate clients.

Cheryl Mills herself, Hillary's longtime chief of staff, was also granted SGE status so she could continue to direct Haiti relief efforts at the State Department while returning to work for the Clinton Foundation after Hillary resigned.

SGE Elizabeth Bagley, who married into the RJR Reynolds tobacco fortune, was a longtime Hillary fundraiser who joined the State Department as a "special advisor to the Secretary" and then "special advisor for Secretary initiatives." Bagley and her husband had kicked in more than $1 million to the Clinton Foundation. At State, she was paid a $129,000 salary (the highest possible) and allowed to continue her other commercial activities.

Ann Gavaghan, a former member of Hillary's Senate staff, was also granted SGE special status. Gavaghan served as the chief of staff in the State Department's Office of the US Global AIDS Coordinator.

One value of SGE status is that ethics rules are looser than those that apply to regular public employees.

SGEs can "work on a matter if you have a personal relationship with one of the parties."[12] They are also able to work for clients with matters before the office they work in. And they can raise money for political candidates (or entities like the Clinton Foundation) "if you do so only during non-duty hours and if you do not use a government resource."[13]

As the *Boston Globe* put it, this kind of arrangement is "fraught with potential conflicts and abuses."[14]

Propublica, a nonprofit news organization, investigated the use of SGE status in the federal government and asked numerous government agencies to send them lists of SGEs at their agencies. According to *Propublica*'s Justine Elliott and Liz Day, many of them did. But the State Department balked. So *Propublica* filed a Freedom of Information Act (FOIA) request. The State Department responded after several months that assembling the list would require "extensive research," finally handing it over four months after that. State Department officials would not explain why they were so reluctant to share the information.

The other tool Hillary used to create payroll opportunities for Clinton friends and allies was the S-class designation. S-class positions were under the direct purview and financial control of the secretary of state and no one else. This allowed Hillary to exclude State Department bureaucrats, Foreign Service officers, or civil servants from involvement or control over certain projects or activities, including everything from economic diplomacy to health care issues. As reporters Jonathan Allen and Amie Parnes put it in a sympathetic portrait of her tenure, Hillary appointed "a cluster of special ambassadors, envoys and representatives and senior advisers who exercised tremendous power to circumvent the department bureaucracy."[15]

Hillary further centralized control over the awarding of government grants, contracts, and consulting agreements by dramatically reducing the independence of USAID, which was part of the State Department apparatus. Dubbed the "Foggy Bottom Smackdown" by some in Washington, Hillary effectively took away power from USAID administrators and in her Quadrennial Diplomacy and Development Review made clear that the agency's budget would remain under the State Department. As the New Republic reported, not only were USAID programs further put under her control, but she populated the agency with loyalists who had little or no relevant experience.[16]

The practice of appointing special status employees throughout the State Department bureaucracy effectively blurred the lines between American diplomatic initiatives and the interests of the Clintons and their friends.

Consider the case of Laureate Education—a typical example of the Clinton Blur in action.

Laureate Education began as part of Sylvan Learning Systems but branched out to become one of the largest for-profit university systems in the world. Founded in Baltimore in 1999, it now comprises a sprawling network of campuses, including six in Saudi Arabia, a dozen in Brazil, three in China, and even one in Cyprus.[17] In Brazil alone, there are 130,000 students paying tuition to attend ten Laureate International schools on forty different campuses.[18]

Laureate recruits students through telemarketing. The call centers are often on the campus themselves and those making the calls are university students.[19] The university system spends more than $200 million a year on advertising, including television commercials, online campaigns, and billboards that dot the developing world.

In early 2010 Bill signed on as "honorary chancellor" of Laureate. The title might have been "honorary," but Bill got paid for his services. How much? It's hard to know. Government disclosure forms did not require him to specify, only that it was "more than $1,000." But part of his job included speaking at half a dozen or so Laureate schools every year, which, based on his typical fee scale, meant perhaps $1 million per year.

Bill sparked tremendous excitement when he showed up in 2012 to address throngs of students and faculty at Laureate schools in Tegucigalpa, Honduras, and Mexico City. He also visited campuses in Germany, Spain, Turkey, Malaysia, Brazil, Peru, and the United States.[20] Bill's face and name have been plastered on Laureate marketing materials and pictures of him have lined the walkways at campuses like Laureate's Bilgi University in Istanbul, Turkey.[21]

The relationship between Laureate chairman Douglas Becker and the Clintons formed in the years before Hillary became secretary of state, when Becker started showing up at Clinton Global Initiative (CGI) events. In 2008 Laureate became a partner with CGI. By 2009 Becker was paying Bill to give speeches at Laureate campuses in Spain, Brazil, and Peru.[22]

Other Clinton friends were soon brought in. Henry Cisneros, who served as secretary of housing and urban development during Clinton's presidency, became chairman of Laureate's National Hispanic University advisory board. Cisneros delivered commencement addresses in San Jose, California, where he praised Laureate as a "pioneer in higher education for Hispanics."[23]

But Laureate's business practices have faced serious legal scrutiny and criminal investigations in some countries. In Mexico, Chile, and Turkey, where Laureate operates, for-profit universities are actually illegal. Laureate has put money into a struggling nonprofit school, getting positions on the board, then getting the school to hire Laureate for a variety of "services," including computer-advisory services and English courses. Laureate has also received funds for the use of its trademark.

According to Chile's economic crimes unit, Laureate's Chilean schools transferred more than $80 million out of the country between 2011 and 2013. A national commission found that there were irregularities regarding Laureate's activities.[24] In its financial filings with the US Securities and Exchange Commission (SEC), Laureate admitted that the service agreements are a way to "efficiently transfer funds out of the universities in these countries."[25]

Becker, in addition to running Laureate, is also the chairman of the International Youth Foundation (IYF). This nonprofit sister organization (whose offices are less than a mile from Laureate's in Baltimore) runs numerous programs through Laureate, including something called YouthActionNet, which has fellows on Laureate's campuses in Brazil, Mexico, Spain, Peru,

Chile, and Turkey.[26] Becker's company announced its YouthActionNet commitment at the CGI annual meeting in 2010. Bill heartily approved: "I am pleased that Laureate International Universities and the International Youth Foundation have partnered on this commitment to empower young social entrepreneurs to take on pressing challenges in their own communities and around the world."[27]

Shortly after Bill became honorary chancellor in April 2010, Hillary made Laureate part of her State Department Global Partnership. In October 2010 the State Department held a gala reception on the twentieth anniversary of IYF's founding. The featured speaker was Maria Otero, the undersecretary of state for democracy and global affairs, who praised the group for "doing such important work."[28]

IYF had already received financial support from USAID before Hillary became secretary of state, going back to 2001.[29] But the amount of its grants has exploded since Bill became chancellor of Laureate. According to IYF tax filings, in 2010 government grants accounted for $23 million of its revenue, compared to $5.4 million from other sources. It received $21 million in 2011 and $23 million in 2012.[30] In June 2011 IYF joined with the State Department and USAID in holding a Youth Partnerships Employability Conference in Washington.[31]

During Hillary's tenure at State, IYF received USAID grants to work in Mexico, Mozambique, Senegal, Tanzania, the Kyrgyz Republic, Uganda, Jordan, the Caribbean, the West Bank and Gaza, and Algeria, and to address "good governance" issues worldwide. In 2012 it also received its first grant directly from the State Department: $1.9 million for work on a Middle East Partnership Initiative.

In January 2013, just before Hillary left her post as secretary of state, the International Finance Corporation (IFC) made a $150 million equity investment in Laureate, the first time the development organization had ever done so. IFC is part of the World Bank. The head of the World Bank at the time was Jim Kim, a Clinton friend and cofounder of Partners in Health, a partner of the Clinton Foundation.

Isn't it troubling that while Bill Clinton was being paid by a private corporation, that corporation was also benefiting from State Department actions? Isn't it troubling that an affiliate of that corporation is also receiving tens of millions in taxpayer money? Isn't it troubling that this seeming conflict of interest was not disclosed?

Troubling State Department conflict of interest questions hardly end here. But now let us turn the camera to the man behind the podium (and Foggy Bottom).

Chapter 7
Podium Economics

Most ex-presidents see the demand for their speechmaking decline as they move farther away from their time in office. The opposite applies to Bill. Indeed, during Hillary's tenure as secretary of state, Bill's speechmaking activity increased and became much more profitable, particularly overseas. In a number of cases, these speeches were paid for by people with an interest in obtaining favors from Hillary.

Does Bill's outsized personality and global popularity really explain his record financial success on the speaking circuit? We have become used to former occupants of the Oval Office making money in their post-presidential years. Ronald Reagan famously gave two speeches for $2 million in Tokyo following his retirement from office. George H. W. Bush gave lectures and joined corporate boards for firms like the investment giant the Carlyle Group. But no one comes close to Bill Clinton.

The really troubling thing about Bill's speeches is the apparent correlation between his fees and Hillary's decisions during her tenure as secretary of state. The timing of the payments, the much higher than average size of some of them, and the subsequent actions taken by Hillary raise serious questions about just what those who underwrote these exorbitant fees were actually paying for.

As noted earlier, Hillary infamously claimed she and Bill were "dead broke" when they left the White House. So while Hillary went to the US Senate, Bill hit the lecture circuit. In 2001 he gave thirty-nine speeches overseas and twenty in the United States. In the following seven years, the Clintons pulled in a stunning $109 million.[1]

As Clinton's presidency receded into the past, his income from speeches, especially big paydays from overseas speeches, declined. But when Hillary became secretary of state in 2009, those high-paying overseas speeches ramped up dramatically. Bill's three best years securing speaking fees over $250,000 occurred while Hillary was at State. In fact, of the thirteen Clinton speeches that fetched $500,000 or more, only two occurred during the years his wife was not secretary of state.

TD Bank, a Canadian financial institution, has paid Bill more than any other financial institution for lectures. More than Goldman Sachs, UBS, JPMorgan, or anyone on Wall Street. TD Bank paid Bill $1.8 million for ten speeches over a roughly two-and-half-year period from late 2008 to mid-2011. Moreover, these payments came at a crucial time, as Hillary wrestled with a controversial decision of enormous financial interest to the bank.

Beginning in 2008 TransCanada Corporation sought US government approval for the $8 billion, 1,660-mile-long Keystone XL pipeline, which was designed to transport 900,000 barrels a day from Alberta's oil sands to Gulf Coast refineries in Port Arthur, Texas.[2] Because the project crossed an international border, authority for granting a presidential permit of approval rested with the US secretary of state.[3]

TD Bank had never paid Bill for a speech until the pipeline project began snaking its way through Washington. It was late 2008 and Keystone XL permits had just been submitted to Washington. Hillary had lost the Democratic nod for the White House, but she was still a powerful US senator. Capitol Hill Republicans were generally supportive of energy projects like

Keystone XL. If there was going to be opposition, it would likely come from liberal Democrats.

The Keystone XL pipeline's single biggest shareholder was none other than TD Bank, which held $1.6 billion in shares. TD Bank was also on the hook for $993 million it had loaned to TransCanada.[4] TD Bank, in a research note, called the pipeline a "national priority" that was essential for the long-term health of the Canadian oil industry.[5]

There had been talk since June 2008 that Barack Obama, having sewn up the Democratic nomination, would pick Hillary as his secretary of state. On November 21, 2008, the *New York Times* reported that Hillary would indeed be his nominee to head up the State Department.[6] Four days later, on November 25 and 26, Bill was in Canada delivering his first of three speeches, for which TD Bank paid him $525,000.[7] But the Clintons were only getting started. Hillary was confirmed as secretary of state on February 21, 2009. In May Bill returned to Canada and gave three more speeches for another $525,000, making appearances in Halifax, St. John, and Toronto. Four months later, on September 13, TD Bank sponsored yet another appearance, this one for $175,000 in Toronto. On November 3, 2009, TD Bank paid him another $175,000 for a speech in Abu Dhabi.[8] On May 20, 2010, Bill spoke for another $175,000 in a speech underwritten by TD Bank, this time in Calgary.[9]

Many of these TD-sponsored events were "private affairs," not open to the public or the press.[10]

At several of the speeches, Clinton was introduced or interviewed by TD Bank vice chairman Frank McKenna. A former Canadian politician and former ambassador to the United States, McKenna is described in the Canadian press as "a good friend of both Bill and Hillary Clinton."[11] His interest in the Keystone XL pipeline went beyond his role as an executive with TD Bank. McKenna also sits on the corporate board of Canadian Natural Resources Ltd. (CNRL), a heavy-oil producer that planned to use the pipeline to move its oil to the United States.[12]

When the pipeline project ran into rough opposition in Washington, McKenna became a vocal advocate. When President Obama decided to delay review of the project until after the 2012 elections, McKenna questioned whether Canadians were being "screwed" by the decision.[13]

Given Hillary's role in green-lighting the project, she naturally became the focus of intense lobbying efforts. In addition to suddenly throwing almost $2 million at Bill, Canadian corporations with an interest in the project hired several senior aides from Hillary's presidential campaign to assist them in their efforts.

The lead lobbyist for TransCanada was Paul Elliott, who had served as the deputy national campaign director on Hillary's 2008 presidential campaign. E-mail correspondence released through the FOIA reveals that US State Department officials advised TransCanada on how to build support for the Keystone Pipeline— even as the department was conducting its review on whether or not to approve it.[14] One of those communicating with Elliott was Nora Toiv, a special assistant to Hillary Clinton.

The chummy nature of the correspondence between Elliott and senior officials in the State Department enraged environmental groups. "I think we've gone way beyond bias," said Damon Moglen, the director of the climate and energy program for Friends of the Earth. "We now see that the State Department has been complicit in this entire affair."[15]

TransCanada certainly seems to have gotten its money's worth from Elliott. Meanwhile the provincial government of Alberta, where the oil sands were located, hired another Clinton aide. Hilary Lefebre, who served as the director of broadcast media strategy for Hillary's presidential campaign, received a $54,000 consulting fee to "blunt" criticism of the project from environmental groups.[16]

Environmental activists continued to accuse the State Department of failing to offer a truly independent review of the Keystone XL project. To offer an environmental assessment, State hired a company called Environmental Resources Management (ERM). But there was a problem: environmental activists pointed out that ERM had financial ties with TransCanada. State Department officials attempted to cover that fact up, redacting the biographies of the study's authors to hide their previous work for TransCanada.[17]

Meanwhile, in May 2011 Bill was paid $280,000 for appearances in Fredericton and Antigonish.[18] The Clinton speech submissions to State Department ethics officials (per the Obama administration memorandum of understanding described in chapter 1) didn't indicate that TD Bank was a major investor in Keystone XL. Three months later, in August, the State Department released a final environmental impact statement that was seen as largely supportive of the pipeline.[19]

Throughout the process, Hillary remained relatively quiet. The political winds for Democrats were difficult. While organized labor favored the deal, environmentalists, Hollywood, and numerous high-dollar contributors opposed it.[20]

By late 2011 events appeared to be reaching a crescendo. As hearings commenced in Washington, Hillary sent word that there should be no Canadians present. "Canadian officials saw the request as a suggestion that

Ms. Clinton supported the project, and didn't want a Canadian presence to further disturb the peace."[21] And there was muted evidence that Hillary was quietly pushing the deal through. At an appearance at the Commonwealth Club in San Francisco, she had been asked about energy policy in general and the Keystone XL pipeline in particular. While explaining that she had not yet decided whether to approve the project, Hillary declared, "we are inclined to do so, and we are for several reasons." She touted the project on the grounds of "energy security." "We're either going to be dependent on dirty oil from the [Persian] Gulf or dirty oil from Canada," she said, leaving the audience with the impression that she favored the latter.[22]

Vocal opposition continued to mount, as President Obama came under increasing pressure from environmentalists. During an October 26 speech, Obama was heckled about the pipeline. "I know your deep concern about [Keystone XL]," he said. "We will address it." In a series of interviews with local media outlets through the Midwest, where the pipeline was supposed to run, he was pressed on the issue.[23] After officials in Nebraska demanded that the pipeline be rerouted to avoid sensitive environmental areas, President Obama decided to delay approval of the project.[24]

In late February 2012 Bill finally issued his statement of support for the project at (of all places) a Department of Energy conference for clean technology start-ups. With a group of bureaucrats and green-energy investors looking on, Bill told the crowd in Maryland that America should "embrace" the pipeline.[25] Later the same afternoon, Hillary was at the House of Representatives Foreign Affairs Committee hearing, discussing the pipeline. Naturally, she was asked about her husband's remarks.

"He's a very smart man," she responded, causing a smattering of chuckles in the crowd. For Canadians, this was another hopeful sign. As the Canadian press put it, "Bill Clinton's comments will almost certainly cause a stir given his wife has already been accused of a pro-pipeline bias by the sea of American environmentalists who oppose Keystone XL."[26]

Obama's edict that the pipeline issue not be settled until after the 2012 elections effectively sealed its fate, at least as it related to Hillary's ability to get it approved. By January 2013 she was gone from Foggy Bottom.

Five months later, in June 2013, TD Bank announced that "it will begin selling its $1.6 billion worth of shares in the massive but potentially still-born Keystone XL crude pipeline project."[27] The bank said in a statement, "TD will gradually sell its $1.6 billion take in Keystone

XL as the first step toward transitioning away from investment in oil sands extraction entirely."[28]

Too bad for TD Bank. But the Clintons got paid regardless. Since she left office, Hillary has used the fact that because she was involved in the process, she can't talk about her views on the Keystone Pipeline. As she told one crowd, "I've said before in Canada as I've traveled around your country avoiding answering questions about the Keystone pipeline because I really can't, having been part of the process." So her involvement prevents her from talking about Keystone, but it didn't prevent her husband from making millions from its largest shareholder.[29] As Charles Calomiris, a professor of financial institutions at the Columbia University Graduate School of Business, explains, the speeches were not really about speeches. What they really wanted was to buy Hillary's goodwill by paying Bill. "I'm not sure it would matter if those speeches had taken place in Clinton's bathtub," he said. "What matters is that they paid him."[30]

While much of the media attention to Clinton's speaking has focused on his fees from Wall Street and pharmaceutical companies, it has been the outsized payments from overseas that have really brought in the money. In 2011 Bill Clinton made $13.3 million in speaking fees for giving fifty-four speeches.[31] But of those speeches paying $250,000 or more, nearly 40 percent, or $5.1 million of those fees, came from just eleven speeches given outside the United States. Overall, these mega-paying speeches for over $250,000 generated nearly $40 million in income for the Clintons from 2001 to 2013.

In short, Bill Clinton's best years—with much higher than average fees being consistently paid by foreign entities—occurred while his wife was at the pinnacle of her power as secretary of state, a perch with enormous influence over issues that directly affected foreign governments.

A few examples make the point.

Beginning in 2009, the Swedish telecom giant Ericsson came under US pressure for selling telecom equipment to oppressive governments, some of which used those technologies to monitor and control their own people. In late 2010 the SEC sent a letter to Ericsson about sales to countries that were considered state sponsors of terrorism by Hillary's State Department.[32] The regimes included Sudan and Syria, where Ericsson sold and maintained telephone-switching equipment, and Iran, where it was selling "commercial grade systems to public network operators for mobile communications."[33]

Hillary was a well-known hawk on Iran and used economic tools against regimes that were considered sponsors of terrorism. According to US diplomatic cables, State Department officials were "regularly and increasingly" raising these transactions involving Ericsson with the Swedish foreign minister.[34]

In April 2011 Ericsson was named in a State Department report for supplying telecom equipment for the oppressive regime in Belarus.[35] Separately, on Capitol Hill pressure was mounting and a bill would later be introduced in December 2011 in the House of Representatives to "stop the sale of surveillance technologies to repressive regimes."[36] In June 2011 the State Department started drawing up a list of which goods and services might be covered under expanded sanctions on Iran and other state sponsors of terrorism.[37]

Meanwhile, Ericsson decided to sponsor a speech by Bill Clinton and paid him more than he had ever been paid for a single speech: $750,000. According to Clinton financial disclosures, in the previous ten years Ericsson had never sponsored a Clinton speech. But now it apparently thought would be a good time to do so.

On November 12, 2011, Bill appeared at a telecom conference in Hong Kong and talked in general terms about the role that telecom plays in our lives. One week later, on November 19, the State Department unveiled its new sanctions list for Iran. Telecom was not on the list.[38]

On December 8, Hillary discussed the issue of telecom companies and their sales to repressive regimes for the first time since Bill's speech. She argued that companies like Ericsson needed to make "good decisions" about whom they do business with but proposed no further action.[39]

In April 2012, President Obama signed an executive order imposing sanctions on telecom sales to Iran and Syria. But those sanctions did not cover Ericsson's work in Iran. The Swedish company said that it was planning to scale down its work in the country because of public pressure, but internal documents obtained by Reuters found that the company planned to honor existing contracts in Iran.[40]

In 2011 much of the Arab world was in upheaval, dealing with the aftermath of the Arab Spring, which had sparked widespread protests across the region. In Egypt and Tunisia, large crowds took to the streets and demanded political change. Many of these protests turned violent.[41] Even countries considered relatively stable, including Bahrain and Yemen, were dealing with violent upheavals.[42]

The events left small but wealthy countries like the United Arab Emirates (UAE) feeling very vulnerable. The UAE was being pressured by the United States to tighten its grip on economic ties with Iran.[43] In May two oil and shipping companies faced sanctions for their trade with Iran. On June 20, 2011, the Obama administration designated six UAE-based shipping firms for sanctions over their business dealings with Iran.[44] Three days later, the United States charged several other parties in the UAE with trading parts for fighter jets and attack helicopters to Iran.[45]

The UAE was in a precarious situation because it feared the Iranian regime. But it feared something perhaps even more: being abandoned by the United States. In a secret State Department cable, the crown prince said his country was "being left out of our [US] Iran sanctions consultations." He explained to a visiting congressional delegation that the royal family was "left wondering what will happen to them in any deal the US and Iran reach through back-channel conversations."[46]

Amid this uncertainty, the royal family decided to pay Bill Clinton $500,000 to come and speak in Abu Dhabi.[47] Bill arrived in Abu Dhabi and stayed at the Emirates Palace hotel.[48]

His speech was on collecting environmental data. "The lack of environmental data hurts," he said. "On top of all environmental issues, the financial crisis is making the world's stability even worse. The only way out, though, is a green economy." [49]

What is striking about the speech is not what Clinton said but the timing of the payment. Even as Bill was being introduced to the audience by the crown prince of the UAE, the prince's brother (the foreign minister) was en route to Washington for meetings with none other than Hillary. Sheikh Abdullah bin Zayed al-Nahyan arrived in Washington on December 12 and met Hillary the day after Bill collected his half million. Based on the Clintons' financial disclosures, it does not appear that the UAE royal family had ever paid for a Clinton speech before.[50]

This was not the first time Bill collected large checks for speeches paid by foreign governments, such as Thailand and Turkey.[51] It certainly wouldn't be the last.

The year 2010 was a tense time for US-Chinese relations. The problems were piling up: the Chinese government reduced its military ties with the Pentagon following US arms sales to Taiwan; Google disclosed that it had been a victim of a Chinese cyber assault; Barack Obama hosted the Dalai Lama in Washington amidst public outcries in Beijing; relations grew stiff when officials disagreed on trade issues and China's alleged manipulation of its currency. Meanwhile, China was flexing its military muscle, sending a submarine to the bottom of the South China Sea where it planted a Chinese flag on the ocean floor to signify China's claim to the mineral-rich area.

At the center of US policy toward China was Hillary Clinton, who was the architect of the Obama administration's strategic "pivot" to Asia.

At this critical time for US-Chinese relations, Bill Clinton gave a number of speeches that were underwritten by the Chinese government and its supporters. That might not be apparent if you look at the Clintons' public financial disclosures. For example, on October 21, 2011, Bill gave a speech before something called the Silicon Valley Information Business Alliance in Santa Clara, California. But who underwrote the speech? According to correspondence between Bill's office and the State Department, the cosponsors were a coalition of Chinese government entities and organizations. Bill received $200,000 for the speech (well above his average for speaking in the United States) and the sponsors were the China Electronic Commerce Association (an entity launched and chaired by an official from the Chinese Ministry of Information Industry);[52] the Suzhou People's government (a municipality around

Shanghai); the China Association of Science and Technology Industry Parks (this third sponsor sounds pretty innocuous, but it is a government-run entity in China); and the California State Friendship Committee, a small California-based organization designed to foster US-Chinese relations.[53]

There were no clear guidelines about what was and what wasn't permissible. After the speech in California, Bill Clinton's office contacted the State Department and sought approval for a speech sponsored by the Shanghai Airport Authority (SAA). Note the flexibility and lack of understanding that it had already approved the speech in California when the State Department wrote back, "[Your correspondence] states that the Shanghai Airport Authority, a state-owned enterprise, would be a 'title sponsor only.' Does this mean that SAA is not contributing any funds to pay for President Clinton's fees? I don't believe we've previously cleared acceptance of fees from PRC-linked entities, but could consider this variation."

The State Department Ethics Office was willing to "consider" a "variation" on guidelines, they wrote to Clinton's office. Ultimately Clinton declined the speech. His office said there was a scheduling problem.

Bill also took a $550,000 payment for an appearance in Shanghai at something called the Huatuo CEO forum, underwritten by Chinese billionaire Yan Jiehe, a man described as "China's baddest billionaire builder." Yan has become wealthy in part through large government construction contracts. His company is perhaps most famous in China for lopping off and flattening seven hundred mountaintops for a construction project. (Yan says, in defense, the number wasn't quite that high.)[54] Yan, who calls Clinton a "close friend," is an outspoken Chinese nationalist, explaining that foreign countries must "not look down on China. . . . I understand that my country, my nation, China is the greatest in history."[55]

Prior to Hillary's appointment as secretary of state, Bill had given only two speeches on the Chinese mainland, for a total of $450,000.

After Hillary's appointment, the Clintons promised both the incoming Obama White House and the US Senate that his speeches and business ties would be vetted by the State Department Ethics Office, as described in chapter 1.

This approach was doomed to fail, because the disclosures to be made were not required to indicate anything other than the name of the donor, certainly not investments or what business they might have with the State Department. An examination of the communication between Bill's office and State Department ethics officers, which was obtained by Judicial Watch through the Freedom of Information Act (FOIA), indicates that Bill Clinton's office never provided anything but a cursory description of who was paying for each speech. TD Bank's ties to the Keystone Pipeline, for example, were never disclosed. Ericsson, in the correspondence concerning that speech, is simply described as a "world-leading provider of telecommunications equipment." No mention is made of its tangles with the State Department at the time. And the department greenlighted 215 speechmaking arrangements as not posing conflicts of interest.[56]

For the ethics officers replying to the Clinton requests, the emphasis was on a speedy response. And then there was the intimidation factor: they were vetting speeches being done by the spouse of their ultimate boss. And the spouse happened to be a former president. For good measure, all correspondence pertaining to Bill's speeches between his office and the ethics office was copied to Cheryl Mills, Hillary's chief of staff and Bill's longtime friend.[57] And who ran the ethics office at the time? That would be the State Department legal adviser, Harold Koh, who had previously been appointed by President Clinton as assistant secretary of state for democracy, human rights, and labor.[58]

Speaking of ethics problems, some of Bill's largest paydays for speaking fees have come from scandal-plagued Nigeria. As we will learn in the next chapter, the Clinton financial ties to the continent of Africa run deep, and often include those with troubling reputations and rich histories of corruption.

Chapter 8
Warlord Economics

I t was an unusually hot July in 2009 when Secretary of State Hillary Clinton landed in Kinshasa, the sprawling capital of the Democratic Republic of Congo (DRC). The DRC (previously named Zaire) had for decades been a house of horrors. Ruled by corrupt dictators, populated by child soldiers, plagued by tribal fighting, and suffering from invasions by neighboring countries, few places on earth are more hellish than the DRC.

As a senator, Hillary had taken the lead in rooting out DRC corruption and violence. In 2006 she was one of the first to sign on as a cosponsor of the Democratic Republic of the Congo Relief, Security, and Democracy Promotion Act of 2006—one of only twelve cosponsors in the Senate. The legislation—which was authored by then senator Barack Obama—included provisions on human rights, corruption, and sexual violence. It also addressed the issue of conflict minerals, the illicit trade in valuable minerals that fuel much of the country's violence. The bill had teeth, giving the US secretary of state real power and authority to combat the country's problems. The bill was passed by the Senate and House, and President George W. Bush signed it into law.[1]

Hillary was also a vocal supporter of the Enough Project, an initiative launched by the liberal Center for American Progress. The project called for an international certification system that would require DRC mining companies and end users to account for their minerals' origins. A similar program had been established several years earlier for the diamond trade. Soon after Hillary arrived in Kinshasa, former NBA star Dikembe Mutombo, who was from Congo, took her on a tour of a hospital built in honor of his late mother. Mutombo worked with both the Clinton Foundation and the Clinton Global Initiative (CGI) on projects in the region.[2]

Hillary spoke with students about her commitment to helping Congo turn things around. "We know that the promise of the DRC is limitless," she told them. "We will help you build a strong, civilian-led government that is accountable and transparent." From Kinshasa she hopped aboard a UN plane (her US aircraft was too big) to visit President Joseph Kabila in the eastern city of Goma. There she talked about efforts to reduce the rapes and sexual violence that had terrorized the population. She talked about the lucrative mining trade in the country, too. "I am particularly concerned about the exploitation of natural resources, like the mining and the timber, where the resources do nothing to help the people of this country," she said in front of the international media.[3]

Her words were strong. But her actions during her tenure as secretary of state came nowhere near the positions she had taken while in the US Senate. As one scholar from Johns Hopkins University put it, the law she had cosponsored was "never implemented" by Secretary of State Clinton.[4] Furthermore, in 2011 the DRC government held national elections that were widely condemned. But the State Department showed little interest in trying to remedy them. When the Congolese government changed its constitution midelection in favor of President Kabila, the State Department called it an "internal affair." When the United Nations Group of Experts linked Congolese militia groups to the neighboring government in Rwanda, it was proof of Rwanda's military intervention into Congo that had contributed to hundreds of thousands of deaths. Some have asserted that Hillary's State Department sought to block or delay the publication of the damning portion of the investigation and "quietly" asked Rwanda to stop its support for the rebellion.[5]

What happened between 2006, when Hillary took those strong positions, and 2009, when she became secretary of state? Did she change her position? And if so, why? We can't ultimately know why she carried out the policies that she did, but we can notice where changes in policies conformed with the interests of Clinton Foundation large donors.

On January 20, 2007, Hillary Clinton sat on a gold-colored sofa in her Washington, DC, home and announced via the Internet that she was forming an exploratory committee and filing with the Federal Election Commission (FEC) to seek the presidency. "I'm in," Hillary declared. "And I'm in to win."[6]

Poll numbers gave her reason to be confident. With George W. Bush's poll numbers in a free fall, there was a sinking feeling in Republican circles that the GOP would have a hard time keeping the White House. And among Democrats, Hillary was the early front-runner.

Pundits, pollsters, and the American public were not the only ones paying attention. Hillary's announcement, in the weeks and months to follow, sent a cascade of foreign dollars flowing into the Clinton Foundation and into the Clintons' own pockets. Significant funds came from foreign investors with massive investments in troubled corners of the world. Securing access to African business opportunities had often required paying bribes to government officials. Now these investors were looking for access and political cover at the highest levels of power in Washington.

A few months after Hillary's presidential announcement, on July 6, 2007, the Clinton Foundation announced that a reclusive Swedish mining investor named Lukas Lundin was committing $100 million through a charity called Lundin for Africa. According to the announcement, "the Lundin for Africa commitment will be aimed, in large part, at approved projects in Africa, where the Lundin Group has significant mining, oil, and gas interests."[7] Lundin lived in Vancouver, Canada, and used a series of offshore trusts to manage his business affairs. A friend of Frank Giustra, Lundin was the head of a sprawling enterprise that cut deals with African warlords and dictators to gain access to valuable minerals and oil. As one longtime observer put it, the company "pursued a strategy of operating in countries under sanctions" and "building assets in countries such as Libya, Iran, and Sudan, where many other competitors were unable to operate."[8]

This kind of business could be enormously profitable if you were willing to look the other way on corruption and human rights. But the strategy also posed enormous risks. By 2007, when he made his commitment to the Clinton Foundation, his company was under considerable political and legal heat in the United States and Europe for some of its business dealings. The Lundin Group was one of only two Western oil companies drilling in the Sudan, which was not only the focus of media attention for massive human rights violations but was also on the US State Department's list of terrorism-sponsoring nations. Human rights activists were pushing for pension funds to divest stock in the company. Even more troubling, the Lundin Group was under investigation by the International Prosecution Chamber in Stockholm for complicity in "war crimes and crimes against humanity." (In 2012, the chief prosecutor decided not to press charges.)[9] In announcing the donation to the Clinton Foundation, the family's spokesman explained, "This is not to soothe a bad conscience but we want a positive impact in countries in Africa where mining is conducted."[10]

That may be true, but it does not explain why the Clinton Foundation saw fit to accept such a large contribution from such a questionable source.

The Lundin Companies were founded by Lukas's father, Adolph, who had made a lot of cash mining in apartheid South Africa after the United Nations applied international sanctions. While other companies had fled the country in the face of international pressure, Lundin stayed. When Adolph died in 2006, Lukas continued where his father left off, working in the darker corners of Africa, where few companies ventured. The Africa Oil Corporation, in which they owned a controlling share, was active in Ethiopia's Rift Valley, a region run by a corrupt dictatorial regime. Lundin also had a spin-off called Horn Petroleum that was drilling in Somalia even though the government there collapsed in 1990 and the country was essentially run by warlords.[11] Lukas Lundin was also chairman of a company called NGEx Resources that was mining in Eritrea, a region that was attempting to break away from Ethiopia.[12] The company also had a heavy stake in gold mining operations in Mauritania and Ghana.[13]

But perhaps the most lucrative mining operations in the Lundin portfolio were in the war-torn DRC, which has known more death, corruption, and fighting than perhaps any other area of Africa.

The Lundins got their foot in the door by striking a bargain with a Marxist warlord. In early 1997 the Congolese rebel leader Laurent Kabila, who had once worked with Che Guevara, was in the middle of a campaign to overthrow Mobutu Sese Seko, the country's longtime strongman ruler. To finance his rebel campaign, he sent a representative to Canada to talk to mining companies about "investment opportunities." His proposal was simple: give me money and I will give you lucrative mining rights in my country once I seize power. One of the first to bite was the Lundin family, which signed an agreement with the rebels and provided them with most of the funds they needed to march into the capital. The Lundins reportedly paid $50 million to Kabila's "finance minister," the first installment of $250 million they would give to the rebels. The rebels wanted cash and by all accounts didn't know what they were doing. Kabila's minister of mines, Kambale Mututulo, had never seen one. "He asked us to send him some books on how to run one," noted one executive who met with him.[14]

For the Lundins, this was an enormously lucrative opportunity. "There are moments in the history of mining when you can make deals like this under excellent terms," said Adolph Lundin at the time.[15]

By the time Lukas Lundin made his $100 million pledge to the Clinton Foundation, the Congo operation was making the company "staggering profits."[16] But for the profits to remain staggering, US policy needed to remain unchanged. The 2006 Congo Relief, Security, and Democracy Promotion Act, which Hillary had cosponsored, placed those investments at serious risk, because they threatened to overturn the political leadership in the country. What benefited Lundin was the status quo in Congo. That status quo was preserved by Hillary's disappointing failure as secretary of state to implement any of the key provisions in the law that she had strongly advocated only a few years earlier—before Lundin made his contribution. According to a July 2012 article in *Foreign Policy*, the law had real teeth and empowered the secretary of state to intervene in a number of important ways. Yet for reasons unknown, Hillary chose not to do so.

This failure to act could at best be described as a sin of omission—though it is a sin compounded by her many promises as a senator to bring real change to the DRC. But Hillary was apparently willing to intervene directly when other well-connected mining companies saw their interests threatened, including foreign mining companies she had no real reason to support. In 2009 a DRC government commission claimed that a Canadian company called First Quantum Minerals Ltd. had won a lucrative concession for a Lonshi mine (worth $1 billion Canadian) through questionable methods. According to the commission, First Quantum won the Lonshi concession without any competitive bidding. The company had allegedly offered "cash payments and shares" to some government officials to get it. DRC officials wanted to cancel the contract and suspend the company's license. But according to *Le Monde Diplomatique*, a prominent French publication, Hillary intervened and tried to pressure the government to restore the company's license. In January 2012 First Quantum received $1.25 billion for its Congolese assets.[17]

Why did the US State Department seek to intervene for a Canadian company doing business in the DRC, especially when 90 percent of the mine's yield ended up in China? We do not know. But it is certainly worth noting that First Quantum was founded by Canadian businessman Jean-Raymond Boulle, a longtime Clinton friend and benefactor. It was Boulle who had put together the diamond deal in Arkansas back in the 1980s when Bill was governor. Hillary wore one of his diamonds to the Clinton inaugural ball.

But Boulle was not the only Clinton donor or ally who was seeking to exploit the DRC's vast mineral wealth.

Former NBA star Dikembe Mutombo has worked with the Clinton Global Initiative as a partner and was appointed by Hillary to the State Department's Young African Leaders Initiative in 2010. In October 2011 he was a member of an official State Department delegation to Sudan. The following month he joined forces with a Hillary presidential campaign bundler named Kase Lawal on a $10 million venture to transport 4.5 tons of gold out of the Democratic Republic of Congo.[18] According to a UN report, the deal involved some of the most notorious war criminals on the planet, including "individuals operating in the Democratic Republic of the Congo and committing serious violations of international law involving the targeting of children or women."[19]

Lawal, a Nigerian and devout Muslim who lived in Houston, was the head of CAMAC, an energy company that did considerable business in Nigeria. He also had a long history with the Clintons. In the 1990s, Bill had appointed Lawal to his Trade Advisory Committee on Africa.[20] When Bill visited Africa in 1998 as president, Lawal accompanied him. Lawal's CAMAC featured on its board former Clinton energy secretary Hazel O'Leary and former Clinton senior White House official Dr. Lee Patrick Brown.[21]

According to a 2012 report in the *Atlantic Monthly*, Lawal leased a Gulfstream V jet from Dallas-based Southlake Aviation and sent his half brother Mickey

Lawal (vice president of CAMAC), along with Reagan Mutombo (Dikembe's nephew) and employees from his company, to Africa to secure the prize. Also involved was a Texas-based diamond trader named Carlos St. Mary. If all went well, the expected profit was a quick $20 million.[22]

All did not go well. The Gulfstream ended up in Goma, Congo. The man they were dealing with to secure the gold was a notorious warlord named Bosco Ntaganda. There are plenty of nefarious criminal leaders in Africa, but Ntaganda belongs near the top of the list. The International Criminal Court indicted him in 2006 for using child soldiers. He was also categorized as a sanctioned individual on the US Treasury Department's Office of Foreign Asset Control list. The consequences: US citizens doing business with him faced the possibility of up to twenty years in prison.

As text messages obtained by UN investigators make clear, Kase Lawal knew he was dealing with the notorious Ntaganda. And from the beginning he knew that the gold was from the DRC. To combat the export of gold by warlords and criminal bans, the DRC government banned unregulated exports of gold out of the country.[23] Lawal denied any involvement in illegal activities.

The "delegation" from Lawal and Mutombo transferred $5 million of the cash and awaited their gold. But then DRC customs officials seized the Gulfstream and arrested everyone onboard.[24]

The owner of the leased jet, David Disiere, got a call in the dead of night informing him that the $43 million jet was loaded with ten boxes of gold but was now being held by authorities in Goma. Detained by Congo authorities for the violation of several laws, Lawal and Mutombo contacted the State Department to get them released. As the Texas diamond trader St. Mary described it later in a legal deposition, "He [Mutombo] said that . . . he had lobbied a lot on our behalf with Washington, D.C. and he indicated that—that Kase was quite impressed with his ability—his ability to lobby at the U.S. State Department on our behalf and was surprised at the number of people that he knew because he was the former ambassador to the Congo under Clinton's administration."[25]

They were released from jail following State Department intervention. No one involved has faced criminal charges in the United States.

Meanwhile, at the same time that Lukas Lundin made his $100 million commitment to the Clinton Foundation, another major foreign investor with much at stake in Africa was doing the same thing.

Less than three months after Hillary announced her presidential bid, Bill was in London for a meeting with a reclusive Saudi sheikh named Mohammed al-Amoudi. Amoudi was the head of a sprawling conglomerate called the Mohammed International Development Research and Organization Companies (MIDROC), which had extensive interests in Ethiopia including mines, agriculture, hotels, hospitals, steel, and cement.[26]

Born in Ethiopia to an Ethiopian mother and a Yemeni father, Amoudi grew up in Saudi Arabia and became the kingdom's second richest man.[27] Much of his wealth derived from his close relationship with Ethiopia's repressive government, which sold him government assets—mines, concessions, and land—for deeply discounted prices. An enormous amount of his wealth was tied up with that government and he took acts likely aimed at helping it stay in power.[28]

On May 14, 2007, in a small ceremony, the sheikh announced that he was committing $20 million to the Clinton Foundation. He started things off with a check for $2 million.[29]

Amoudi was familiar with the money ways of Washington. His lobbying firm in Washington included Senators George Mitchell, Lloyd Bentsen (who had been treasury secretary when Bill was president), and Bob Dole as paid advisers.[30]

In May 2007, when he made his commitment to the Clinton Foundation, the Ethiopia Democracy and Accountability Act (H.R. 2003) had just been introduced by Congressman Donald Payne. The bill quickly acquired eighty-five cosponsors in the House and passed on October 2, 2007. The United States was sending hundreds of millions in taxpayer money to Ethiopia every year: the bill called for tying that aid directly to progress on human rights. For Amoudi's interests, a bill pressuring the regime that had given him so much to reform would be a disaster. Amoudi's business interests were protected by the ruling regime in Ethiopia. Indeed, some of his businesses had been purchased at bargain-basement prices during the privatization of government assets. A democratic election bringing in new leadership would put them at risk.

As the bill moved to the US Senate, many looked to see where Senator Clinton would come down. After all, she was the clear frontrunner for the Democratic presidential nomination at the time and chair of the Senate Armed Services Committee.

An Ethiopian human rights organization sent a letter in 2009 to former president Clinton at the Clinton Foundation warning that the donation was an attempt to influence US policy toward Ethiopia. "We have reason to believe that the huge donation to the Clinton

Foundation was made on behalf of the Ethiopian government. . . . Although we believe in philanthropy, there is something troubling with this picture. By all accounts, Sheikh Amoudi, the owner of Ethiopia's famous Sheraton Hotel, is not known for much philanthropy."

The letter, a copy of which was also sent to Hillary at the State Department, further noted what observers in other countries had seen. "Local AIDS organizations that appealed to the billionaire [Amoudi] for paltry sums were turned down," the Ethiopians wrote to Clinton. "So why would a wealthy man from one of the poorest countries in the world say no to organizations in his country and yet easily cough up $20 million for an American organization 10,000 miles away? Is this just a coincidence that the donation was made at the start of U.S. presidential elections?"[31]

The letter also asserted that the Clinton Foundation had a close working relationship with the oppressive government. "The work of the Clinton Foundation in Ethiopia is loosely intertwined with government operations. We urge you to go beyond the government and to seek out independent community organizations that are closely working with the poor."[32]

Neither Bill nor the foundation ever responded. Instead, as we will see, when Hillary became secretary of state, Amoudi's companies received special benefits from the US State Department, including taxpayer funds.

Much of Amoudi's wealth came from his relationship with Ethiopia's longtime dictator, Meles Zenawi. A diminutive man with a goatee and arched eyebrows, Zenawi had joined a rebel group fighting the Marxist Mengistu regime. He quickly rose through the ranks. When they seized power in 1991, Zenawi was thirty-six and became head of the country.[33]

It is hard to overstate how closely Amoudi's wealth was tied to Zenawi's rule in Ethiopia. (When Zenawi died in 2012 of a mysterious stomach ailment, Amoudi would say, "I lost my right hand.")[34] Amoudi had been able to buy 70 percent of Ethiopia's National Oil Corporation from the government. One of the sheikh's companies, Saudi Star, was given leases on tens of thousands of acres of Ethiopian land.[35] The sheikh controls Ethiopia's steel production and is the country's exclusive gold exporter, with one of his mines (also purchased from the government) producing more than ten thousand pounds of gold and silver per year.[36]

Zenawi's policies pushed local people off their lands, decimated forests, and encroached on game reserves.[37] The list of his offenses is immense, reported Britain's

prestigious *The Lancet,* including politically manipu-
lating the foreign aid the United States and other countries provide: "badly needed food and agricultural
aid that had been given by foreign donors was being
denied to hungry village communities not allied with
the ruling party."[38]

Zenawi was a shrewd technocrat known for "impris-
oning his political opponents, withholding development
assistance from restive areas, stealing elections, and
cracking down on civil society NGOs." He sentenced
journalists (including two Europeans) to lengthy jail
terms. As *The Atlantic* put it, "From a human rights
perspective, Zenawi's rule has been abusive, heavy-
handed, and self-interested."[39]

On the plus side, under his rule Ethiopia also experienced rapid economic growth. And it was this economic growth that had led Bill Clinton to praise him
as part of a " 'new generation' of African leaders."[40]
Zenawi's ability to curry favor with some in the West
while being a brutal dictator at home led one observer
to note, "He was a charmer in Geneva and London. He
was a stern, even brutal, autocrat at home."[41]

Despite his mixed record, many in the West—
including the Clintons—embraced and legitimized
him. According to a leaked State Department cable,
in 2007, on his way to attend the G20 summit in

Pittsburgh, Zenawi was invited to attend Clinton Foundation events in New York.[42]

When Hillary Clinton became secretary of state in January 2009, Ethiopian officials interacted confidently with US diplomats. Despite public statements coming from Washington about promoting human rights in Ethiopia and Africa, Ethiopian officials remained unfazed. In February 2010 Hillary's undersecretary of state, Maria Otero, met with the dictator and raised questions about the plight and arrest of an opposition figure named Birtukan Midekssa. Zenawi told her that Midekssa will "vegetate in jail, forever," according to leaked State Department cables obtained through WikiLeaks. As far as opposition groups were concerned, he said, "we will crush them with our full force."[43]

It was a shocking display of disrespect, given that the United States was sending his government half a billion dollars a year. As *Foreign Affairs* put it, "Washington has expressed its concern about these issues to the Ethiopian government, and the Ethiopian government has reacted not only negatively but also insultingly— despite receiving $533 million in U.S. assistance in fiscal year 2010."[44]

Zenawi aggressively went after not only domestic political opponents but also American organizations, like the US Chamber of Commerce and Jimmy Carter's Carter Center, that were working in the country. According to another WikiLeaks State Department cable, diplomats raised concerns with Zenawi about his new policy requiring organizations like the US Chamber of Commerce and the Carter Center to seek government approval to use US money sent from the United States in Ethiopia. Zenawi said as far as the Carter Center was concerned, "Maybe we are better off if they do not come." He was equally dismissive when diplomats raised questions about how the government restricted access to Western food aid in certain regions for political reasons.[45]

In 2012 Ethiopia was among the top sub-Saharan African recipients of US aid, with $707 million in planned aid. As secretary of state, Hillary was required to evaluate whether countries receiving American aid were transparent in how the money was spent. "The Department of State, Foreign Operations, and Related Programs Appropriation Act prohibits U.S. assistance to the central government of any country that does not meet minimum standards of fiscal transparency." Unless, that is, Hillary decided to grant the country a waiver.[46]

State Department officials determined that Ethiopia failed to meet the transparency requirement. According to leaked cables from the embassy,

Ethiopia does not, however, have specific laws or regulations governing the public disclosure of revenues and expenditures in national budgets. There are no independent auditors of government budget data, so information is taken at face value. International economists generally focus their criticism on the number of extra-budgetary items that are omitted from the national budget. Notably, the national budget does not include over 100 state-owned enterprises or the over 70 "endowment" companies owned by the ruling political party.

The list of offenses continued and concluded by noting, "In the past year, there have not been any events that affected Ethiopia's budget transparency and the Government of Ethiopia has not made any steps towards improving its fiscal transparency." When US diplomats asked the Ethiopian minister of finance about the national budget, he "maintained that he does not have access" to complete books either. Diplomats raised the "message to GOE [Government of Ethiopia] officials regarding Ethiopia's need to comply with USG [US government] fiscal transparency guidelines; however, this message has fallen on deaf ears and only seems to aggravate relations."[47]

Despite the lack of compliance and the apparent lack of interest in moving toward transparency, Hillary granted the government of Ethiopia a waiver, which allowed it to avoid transparency requirements.[48]

Someone who has directly benefited from US assistance to Ethiopia is Sheikh Amoudi. Amoudi owned Ethiopia's Dashen Bank, which he used to finance his other companies and projects. According to Dashen's annual reports, the bank reaps financial reward through the USAID's Development Credit Authority, which is funded by US taxpayers and provides Ethiopian loan guarantees.[49] The USAID also brokered a long-term contract in November 2009 specifically for Almeda Textiles (which is owned by Amoudi) to import textiles into the United States.[50]

When Hillary was appointed secretary of state, she brought in a group of advisers to shape American policy toward Africa. But two individuals largely responsible for forming it didn't have a direct portfolio at State. Husband Bill was considered to be Hillary's closest Africa adviser. He had good contacts with several African presidents and traveled there regularly.[51]

The other key unofficial adviser was former ambassador Joe Wilson, regarded as Hillary's "grey eminence for Africa."[52] Wilson had served as ambassador to several countries in Africa. In 1997 he was appointed special assistant to President Clinton and senior director for African affairs in the White House.

Wilson had the responsibility to "plan and execute" then president Bill Clinton's first trip to Africa, which supposedly raised his consciousness concerning the continent.[53]

Wilson is perhaps most famous for the role he played in a controversy involving his wife, Valerie Plame, a former CIA agent who had been outed by officials in the Bush administration. Wilson charged that this was an intentional act of retaliation against him for debunking the administration's claims about Saddam Hussein's seeking yellowcake uranium in Africa. It later turned out that the leak of Plame's identity came from the State Department, not the White House. Nevertheless, husband and wife made something of a career out of the episode: Plame published a book about her experience, which in turn became a movie starring Sean Penn and Naomi Watts. Wilson's claims about the yellowcake uranium were later debunked by the Senate Intelligence Committee.[54]

Wilson was close to the Clintons. "He was very active with the Hillary Clinton [presidential] campaign," his wife noted. Wilson penned articles declaring that in contrast with then senator Obama, Hillary had real-world diplomatic experience. On the campaign trail in Portland, Oregon, in April 2008, he said that Hillary was "easily the better candidate." Joe Wilson also traveled with Bill Clinton to Africa as part of a Clinton Foundation delegation.[55]

Once Hillary was nominated for secretary of state, many believed she wanted to appoint Wilson to a senior State Department post for African affairs. But the reality of facing a difficult Senate confirmation deterred her. Many Republicans strongly disliked him. Still, Wilson was a strong presence at the State Department despite his lack of an official post. "Wilson's presence in the wings is still strongly felt and the future incumbent in this post will constantly have him under their feet," noted one African business publication.[56]

In January 2007 Wilson became vice chairman of a New York–based investment firm called Jarch Capital.[57] A holding company focused on natural resources like oil, uranium, and gold, it specialized in cutting deals in countries where it expected "sovereignty changes." That's a nice way of saying countries that are at war.[58]

"Ambassador Wilson will be instrumental in the growth of Jarch as it expands in Africa, sometimes in politically sensitive areas," noted the company in a press release. In other words, like Adolph Lundin did in Congo, Jarch would be striking deals with warlords fighting local governments, hoping to cash in when power changed hands. (As Jarch founder Philippe

Heilberg, a former Wall Street banker, explained his strategy of cutting deals with warlords, "You have to go to the guns, this is Africa.")[59]

The venture was clearly off the grid as far as the Bush State Department was concerned. As *Harper's* quoted a knowledgeable observer in 2007, "The State Department isn't supportive of Jarch's involvement because it knows that once Americans go after oil in the south any hope of a national unity government collapses."[60]

But Jarch Capital pressed on anyway. Wilson was of particular help because he had dealt with Sudanese warlords while he had served in the Clinton administration. He knew the region, and was a master negotiator. These skills proved extremely valuable to Jarch.

Jarch was close to several warlords operating in the Sudan. In 2009, shortly after Hillary was appointed secretary of state, Jarch took out a fifty-year lease on 400,000 hectares (or one million acres—about the size of Vermont) in Unity State, South Sudan.[61] In addition to the rights to farm the land, it procured oil and uranium rights as well. As the *Financial Times* put it, the deal had "a decidedly 19th century flavor to it."[62]

Sudan was in the middle of a civil war and the United States had placed restrictions on US companies wanting to do business in the country. So Jarch set up a subsidiary, Jarch Management, which was registered outside of the United States, "making it easier to circumvent such restrictions."[63]

Jarch acquired the land by striking a bargain with Gabriel Matip, the eldest son of General Paulino Matip Nhial, who was deputy commander in chief of the Sudan People's Liberation Army (SPLA) and former head of the South Sudan Defense Force (SSDF). The general was also put on the Jarch advisory board. SSDF bragged, "This company is set to become the largest producer of oil and gas in South Sudan."[64]

Wilson's firm continued signing up warlords and enriching their family members in exchange for lucrative leases on rebel-held territory. In 2010 it signed up Sudanese General Gabriel Tanginya as an "adviser" and leased a huge area of his native Jonglei state in what was called "Africa's largest land deal."[65] Tanginya, who has been accused of instigating violence against civilians in southern Sudan, was apparently a very welcome addition to the firm. Jarch declared that General Tanginya "will give the Company much needed expertise in Jonglei and expand its expertise in Greater Upper Nile."[66]

By the time there were national elections in 2011, the newly minted vice president of South Sudan was Riek Machar, who was also an adviser to Jarch. Machar had been a rebel leader and later apologized for his role in the Bor Massacre, in which thousands of people had been killed.[67]

As South Sudan struggles with factional fighting following its independence in 2011, Jarch Capital–linked warlords are in the thick of the fight. General Peter Gadet, a former member of the Jarch Capital advisory board, is the target of international sanctions. According to the BBC, the international sanctions are in response to "reports of atrocities committed in the first half of 2014."[68]

The cluster of donors and advisers to the Clintons who rely on warlords and corrupt dictators is not confined to the Democratic Republic of Congo, Ethiopia, or Sudan. It extends further south on the continent and includes a longtime Clinton benefactor with close ties to the corrupt regime in Nigeria.

Nigeria is widely recognized as one of the most corrupt countries in the world. It has also been one of the most lucrative countries for the Clintons. Over the course of more than fifteen years, they have collected large speaking fees, campaign-related funds, and large contributions for the Clinton Foundation from those who have made fortunes by working in the corrupt world of Nigerian politics.

In his first eight years on the global lecture circuit, Bill had never been paid to speak in Nigeria. But once Hillary was appointed secretary of state, he booked two of his top three highest-paid speeches ever by traveling to Nigeria, pulling in a whopping $700,000 each.[69]

The two speeches were allegedly underwritten by Nigerian media mogul Nduka Obaigbena, who owns Nigeria's *ThisDay* newspaper. Obaigbena, a solidly built man "with a taste for bespoke Lanvin suits," professes "to live modestly and discreetly," all the while maintaining a home in Lagos, a large estate in Nigeria's Delta State, and a sleek penthouse at the Ritz Carlton in Washington, DC.[70]

Obaigbena casts himself as a rebel fighting Nigeria's corrupt political establishment. But he's known more for his lavish parties and concerts, which have brought Beyoncé and Jay-Z, as well as Bill Clinton, to Nigeria at enormous expense. Often these lavish events come at a price for ordinary Nigerians. When Clinton appeared at a *ThisDay* award event in 2013, he handed out checks to schoolteachers as a reward for their work. But while Clinton collected his fee, the teachers saw their checks from *ThisDay* bounce.[71]

Obaigbena is close to the Nigerian government of President Goodluck Jonathan, to whom he serves as an unofficial adviser. Jonathan has been accused of corruption by numerous international organizations. (As the Associated Press puts it, Obaigbena has "close ties to major business leaders and those in the ruling People's Democratic Party.") Hillary's State Department said that Jonathan's tenure is marked by "massive, widespread, and pervasive corruption" at all levels of the Nigerian government.[72] And yet, as with Ethiopia, Hillary granted the country a waiver for corruption so it could continue to receive US assistance. Back in 2006, when Jonathan was the governor of Bayelsa State, he authorized the transfer of $1 million from the government's poverty alleviation fund to Obaigbena's organization so he could bring Beyoncé to Nigeria.[73]

One longtime Clinton benefactor is businessman Gilbert Chagoury, who has also been implicated in corruption and bribery in Nigeria. Born in Lagos, Chagoury comes from a Lebanese family and has dual citizenship in Lebanon and the United Kingdom. He built a financial empire in Nigeria with the help of General Sani Abacha, a Nigerian dictator whose five-year tenure was "known for its corruption and brutality."[74]

Chagoury served as a "front for the general's extensive business empire." And the two had a business partner in their activities: Marc Rich, the fugitive oil and commodities broker. Chagoury apparently worked with Rich to sop up oil assets in Nigeria and sell them on the oil market for the benefit of General Abacha and his associates. The Nigerian media declared in 1999 that the "Gilbert Chagoury-Marc Rich alliance remains a formidable foe."[75]

Abacha and Chagoury met when the future dictator was a young army officer. After Abacha carried out a coup in 1993, Chagoury received prized oil concessions and government construction contracts.[76] In exchange, Chagoury helped the general siphon off money and get it out of the country. Abacha's rule was highly criticized in Washington, where hundreds of millions of dollars in foreign assistance were disappearing into European bank accounts.[77] During his rule, Abacha funneled billions of dollars to foreign bank accounts. Nigeria's lead anticorruption prosecutor at the time, Nuhu Ribadu, put Chagoury at the center of the scheme. "You couldn't investigate corruption without looking at Chagoury," he said. According to Ribadu, Chagoury helped steer more than $4 billion into bank accounts in Switzerland, Luxembourg, Liechtenstein, and the Isle of Jersey.[78]

Recognizing that it helped to have highly placed friends in Washington, Chagoury started funneling money to the 1996 Clinton reelection campaign and the Democratic National Committee. He contributed

$460,000 to a Miami-based voter registration group tied to the DNC. (Because Chagoury is not an American citizen, he is unable to legally contribute directly to a campaign.) As the *Washington Post* put it, the nearly half-million-dollar contribution was given to "curry favor with Clinton's administration on Abacha's behalf."[79]

Apparently it worked: in 1996, Chagoury and his wife attended the White House Christmas party.[80] More significantly, Bill effectively changed US policy toward Nigeria with a single sentence. The United States government had been pressuring Abacha to step down and hold elections. Abacha was expected to go. But President Clinton said in 1998, "If [Abacha] stands for election, we hope he will stand as a civilian."[81] In short, Clinton signaled that Abacha could stay; he simply needed to run as a civilian. The *New York Times* called it a "shift" in US policy.

When Abacha died in 1998 (allegedly in the company of two prostitutes), the Nigerian government and European authorities began investigating the missing money.[82] They quickly fingered Chagoury. In 2000 he was convicted in Geneva, Switzerland, of money laundering and "aiding a criminal organization in connection with the billions of dollars stolen from Nigeria during the Abacha years," as PBS's *Frontline* put it. (As part of a plea deal the conviction was later expunged.)[83] Chagoury cut a deal with the Nigerians and Swiss, returning $300 million of his own profits in exchange for legal immunity. Subsequently, the tiny island state of St. Lucia appointed him as its envoy to the United Nations Education, Social and Cultural Organization (UNESCO), bringing him diplomatic immunity and preventing prosecution in other European countries.[84] Why St. Lucia bestowed this honor on him is unclear.

Chagoury's apparent complicity in the looting of Nigeria by a brutal dictator might be enough to deter most people from doing business with him. But not the Clintons. If anything, their relationship has blossomed. Clinton has recently been described as Chagoury's "close friend."[85]

Since his conviction in Europe, Chagoury has donated millions to the Clinton Foundation. In 2009, shortly after Hillary became secretary of state, he pledged a whopping $1 billion to the Clinton's legacy project.[86] During a speech Bill delivered in St. Lucia, the island's prime minister extended thanks to Chagoury for arranging the visit.[87] He was also an invited guest to Bill's sixtieth birthday party and attended the wedding of Bill's longtime aide Doug Band. The Chagourys were also active in Hillary's 2008 presidential bid. Michel

Chaghouri, a nephew in Los Angeles, was a bundler for the campaign and served on the campaign staff.[88] Numerous other relatives gave the maximum $4,600 each to her campaign.[89]

Chagoury's legal troubles continued. In April 2010 Gilbert Chagoury and his brother Jack were indicted by the US Justice Department in a massive bribery scandal involving $6 billion and Halliburton. Bribes had allegedly been paid to secure contracts in Nigeria. Eventually Chagoury and his brother were dropped from the case, and Halliburton settled with the federal government for $35 million.[90]

Bill has lavished praise on Chagoury over the years. In 2005 Chagoury was presented with the Pride of Heritage award from the Lebanese community by Bill.[91] And in 2009 the Clinton Global Initiative gave Chagoury's company an award for sustainable development.[92] In 2013 Bill showed up in Nigeria for a public ceremony involving one of Chagoury's construction projects.

Why the Clintons continue to associate with, take money from, and have transactions with Gilbert Chagoury remains a mystery. No less an expert than Marc Rich, who had years of experience working with Chagoury and Nigeria, once described the country as "the global capital of corruption."[93]

The Clinton Foundation has made its work in Africa a centerpiece of its global work on HIV/AIDS and development. Unfortunately, many of those who are paying it and providing it with funds have profited off the worst excesses on the continent. One has to wonder why the Clintons would permit themselves to be so closely tied to such a corrupt group of individuals.

Chapter 9
Rainforest Riches

HILLARY, BILL, AND COLOMBIAN
TIMBER AND OIL DEALS

I n early June 2010 Bill Clinton met Frank Giustra in Colombia to launch a $20 million fund for small businesses.[1] The two had visited Colombia together numerous times: for paid speeches, to look in on Giustra's growing investments there, and to launch a Clinton Foundation project in the country.

Giustra was invested in natural resources in Colombia. And he was looking to expand his holdings in oil, natural gas, coal, and timber. The country had been plagued by violence and narcoterrorism for decades and was slowly coming out of it, thanks in part to a large infusion of American foreign aid. (Colombia was the fourth largest recipient of US foreign and military aid in the world.) It was also desperate to get a free-trade agreement passed in the United States to jump-start its economy.

What that meant was that Hillary, as secretary of state, held much of the country's future in her hands. And as some unseen power of timing would have it, Hillary was set to arrive in Colombia the very next day. In her memoirs, Hillary called the fact that she and her husband were both in the country "a happy coincidence in our hectic schedules."[2]

It was the waning weeks of Colombian president Alvaro Uribe's tenure in office. The thin, bespectacled Uribe had first been elected in 2002 on a platform of fighting terrorism and violence. When he took office, he later wrote, "Vast swathes of Colombia were under total dominion of the *narcoterroristas*."[3] For Uribe the fight was personal: his father had been killed by Revolutionary Armed Forces of Colombia (FARC) terrorists in the 1980s. During his eight years in office, he had achieved an impressive record of success. But term limits prevented him from running again. (He tried holding a popular referendum that would get him another term, but Colombian courts rejected it.) He would be out of office by August 2010 but still had substantial powers until the next election.

Hillary was popping over to Bogotá from nearby Ecuador aboard a US government plane. After her aircraft touched down at Colombia's Catam Military Airport, she was greeted by US ambassador William Brownfield and Colombian foreign minister Jaime

Bermudez. Hillary expressed her strong support for the Uribe government and closer ties with Colombia. "The United States will continue to support the Colombian people, the Colombian military and their government in the ongoing struggle against the insurgents, the guerrillas, the narco-traffickers who would wish to turn the clock back," she said.[4]

These were not meaningless niceties. Only a couple of months earlier, three influential Democratic senators—who were also Hillary's friends—had written to her about cutting aid to Colombia. Russ Feingold of Wisconsin, Chris Dodd of Connecticut, and Patrick Leahy of Vermont had penned a letter saying it was time to back away. "Given U.S. record budget deficits, we cannot afford to continue assistance that is not achieving sufficient results," they wrote. They also dinged Uribe on human rights. "In particular," they said, "human rights abuses by Colombian military personnel supported by the U.S. continue, and those responsible are rarely brought to justice."[5]

Nor were they alone. Foreign aid for Colombia was never a popular subject among Democrats, who were worried about human rights and labor rights conditions in the country.[6]

From the airport Hillary headed into Bogotá and met Bill at a restaurant in the northern part of the city.

With a few friends (it is unclear if Giustra was also there) they enjoyed cappuccinos and a steak dinner.

The next morning, June 9, Bill headed to Casa de Nariño, the presidential palace, for a quiet meeting with President Uribe. They met for approximately an hour and had what the media called an "animated dialogue."[7]

Bill left Casa de Nariño before noon. Hillary arrived for lunch with the president, after which they signed a series of science and technology agreements. Most importantly for Uribe, Hillary also lent her vocal support to a trade agreement between the United States and Colombia. "First, let me underscore President Obama's and my commitment to the Free Trade Agreement," she told RCN Television. "We are going to continue to work to obtain the votes in the Congress to be able to pass it. We think it's strongly in the interests of both Colombia and the United States. And I return very invigorated . . . to begin a very intensive effort to try to obtain the votes to get the Free Trade Agreement finally ratified."[8]

Uribe could not have been more pleased. It is also worth noting that her support for this agreement represented a complete reversal of her position—and Obama's—from the 2008 campaign.

Days after Hillary left Bogotá, Prima Colombia Properties, which Frank Giustra has ownership interest in through a shell company called Flagship Industries, announced that it had acquired the right to cut timber in a biologically diverse forest on the pristine Colombian shoreline. The International Tropical Timber Organization (ITTO) calls this property "one of the world's largest untapped hardwood timber supplies."[9] Through its Colombia-domiciled subsidiary REM International CISA, Prima entered into an exclusive agreement with the Colombian government giving it the right to "harvest 1,050,000 cubic meters of hardwood" on the west coast of Colombia.[10] The timber would be cut along picturesque Huaca Beach in Choco and shipped to China.[11]

Days later, Pacific Rubiales Energy, a company for which Giustra was the Canadian face, announced that the Uribe government was giving the company the right to drill for oil on six lucrative plots.[12] Pacific Rubiales acquired the largest exploration acreage in the Putumayo Basin, which sits at the center of Colombia's oil belt. The other plots were in the giant reserves east of Ciusiana-Cupiagua, and three blocks in the Llanos Basin, a prolific oil-rich area at the foot of the Andes mountains.

It was a stunning success, given that Pacific Rubiales was a relatively new company with little track record in the country. But these lucrative concessions helped the company grow quickly. As German Hernandez, who oversees business operations for the company, explained in 2011, "[A few years ago] we were fewer than 20 people, practically living in tents with mosquito netting. . . . Today we are the number one project in the petroleum industry in Colombia."[13] By the end of 2010 the company was producing a net of seventy thousand barrels of oil equivalent per day in Colombia, and boasted a market cap of over $8.3 billion.[14]

According to Pacific Rubiales cochairman Serafino Iacono, Giustra's role at the company is to provide "valuable financial capital and *political capital* [emphasis added] along the way."[15]

Pacific Rubiales signed up as an early contributor to the Clinton Foundation.[16] Pacific Rubiales and underwriters contributed over $4 million to the Clinton Giustra Sustainable Growth Initiative (CGSGI).[17] And as we have seen in several other cases, the company's decision to give to a charity thousands of miles away to fund work in Colombia struck local charities as odd. They, along with labor-backed social welfare organizations, had been clamoring for the company to provide donations for several health and welfare initiatives. They also wanted the company to raise the salaries of employees. These efforts were rebuffed. Instead of flowing to local charities, the bulk of the company's charitable contributions were given to the Clinton Foundation.[18]

Pacific Rubiales, despite its announced commitment, does not appear on the Clinton Foundation list of donors. Repeated phone calls and e-mails to Pacific Rubiales to determine whether it honored their commitment have not been returned as of this writing.

Giustra's run of good business news in the summer of 2010 was not finished. Less than two weeks after Hillary left, yet another of Giustra's companies, Petroamerica, announced that Colombian regulators had designated the company a "restricted operator," which meant it was eligible to explore for and produce oil.[19] Petroamerica had been founded only a few months earlier, in late 2009, by what a Canadian business journal called "a group of part-time managers and directors."[20] Now, courtesy of the Uribe government, it was sitting on some very big prospects in Colombia. "Of all the resource projects that I am involved with, this is the one I am most excited about," Giustra told one business publication.[21]

The Clinton Foundation was integrated into US State Department energy initiatives in Colombia. According to a leaked State Department memo, on November 8, 2009, a US government delegation arrived in Colombia to explore the rapid expansion of energy and mining loans backed by the US government in Colombia. "The energy sector in Colombia has big plans to expand and the Export-Import Bank (ExIm) and the U.S. Trade Development Agency (TDA) want to be a part of this expansion by providing financial backing and trade capacity building assistance." When TDA representative Patricia Arriagada arrived in Colombia, she met with mines and energy minister Silvana Giaimo. According to a leaked State Department cable, in that meeting Arriagada was "accompanied by Manuel Olivera, local director of the Clinton Foundation."[22] The memo mentions no other nonprofit organization involved in these discussions.

As a result of that delegation, the US government expanded energy and mining loans in Colombia.[23] One of the big projects funded by the US Export-Import Bank was a $280 million liquid natural gas (LNG) barge that was to be used to transport LNG from Colombia to China. The barge was being built for Giustra's company, Pacific Rubiales.[24]

Giustra had other projects in Latin America that received US taxpayer money. Giustra's Endeavour Mining arranged for Export-Import funding in September 2010 as part of an $858 million package of loans for a copper mining project in Mexico called Baja Mining.[25] (According to an Endeavour PowerPoint marketing presentation, it "closed" the deal.) The project involved developing an underground copper-zinc mine near the Mexican town of Santa Rosalia. Endeavour was an adviser on the deal, but Baja Mining was also a "core investment" for the firm, according to one investment document.[26] US taxpayers were on the hook for approximately $420 million.[27]

The Baja investment didn't go well—at least for American taxpayers. According to the Office of the Inspector General at the Export-Import Bank, the project was plagued with cost overruns. The report also suggested that "corporate malfeasance" had taken place. As the report put it, "Our inspection revealed evidence of inappropriate conduct by several parties including the Borrower's failure to make timely disclosure of significant cost overruns, inaccurate representations, allegations of fraud related to one of the project's local vendors, management impropriety, and an overarching lack of governance." The report noted further that the Export-Import Bank had failed to perform proper due diligence when approving the deal. The project apparently fell into default within six months of financial closing.[28]

The full extent of taxpayer funds spent and US government power exerted that helped Giustra cannot be fully known. In Colombia, as in other countries, he uses a web of companies, shell companies, foreign affiliates, and offshore entities that make tracking his investments extremely difficult. In addition to the investments mentioned in this chapter, he also controls a private company called Blue Pacific, which "owns ports under construction in Cartagena and Barranquilla, as well as power plants, farms, mines, and other infrastructure assets" in Colombia.[29]

Colombia had long been a focus of interest for the Clintons. During his presidency, Bill won praise from the Colombians for pouring aid into the country to fight both drug cartels and a revolutionary insurgency. In 2000 he had initiated Plan Colombia, an ambitious program to escalate the war on drugs that came with more than $1.3 billion in aid.[30]

Once he was out of office, his attention shifted from the war on drugs to Colombia's ambitions to sign a free-trade agreement with the United States. The Colombian government wanted a free-trade agreement so that it could sell its products, including natural resources, in the US market tariff free. President George W. Bush and Republicans in Congress generally favored the deal. Opposition mostly came from Democrats (and organized labor) who felt the move would hurt wages for US workers. Democrats also argued that Colombia's human rights record was poor.[31]

For Colombians themselves, it was clear that, as the leading Colombian newspaper, *El Pais*, put it in 2006, "The support of Senator Hillary Clinton and her husband, former President Bill Clinton, will be decisive."[32]

The story began, as it often does, with a lucrative speech. In June 2005 a South American business group called Gold Service International offered Bill $800,000 to deliver four speeches in South America. Gold Service was a keen supporter of the proposed US-Colombia free-trade agreement, because it would boost Colombian exports to the United States.

This was a lot of money at that time. Though Bill's fee would go up appreciably when his wife became secretary of state, his average payment through 2010 was $150,000.

Giustra loaned Bill his jet, and Bill made stops in Mexico City and Bogotá, and then gave two speeches in São Paulo, Brazil.[33] As Andres Franco, the group's chief operating officer, explained, "he was supportive of the trade agreement at the time that he came." And Bill spoke openly about his support for it.[34]

Meanwhile, Bill made efforts to bring Giustra and Uribe together so that the Canadian investor could expand his operations in Colombia. Thus, in September

2005 Bill hosted a "philanthropic event" with Uribe. And as he often did, he mixed philanthropy with business. According to the *Wall Street Journal*, the purpose of the meeting was to introduce the two men. As the *Journal* reported, Uribe and Giustra "put up two chairs in a hallway and talked for about ten minutes. . . . Later in the day, a top Clinton aide told Mr. Giustra that he heard the meeting with Mr. Uribe went well."[35]

In January 2007 Giustra's new company, Pacific Rubiales, signed a pipeline deal with Ecopetrol, the state-owned Colombian energy company. One month after the deal was sealed, Bill, Giustra, and Uribe met at the Clintons' home in Chappaqua, New York. In March, they met again, this time in the Colombian port city of Cartagena.[36]

All along, Democrats remained opposed to military assistance to Colombia as well as the Colombian free-trade agreement.[37] But Senator Hillary Clinton's views on the matter remained ambiguous. As one Latin American financial publication put it, when it came to her positions on trade "we find a bit of everything." She was in favor of the North American Free Trade Agreement (NAFTA) and supported trade deals with Chile, Peru, and Singapore. But she was against the Central American Free Trade Agreement and extending trade preferences with other South American countries.[38]

So the Colombians continued their courtship by various means.

In June 2007 President Uribe arrived in New York City to headline a dinner event at a posh hotel. The event was titled "Colombia Is Passion." In fact, the night was largely about Bill. Uribe presented him with the "Colombia Is Passion" award for "believing in our country and encouraging others to do the same."[39]

As *Newsweek* reported,

Eager to repair its image in the United States and help boost support for a controversial United States-Colombia free-trade agreement, the beleaguered government of Alvaro Uribe came up with a clever PR move: give Clinton an award at a banquet, where the popular former president would say nice things about the country.

The dinner included a video depicting Bill as a Colombian hero. Uribe even praised him as the country's unofficial minister of tourism. Bill praised Uribe in turn and declared that, while there was currently a debate in Washington about the free-trade agreement, "[w]e need to remember that we are friends."[40] Then he invited Uribe to be a "featured attendee" at the annual Clinton Global Initiative meeting in New York that September.

As it happens, publicity for the awards ceremony had been handled by Burson-Marsteller Worldwide, a PR firm then headed by Mark Penn, a longtime political adviser and pollster for the Clintons.[41] Penn, who was also serving as Hillary's campaign manager for the 2008 run, was advising the Colombians on how to get the free-trade deal through Congress. Uribe paid Penn's firm $300,000.[42]

Penn's ties to the Colombians proved too embarrassing and he resigned as Hillary's campaign manager. For good measure, the Colombians let Burson go, too.[43]

Also on the Colombian payroll was Hillary's campaign spokesman Howard Wolfson's lobbying firm, Glover Park. The firm was paid $40,000 a month. While Wolfson didn't work directly on the Colombia account, he did have an equity stake in the firm.[44]

The trade deal and Penn's consulting arrangement soon became issues in the Democratic primary. Courting the labor vote, Barack Obama had come out strongly against a free-trade deal with Colombia. So did Hillary. In the sort of overheated rhetoric we often hear on the campaign trail, she was uncompromising. "As I have said for months, I oppose the deal. I have spoken out against the deal, I will vote against the deal, and I will do everything I can to urge the Congress to reject the Colombia Free Trade Agreement."[45]

Uribe, sensing the trade pact was imperiled by American politics, lashed out at Obama—but not at Hillary. "I deplore the fact that Senator Obama, aspiring to be president of the United States, should be unaware of Colombia's efforts," he said. "I think it is for political calculations that he is making a statement that does not correspond to Colombia's reality."[46]

Given that both Hillary and Obama were publicly opposed to the trade deal, either way it looked ominous for Uribe. As one economic consultancy put it, "we are concerned that a Democrat win of the presidency may stymie the FTA for even longer."[47]

Obama, of course, went on to win the nomination and the presidency. And Hillary, as his newly minted secretary of state, was quick to change course on the trade pact. In early 2009, while the Obama administration was reportedly still figuring out its trade policy, Hillary let Uribe know she was "very proud to be working with Colombia" on the trade deal. As Colombian foreign minister Jaime Bermudez Merizalde told the BBC after he met with Hillary in February 2009, "What we talked about was that we have to work together to see how this issue can be handled in Congress."[48]

Hillary had come out swinging in favor of the trade pact when she met with Uribe shortly after Bill in June 2010. By early 2011 she was helping lead the effort to pass the deal. "There are still negotiations that are taking place," she told reporters after meeting with Colombian vice president Angelino Garzon. "We don't want to send an agreement just for the sake of sending an agreement. We want to send an agreement and get it passed."

"Secretary Clinton's remarks represent the clearest signal the administration has sent with respect to its intentions to move the Colombia agreement forward in a specific time frame," said National Foreign Trade Council president Bill Reinsch.[49]

It did not go unnoticed that this represented a complete policy reversal on Hillary's part. She justified the shift on the grounds that the human rights and labor situation in Colombia had improved. Hillary claimed in a press conference that "[w]e have seen improvements in the human rights situations in a number of countries," and cited Colombia, among others.

But Hillary's words concerning labor union conditions contradicted her own department's most recent human rights report.[50] The number of trade unionists killed had actually gone up in 2010.[51]

Hillary also claimed that the trade agreement was now a good deal for everyone. "The U.S.-Colombia Free Trade Agreement would allow our businesses to sell goods in Colombia duty-free—the same way

Colombian goods have entered the United States for many years—and it comes with important new guarantees on labor and human rights."[52]

That view was not shared by the AFL-CIO, which declared in 2011, "Colombia remains the most dangerous place in the world for union members."[53] Human Rights Watch reported that there had been "virtually no progress" since 2006 in obtaining convictions for union violence, and the press cited thirty-eight recent murders of trade unionists in the few months after Colombian elections in 2010.

The trade pact with Colombia was approved by Congress and President Obama signed off on it. The pact benefited US businesses trying to sell products in Colombia and also boosted Colombian exports to the United States. The Colombian government and business community has hailed it as an important victory for the Colombian people.

In February 2012 Bill and Giustra were back in Colombia together for meetings and some golf. Bill was playing in a golf tournament (the Pacific Rubiales Open, no less), which was a fundraiser for the Clinton Foundation. Bill met with President Juan Manuel Santos.

Since then, Giustra's interests in Colombia have run into trouble. For instance, the manner in which energy concessions were handed out has come under fire.

There have been media claims of a "juicy concession" for Giustra from the Colombian government obtained with the help of Bill Clinton.[54] Colombian senator Jorge Enrique Robledo claimed the Uribe government showed favoritism to Pacific Rubiales during the process of granting Colombian oil concessions.[55]

Pacific Rubiales has been the subject of repeated complaints about "deplorable conditions" for workers. The complaints included "contracts, work hours, pay, democratic guarantees, housing, hygiene, transportation and the right to organize." When leaders from the country's petroleum workers union Unión Sindical Obrera (USO) tried to mediate, Pacific Rubiales reportedly blocked the public highways in the region to prevent them from arriving.[56]

Another of Giustra's companies, Prima Colombia Hardwood, has also run into problems. In May 2011 the Ministry of Environment began monitoring the logging being done by Prima Colombia. According to published reports, the company needed to answer for ten environmental violations, including erosion of the natural wildlife habitat, shifting water currents in the area, and the alteration of the vegetation cover. The National Environment Licensing Authority (ANIA) subsequently decided to deny all environmental permits required by Prima Colombia.[57]

Chapter 10

Disaster Capitalism
Clinton-Style

On the afternoon of January 12, 2010, a devastating 7.0 earthquake shook the island nation of Haiti. In less than a minute, the violent tremors leveled an estimated 25,000 government and commercial buildings, more than 100,000 homes, and killed approximately 230,000 people.

When the earth stopped quaking, more than 1.5 million people were left living in makeshift tent camps. "In 30 seconds, Haiti lost 60 percent of its GDP," said Haitian prime minister Jean-Max Bellerive. For a country whose history was plagued with natural disasters, corrupt leaders, and abject poverty, it must have seemed like the exclamation point on some sort of cruel natural joke.

The international charitable response from groups like the Salvation Army and the Red Cross was generous, as millions of people around the world wrote checks or donated via their cell phones. Foreign governments committed funds, too.

Days after the earthquake, Hillary Clinton was en route to Port-au-Prince to inspect the damage. To accommodate her, all flights to and from the island were halted for three hours. Hillary arrived on a Coast Guard C-130, along with American relief workers and a supply of toothpaste, mustard, and cigarettes her staff had purchased from US supermarkets the night before. She did not leave the airport, to avoid impeding rescue efforts, but declared her deep sympathy for the people of Haiti and offered assurances that America would be Haiti's "friend, partner, and supporter," with the State Department and USAID taking a front and center role in the relief effort.

Bill Clinton was soon on the ground in Haiti, too. He had been appointed a United Nations special envoy to the island in 2009 and traveled to Haiti regularly. With a cluster of cameras around him, Bill teared up as he described what he saw.

The Clintons' close friend and confidante, Cheryl Mills, who was Hillary's chief of staff and counselor at the State Department, was assigned responsibility for how the taxpayer money, directed through USAID, would be spent.[1] Within days, the State Department conceived and created a funnel that would direct the aid and relief money that would soon flood into the country. The Interim Haitian Relief Committee (IHRC) was given the task of executing an action plan developed with the help of Haitian authorities and countries that were donating funds to the rebuilding effort. It was supposed to prioritize the rebuilding of Port-au-Prince, with a focus on restoring the economy and government services.[2]

Bill was promptly appointed cochair, along with Bellerive. Together, they constituted IHRC's Executive Committee, giving them concentrated decision-making power. In this role Bill was ultimately responsible for the approval of any projects that would be funded by US taxpayer dollars or international organizations. Clinton and Bellerive would prove to work effectively together. As we will see, Bellerive would later go into business with members of the Clinton family in Haiti.

In public statements, Bill waxed romantic about how they would rebuild Haiti, like a phoenix from the ashes, in a grand vision of social engineering. "I want them to close their landfills," he told *Esquire* magazine, "recycle everything and use the rest for energy. Wouldn't it be great if they become the first wireless nation in the world? They could, I'm telling you, they really could."[3]

It is hard to underestimate the role that IHRC would play in the disbursement of funds. As the State Department itself noted, in addition to reviewing project applications and deciding if those projects would be funded, "IHRC is the planning body for the Haitian recovery." In particular, as the US Government Accountability Office (GAO) put it, IHRC was supposed to "coordinate donors, conduct strategic planning, approve reconstruction projects, and provide accountability."[4]

With the massive expenditure of US taxpayer money, some things have improved in Haiti. Some roads are considerably better than they were before. A large amount of debris has been removed. But beyond that, by the measure of promises made by the Clintons, the efforts to rebuild Haiti, which were largely controlled by Bill and Hillary Clinton, have been a massive failure.

Five years after the earthquake, Haiti is not a "wireless nation." Billions of dollars have indeed been poured into the country, with Hillary and Bill having much of the say in how the funds were allocated. But according to GAO, IHRC ignored the action plan and funding priorities that had been set up by the Haitian government and donor countries.[5] Moreover, much of the taxpayer money intended for practical rebuilding was squandered.[6] Funds for reconstruction have ended up in worthless projects—while in several cases Clinton friends, allies, and even family members have benefited from the reconstruction circumstances.

Natural disasters often create enormous opportunities for politically connected contractors to make money courtesy of the rebuilding effort. Author and critic Naomi Klein calls it "disaster capitalism."

Disaster capitalism need not be all bad. You do need qualified professionals to go into devastated areas and begin the process of providing immediate relief and rebuilding infrastructure. An example of where such efforts went well was in Indonesia, following the tsunami that devastated the region in 2004. Communities that were cut off from the rest of the country saw their services and infrastructure restored, and crime and corruption were generally kept under control, according to the World Bank.[7]

In the case of Haiti, the process was handled very differently. IHRC, for example, was supposed to have a Performance and Anticorruption Office (PAO) to monitor reconstruction efforts and investigate allegations of corruption. But it was eleven months before a single employee was even hired as part of PAO.[8] What's more, IHRC was never fully staffed, and much of the decision making was left in the hands of key employees of the Clinton Foundation.[9]

Less than a month after the earthquake hit, US ambassador Kenneth Merten sent a cable from Port-au-Prince to State Department headquarters titled "THE GOLD RUSH IS ON."[10] A flood of eager businessmen were rushing to the capital looking to obtain government contracts. But securing contracts and business apparently required knowing the right people. Put simply, it was widely believed you needed access to the Clintons.

Florida-based contractor J. R. Bergeron was one of several business owners jockeying to land lucrative contracts to help with disaster cleanup. To compete for cash in what Bergeron called "the Super Bowl of disasters," he understood the Clintons to be the referees.[11] His company, Bergeron Emergency Services, invested more than a million dollars to move employees and equipment to Haiti even before landing a contract. But Bergeron knew he would have to do more than just demonstrate expertise and readiness. As he later observed, "posturing and aggressive self-promotion in Haiti was an inevitable part of this high-stakes competition. . . . Politics plays a large role."[12]

Bergeron hired two lobbyists, giving them the job of "reaching out to officials of the Clinton Foundation's Haiti earthquake relief efforts and the U.S. Agency for International Development."[13] They were Mitch Berger and Alex Heckler; Heckler had served on Hillary's national campaign finance committee. Bergeron also says he made a donation to the Clinton Foundation. (Records indicate he gave less than $250.) He failed to obtain any contracts.

The realities seemed clear. As one individual told the *Wall Street Journal,* "if you don't have Clinton connections you won't be in the game."[14]

But those with impeccable Clinton credentials apparently didn't need to hire lobbyists.

Merten's cable specifically mentioned the arrival of longtime Clinton friend and confidant General Wesley Clark in the weeks after the earthquake.[15] Like Bill, Clark was from Arkansas and had been NATO commander during Bill's presidency. Indeed, Clark had been one of Clintons' favorite generals and received several military promotions when Bill was in the White House. As the *New Yorker* points out, Clark's last three army jobs, including two at the highest rank, were awarded to him without the army's recommendation.[16]

When Clark sought the Democratic nomination for president in 2004, Bill strongly backed his candidacy. When Hillary ran for president in 2008, Clark raised money for her campaign. Clark also serves on an advisory board of the Clinton Global Initiative (CGI). Much later, in 2013, he signed the first fundraising letter for a superpac backing a 2016 Hillary presidential bid.[17]

According to Merten's cable, Clark quickly scored a meeting with Haitian president René Préval.[18]

Clark had come to Port-au-Prince in search of a home-building contract for a south Florida company called Innovida, a manufacturer of building materials. (Clark sat on the board of the company along with former Florida governor Jeb Bush.) Clark was a big cheerleader for the company. "It can do more for housing in Haiti, better and faster, than any other technology out there," he said. Innovida's ties to the Clintons ran even deeper than Clark. According to the *South Florida Business Journal*, Innovida's CEO Claudio Osorio was a "big fundraiser" for the Hillary 2008 campaign and had contributed to CGI.[19]

Innovida had little track record of actually building homes. Yet the company saw its project fast-tracked by the Haitian government and the State Department.[20] Innovida received a $10 million loan from the US government to build five hundred houses in Haiti.

Sadly, the houses were never built. In 2012 Osorio was indicted and convicted of financial fraud. Prosecutors would later accuse Osorio, who drove a Maserati and lived in a Miami Beach mansion, of using the money intended for relief victims to "repay investors and for his and his co-conspirators personal benefit and to further the fraud scheme."[21] He was ultimately sentenced to twelve years in jail. Innovida collapsed.

It is hard to overstate the power the Clintons wielded in the disbursement of US taxpayer money for Haitian relief. *Esquire* magazine called Bill the "CEO of a leaderless nation," because of his role as the cochair of IHRC.[22] The *Miami Herald* repeatedly referred to Bill as the "co-czar of the recovery effort."[23] Others called him "president of Haiti" or "viceroy" because of his powers. Hillary, as secretary of state, had ultimate control over the dispersement of US taxpayer aid dollars.[24]

Many Haitians believed the Clintons further demonstrated their power in Haiti when Garry Conille became prime minister in October 2011. Conille had worked for Bill as a speechwriter and as his UN special envoy chief of staff.[25] Conille's appointment was seen as a compromise, and the fact that he was backed by Bill Clinton was touted by some Haitians as one of the reasons for his selection.[26]

What happened in Haiti was the classic Clinton Blur, mixing philanthropy, politics, and business.

Bill arrived in Port-au-Prince wearing several hats and pursuing myriad agendas, both public and private. As the *Economist* succinctly noted,

The strange multi-dimensional role that Mr. Clinton plays as co-chair of the IHRC, special UN

envoy, former US president, spouse of the US secretary of state, and head of his own foundation
which supports projects in the country, will continue to lead to confusion about who he advocates
for and to whom he ultimately answers.[27]

Pushback from within IHRC came almost immediately. In October 2010 Jean-Marie Bourjolly, a member
of IHRC, wrote a memorandum to the cochairs and the
other commission members cautioning that by "vesting
all powers and authority of the Board in the Executive
Committee [Clinton and Bellerive], it is clear that what
is expected of us [the rest of IHRC] is to act as a rubber-
stamping body."[28] Bourjolly's concerns were not appre-
ciated. Indeed, his memorandum was not included in
the official minutes of the October IHRC meeting.

Other commission members and employees confirmed that Bill and Hillary got what they wanted
when it came to Haiti projects and contracts. As one
employee noted, projects were approved because "they
were submitted by USAID and State." Moreover, "as
long as USAID is submitting it and USAID is paying
for it, they would be approved."[29]

In December 2010 nine of the fourteen Haitian
IHRC members wrote an official complaint to Clinton
and Bellerive; they felt "completely disconnected from

the activities of the IHRC." IHRC was moving forward on projects that didn't seem to conform to the action plan that the Haitian government and donor nations had agreed to in the months following the tragedy. The members warned that "we risk ending up with a variety of ill-assorted projects, some of which are certainly interesting and useful taken individually, but which collectively can neither meet the urgency nor lay the foundation for the rehabilitation of Haiti, and even less its development."[30]

The GAO echoed those concerns, noting in May 2011, "funding for approved projects is uneven across sectors and is not necessarily aligned with Haitian priorities."

Bill's role as unofficial "viceroy" raised questions in the Haitian community because of the Clintons' penchant for mixing politics with crony business arrangements in Haiti. Back when Bill had been appointed special envoy for the United Nations in 2009, the *Haiti Observateur* challenged both Clintons to "come clean about [Bill's] relationship to the former Haitian president and he and his wife's business dealings in Haiti."[31]

"There have been whispers and rumors for quite a while about the Clintons' choice connections to the former president and particularly the telephone business in Haiti," the paper said.

As president in 1994, Bill Clinton had sent troops to Haiti to return to power Jean-Bertrand Aristide, the duly elected president who had been forced out in a 1991 coup. While president, after he was restored to power, a special deal was granted to a small US-based company called Fusion Communications. (The prime minister of Haiti at the time was Aristide friend and ally René Préval, who was president at the time of the earthquake.) The Haitian government–owned telecom company, Teleco, granted Fusion long-distance minutes from the United States to Haiti at a deeply discounted price. With a large number of Haitians living in the United States and calling home, this was a big market.

Fusion was a relatively small player in the long-distance telephone market. But it was top-heavy with operatives and politicians closely aligned with Bill and Hillary. The board of directors included Tom "Mack" McLarty, Bill's former chief of staff, and was headed by Marvin Rosen, who had been chairman of the Democratic National Committee's finance committee during Bill's 1996 reelection campaign. It was under Rosen's tenure that the notorious White House fundraising coffees, rental of the Lincoln Bedroom to large contributors, and foreign donations from China and Asia had occurred.[32] Also on the board was Ray

Mabus, a former Mississippi governor whom Bill had appointed ambassador to Saudi Arabia.[33]

Teleco's special arrangement with Fusion was supposed to be public, in keeping with the regulations and laws of the FCC. But the company worked hard to keep it secret. As *Wall Street Journal* columnist Mary Anastasia O'Grady, who broke the story, wrote, "By law the agreement is a public document but Fusion wouldn't give it to me until the FCC required them to do so." It took her eight years to get a copy of the contract.[34]

It's easy to see why. The contract gave Fusion access to the Haitian telephone network at a rate of twelve cents a minute, even though the official FCC rate was fifty cents a minute. In short, it was a sweetheart deal. Fusion says it "never made any improper payments or engaged in any improper activity with regard to its relationship with Teleco." But of course, it didn't have to.[35]

After the 2010 earthquake, more than a decade later, there were new telecom prizes available in Haiti. The system was set up so that decisions on doling out contracts and projects went through the Clintons.

In the months following the earthquake, the Clintons began pushing the idea of a wireless mobile phone money-transfer system for Haiti. The idea was to enable friends and relatives to send money directly to people in the quake-ravaged country. Hillary's USAID was quick to send taxpayer money via a grant; it also organized the effort. The Bill Gates Foundation also came on board. The Haiti Mobile Money Initiative also offered incentive funds to companies who would establish mobile money services in the country.

The initiative's big winner was Digicel, a mobile phone company owned by Irish billionaire Denis O'Brien. Digicel received millions in US taxpayer money for its TchoTcho Mobile system. (*TchoTcho* means "pocket money" in Creole.) The USAID Food for Peace program, under direct control of the State Department through Cheryl Mills, chose the TchoTcho system for its money transfers. Haitians were given cell phones and a free TchoTcho account. When Haitians used the system, they paid O'Brien's company millions in fees. They also became users of O'Brien's TchoTcho program.[36]

O'Brien had bought the company in 2008. After the project's launch, Digicel's mobile phone subscriptions soared and its profit margins rose, winning praise from investors.[37] By 2012 Digicel had 77 percent of the Haitian mobile phone market, a rise fueled in part by the fact that it was a digital bank supplier.

Was the mobile money system a good idea? Very possibly it was. But the trouble was not in the idea itself;

rather, it was the fact that it was helping make O'Brien lots of money. From April 2011 to March 2012 Digicel's revenues increased 14 percent and its subscriber base jumped 27 percent. By September 2012 Haiti had overtaken Jamaica as Digicel's most profitable market. The Haitian market became key to the success of Digicel. O'Brien granted himself $300 million in dividends from Digicel in 2012.[38]

O'Brien was in turn making money for the Clintons.

O'Brien arranged at least three lucrative speeches in Ireland, for which Bill was paid $200,000 apiece, as well as a speech in Jamaica. Bill's October 9, 2013, speech at the Conrad Hotel in Dublin was his third in three years, "and was mostly facilitated by billionaire Irish tycoon Denis O'Brien," noted *Irish Central*. "Last year Clinton delivered the keynote address at the Worldwide Ireland Funds annual conference in Cork. . . . The year before he was flown over to Ireland on O'Brien's private jet to deliver a speech at the Global Irish Economic Forum in Dublin Castle."[39]

The timing of these paid speeches is also notable. The Haitian Mobile Money Initiative (HMMI) was announced in June 2010. Three months later, on September 29, Bill gave a speech at Dublin castle sponsored by O'Brien. The next day, Digicel filed notice of its intent to compete for HMMI contracts.

In January of the following year, Digicel became the first company to be awarded funds for participation in HMMI.

On October 8, 2011, Bill gave a speech for the Global Irish Economic Forum, again facilitated by O'Brien. The following day, Digicel was awarded $100,000 through HMMI, which it was to split with fellow cell provider Voila. Two weeks later, Clinton gave a speech in Jamaica for $225,000 on "Our Common Humanity." The speech was sponsored by Whisky Productions, in partnership with O'Brien's Digicel.[40]

On December 2 of the same year, USAID paid the first installment of what would eventually be more than $2 million of taxpayer money into O'Brien's Digicel Foundation, based in Jamaica. According to government databases, Digicel had never received taxpayer money before.

The interlay of money and favors also included the use of O'Brien's jet. When Frank Giustra's jetliner was not available, Clinton used O'Brien's, a modest Gulfstream 550 that seats twenty.[41]

In addition to forking over these immense speaking fees, O'Brien was also a major contributor to the Clinton Foundation, pouring between $1 million and $5 million into the Clintons' legacy project sometime in 2010 or 2011.

The Clintons lavished praise on O'Brien for his generosity and business acumen. In 2012 Bill named O'Brien a Clinton Global Citizen, an annual award offered by CGI. O'Brien received his award before a cheering crowd as Bill praised him for his visionary leadership ability. Bill also praised him in an article he penned for *Time* magazine titled "The Case for Optimism."[42]

Ironically, Bill was conferring this award after an Irish government tribunal issued a scathing report concerning how O'Brien had made his fortune in the early days of the Irish wireless industry. The tribunal found that in the 1990s O'Brien had purchased properties for a government official named Michael Lowry, who was responsible for Irish telecom policy. The properties included land in Mansfield, England, and a home in Cheadle, England, that were purchased with funds from O'Brien's Credit Suisse account in London. In exchange, the tribunal found, "Lowry went to considerable effort to assist Denis O'Brien in securing the mobile phone license" that would end up making him a very rich man. For his part, O'Brien denies ever giving money to government officials and he was never formally charged by authorities.[43]

But it wasn't just connected businessmen who were benefiting from the rebuilding of Haiti. Clinton family members did, too. Bill and Hillary had been look-ing for investors to come to Haiti. But it was a risky prospect, given the infrastructure problems, social and political instability, and endemic corruption. One pos-sible bright spot was mining. Haiti is rich in natural resources—there is an estimated $20 billion in gold, silver, and other precious minerals under the rocky Haitian soil.

In 2012 the Haitian government decided to do some-thing it had not done in more than half a century: grant permits for open-pit gold mining.

One of two recipients was a small North Carolina start-up called VCS Mining. The company had little track record of mining operations in Haiti, or anywhere else for that matter. But its leadership would later boast a board member with a familiar last name: Tony Rodham, Hillary's youngest brother. Rodham would join the board of advisors less than a year after VCS was granted the mining permit. Another member of the board: former Haitian prime minister (and IHRC cochairman with Bill) Jean-Max Bellerive.

The Haitian government gave VCS a "gold mining exploitation permit" (in the company's words) for a project in Morne Bossa, which could be generously renewed for up to twenty-five years. "This is one of two permits issued today, the first permit of their kind issued in over five decades," the company proudly noted.

Rodham had no background in mining. More than half of his bio on the VCS Mining website concerned his ties to his sister and her husband.[44]

Not surprisingly, the deal provoked outrage in the Haitian senate. The mining concession was a sweetheart deal. For one thing, the royalties to be paid to the Haitian government were only 2.5 percent, which mining experts noted at the time was "really low." "Anything under five percent is just really ludicrous for a country like Haiti," said mining royalties expert Claire Kumar. "You shouldn't even consider it."[45]

The episode resulted in a resolution by the Haitian parliament challenging the secrecy of the process and calling for a moratorium on new mining permits. The resolution passed the Haitian senate unanimously.[46]

VCS Mining is continuing to build on its mining concessions in Haiti.

Meanwhile, connected businessmen continued to reap benefits from the reconstruction efforts.

For contracts to remove debris in Port-au-Prince, USAID went with Washington-based CHF International. As *Rolling Stone* put it, CHF became "one of the largest USAID contractors in Haiti and enjoys a cozy relationship with Washington."[47]

It turns out that the company's CEO, David Weiss, had been the deputy US trade representative for North American affairs during the Clinton administration. (He was also a 2008 Hillary for President campaign contributor.) In addition, the corporate secretary of the board of directors is Lauri Fitz-Pegado, who was a protégé of Clinton commerce secretary Ron Brown. Fitz-Pegado had served in a series of positions in the Clinton White House, including assistant secretary of commerce.

CHF received particular scorn from journalists on the ground in Haiti. According to *Rolling Stone*, the firm operated out of "two spacious mansions in Port-au-Prince and maintains a fleet of brand-new vehicles, [and] is generally considered one of the most ostentatious" groups working out of Haiti.[48]

USAID contracts also went to consulting firms like New York–based Dalberg Global Development Advisors, which was also an active participant in and financial supporter of CGI. In spring 2010 Dalberg received a $1.5 million contract to identify relocation sites for Haitians displaced by the quake from their homes and communities.

USAID's inspector general reviewed the firm's recommendations and found them generally sloppy and unusable. As *Rolling Stone* reported, "One of the sites they said was habitable was actually a small mountain. . . . It had an open-sided pit on one side of it, a severe 100 foot cliff, and ravines. . . . It became clear that these people may not even have gotten out of their SUVs."[49]

One early initiative pushed by both Bill and Hillary was to provide transitional housing for those left homeless by the earthquake. The plan was to give grants and funds to build approximately twenty thousand temporary shelters for $138 million. But nearly a year later, an April 19, 2011, audit by the USAID Office of the Inspector General (OIG) found that only 22 percent of the shelters had been built and that many of those were "substandard."[50]

The results were no better when it came to providing new permanent homes.

In December 2010 Bill and Hillary approved a "new settlements program" that called for fifteen thousand homes to be built in and around Port-au-Prince. But by June 2013, more than two and a half years later, the GAO audit revealed that only nine hundred houses had been built. The goal was subsequently cut to twenty-six hundred. At the same time, the cost of the project almost doubled, from $53 million to $90 million.

Even projects run through the Clinton Foundation and not the federal government achieved disastrous results.

When Bill decided that the United States needed to secure temporary housing for Haitian schoolchildren (a legitimate priority), Clayton Homes approached the Clinton Foundation and offered to help. The company was still in trouble with the Federal Emergency Management Agency for sending thousands of bad trailers to the US Gulf Coast after Hurricane Katrina. A class action brought against Clayton Homes and others was eventually settled.[51]

In Haiti the Clinton Foundation paid $4 million of private money for what were called "hurricane proof trailers" that were "structurally unsafe," and in some instances were found to have high levels of formaldehyde, with insulation coming out of the walls. The fumes, mold problems, and stifling heat made students sick. Many trailers ended up abandoned because they were poorly designed and ill suited to the Haitian climate.[52]

From Chappaqua, New York, Bill dreamed up the idea of a housing expo in Haiti that would bring architects and design firms from around the world to create sustainable homes using composite materials.[53] The project was dubbed Building Back Better Communities (BBBC). Each builder erected a sample home for Haitians to live in. These buildings and designs were expected to be adopted for widespread use in the earthquake-ravaged country. But fourteen months later, "most of the model homes sat empty," providing shelter for squatters and the occasional goat.[54]

"It was a waste of money with no respect for the builders," Gabriel Rosenberg of GR Construction, a Haitian firm, said in a telephone interview. "We invested about 25,000 dollars. We expected to sell those houses."[55]

"It was the biggest joke I've ever seen," complained John Sorge, with the firm Innovative Composites International (ICI). "It was a hoodwink to promote the government . . . the whole Expo was a farce."[56]

By far the largest and most ambitious project for Hillary and Bill was their plan to build a clothing factory in northern Haiti. The area had been untouched by the earthquake, but they authorized the use of US taxpayer funds for rebuilding to create what would be called the Caracol Industrial Park.[57]

The Clintons had actually been pushing this project for some time. Cheryl Mills, Hillary's right hand at State, was "credited with leading the effort for more than a year," wrote the *Cleveland Plain Dealer*.[58] Originally a straightforward plan for economic development, the project gained new momentum as a means to both uplift the Haitian economy and house homeless workers. In the end, the complex project required hundreds of millions in US taxpayer money and special legislation passed through Congress granting tariff-free access to US markets.

Ostensibly designed for the benefit of the Haitian people, Caracol has shown mixed results. As we have already seen, the best intentions often go awry in a place like Haiti. One thing is clear, however: the most obvious beneficiaries of the deal were three family-owned companies with a long history of supporting the Clintons.

To start things off, a major clothing manufacturer had to be induced to build a factory. Sae-A, a South Korean textile company, was lured to Haiti with a State Department commitment of $124 million for a power plant and basic infrastructure, as well as for employee housing. The Inter-American Development Bank promised another $100 million. The Haitian government gave Sae-A a fifteen-year break on taxes. Meanwhile, in the spring of 2010, Hillary, Bill, and Cheryl Mills pushed for and secured the passage of the Haiti Economic Lift Program (HELP), a law that would allow textiles to enter the United States from Haiti tariff-free.

Construction then began. However, before the omelet could be made, a few eggs had to be broken.

Three hundred sixty-six farmers, relatively prosperous by Haitian standards, were evicted from their land to make way for the factory. The earthquake didn't get them—but the factory did. "We watched, voiceless," Jean-Louis Saint Thomas, an elderly farmer, said. "The government paid us to shut us up."[59]

The construction contract for employee housing went to a Minnesota-based firm called Thor Construction. In addition to the contract rate, the firm received "danger pay" and "hardship pay," increasing its take by over 50 percent. Thor Construction executives, including the CEO, are heavy contributors to Democrats.

The parameters of the job soon changed. The original estimate was that the worker houses would cost $8,000. But due to cost overruns, the price tag quickly jumped to $23,409. The original plan was to build twenty-five thousand homes. In the end, according to the GAO, little more than six thousand were constructed.[60]

In July 2012 Hillary and Bill showed up in Caracol for the factory's grand opening, even as rubble still clogged the streets in the capital city of Port-au-Prince.[61] The Clintons were joined by actors Sean Penn and Ben Stiller, billionaire businessman Richard Branson, and fashion icon Donna Karan to celebrate the factory's opening. Hillary touted it as a great day for Haiti. Bill teared up.

For his part, Bill Vastine, a member of the USAID Shelter Team that established the project's original parameters, was aghast at the results. "If the American people saw the cost of this, they'd say 'you've got to be out of your mind,'" he told a reporter in 2014.[62]

Perhaps those happiest were the US retailers—all of whom enjoy long-standing connections with the Clintons—who would benefit from selling the low-cost products coming out of Caracol.

These included GAP, whose chairman and CEO Robert Fischer sat on the Hillary for President finance committee. The Fischer family had been longtime Clinton financial supporters.

Another big beneficiary: Target Stores, which was founded and is still controlled by the Dayton family. The Daytons have also been longtime Clinton financial supporters.

Wal-Mart also received tariff-free clothing from the factory. Hillary had sat on the Wal-Mart board back when Bill was governor of Arkansas. While some Walton family members do not share the Clintons' politics, several have written checks to a pro-Hillary superpac since the factory opened.

Regrettably, Caracol has failed to live up to its hype. The project's sponsors claimed that it would create sixty thousand jobs. The actual number: about three thousand. The daily wage for workers is two hundred gourdes, which is roughly five dollars. For workers at the factory this is obviously better than nothing. But it is hard to believe such meager results were justified at such great expense.[63]

In sum, little of the money that has poured into Haiti since the 2010 earthquake has ended up helping Haitians. And how that money was spent was largely up to Hillary and Bill.

This fact has prompted two Haitian lawyers to petition Haiti's Supreme Court of Auditors and Administrative Disputes to demand an audit of Bill Clinton's tenure on IHRC. The lawyers, Newton Louis St-Juste and André Michel, have asked for information "to determine the relationship between the former Head of State William Jefferson Bill Clinton and the firms that benefited from contracts during and after his term as head of the IHRC."[64]

In the meantime, the rubble-strewn streets of Port-au-Prince are still populated by those who saw their homes destroyed in 2010. These victims' net worth hasn't changed but that of the Clintons and their associates surely has.

Chapter 11
Quid pro Quo?

O n December 9, 2009, the State Department beamed out a video message from Secretary of State Hillary Clinton. The occasion was "International Anti-Corruption Day." Seated in front of the camera, she spoke about the important fight against political corruption around the world and praised the Organization for Economic Cooperation and Development's (OECD) work combating bribery and graft. The OECD is an international body of the world's largest economies. Hillary herself chaired the group in 2011, on its fiftieth anniversary. In the video, Hillary lauded OECD's Anti-Bribery Convention as "a milestone in global efforts to encourage responsible and accountable governance." She went on to declare that the United States "fully supports the OECD's anti-corruption agenda."[1]

Fighting corruption and bribery in the developing world was an important focus during Hillary's tenure. As a State Department spokesman explained, she "elevated corruption as a major focus of U.S. foreign policy. She also has promoted the importance of international anti-corruption agreements, including the OECD Anti-Bribery Convention."[2]

The OECD Working Group on Bribery specifically explains that "individuals and companies can also be prosecuted when third parties are involved in the bribe transaction, such as when someone other than the official who was bribed receives the illegal benefit, including a family member, business partner, or a favorite charity of the official."[3]

How does she reconcile her anti-corruption stance with the many transactions involving her and her husband that arguably present serious conflicts of interest, even in the best possible light? How can she maintain that her decisions were unaffected by the millions given to her husband and their family foundation, even if there were no explicit agreements? How does she not see herself as part of the problem?

Based on the OECD's definition of bribery, there does not need to be an explicit quid pro quo. As the US Sixth Circuit Court noted in a 2009 corruption case, a quid pro quo does not require "a particular, identifiable act" when the funds were transferred. "Instead, it is sufficient if the public official understood that he or she was expected to exercise some influence on the payor's behalf as opportunities arose."[4] Friends, money, and politics are a dangerous cocktail. The Clintons should know to avoid this kind of drinking while driving US policy.

Large commitments have been made by foreign businessmen with records of making payments to government officials to gain influence. Gilbert Chagoury, for example, who has sponsored speeches by Bill and committed $1 billion to the Clinton Global Initiative, has a long history of association with corrupt transactions in Nigeria. Denis O'Brien, who has also arranged speeches and written checks to the Clinton Foundation, was implicated in enriching government bureaucrats in Ireland to help his cellular business.[5]

The Clintons themselves have a history of questionable financial transactions. During their first presidential campaign in 1992, concerns were raised about their position in a real estate development in Arkansas known as Whitewater. There was also the matter of Hillary's miraculous profit from cattle futures, which turned a $1,000 investment into $100,000. No one ever proved that these transactions were illegal. But a cloud hovered over their heads and, when Bill became president, he and Hillary brought it with them to Washington.

In Bill's first term as president, as both he and Hillary faced myriad allegations concerning unethical conduct, his legal defense fund accepted an anonymous donation of $450,000 through a Little Rock restaurateur named Charlie Trie. Clinton and Trie were close friends. Shortly after the 1992 election, Trie began channeling money to the legal defense fund and into the DNC's so-called soft-money accounts for the president's reelection. The DNC became so concerned that the money might be coming from China that it hired private investigator Terry Lenzner to investigate.

As Lenzner later wrote, "I could see why they were concerned; red flags were obvious. For example, the money orders had different names on them, but the word 'presidential' was misspelled on all of them—in the exact same way and in the same handwriting."[6] Lenzner discovered that many of these donations were from people who were making only $20,000 to $30,000 a year and could not possibly be the source of these large contributions. Accordingly, Lenzner recommended the DNC return the donations. The DNC agreed. But Bill initially refused. It was only after the cochairs of his legal defense fund (a former attorney general and a Catholic priest) both threatened to resign that the donations were sent back.

Following the 1996 election, the DNC was forced to return some $2.8 million in illegal or improper donations, most of it from foreign sources. Of that amount, almost 80 percent was raised or contributed by Trie and another Clinton friend, John Huang. Like Trie, Huang had known Clinton for years and worked for the Lippo Group, an Indonesian conglomerate. Huang took a post as a DNC fundraiser and quickly set about soliciting large sums of money from foreign sources. Huang arranged for South Korean businessman John H. K. Lee to have dinner with President Clinton—in return for a $250,000 donation.[7] He also arranged for Yogesh K. Gandhi, who claimed to be related to Mahatma Gandhi, to meet in the White House with the president and be photographed being presented with an award—in exchange for $325,000. Both donations had to be returned after the stories became public.[8]

Meanwhile, more than one hundred "White House coffees" were held in 1995 and 1996 at which large-dollar contributors paid for face time with the president. White House officials initially denied that these were fundraisers, but schedules from Harold Ickes, the deputy chief of staff in the White House, referred to them as "political/fundraising coffees." White House officials even tracked the "projected revenue" of these events, including who paid and how much.[9] Then there was the evidence that, for the right contribution, you could spend the night in the Lincoln Bedroom.[10]

The Clintons aren't stupid people. They know the law and take pains to operate within it. Besides, corruption of the kind I have described in this book is very difficult to prove. We cannot ultimately know what goes on in their minds and ultimately prove the links between the money they took in and the benefits that subsequently accrued to themselves, their friends, and their associates. That said, the pattern of behavior I have established is too blatant to ignore, and deserves legal scrutiny by those with investigative capabilities that go beyond journalism.

Over the last dozen years, the Clintons have been involved in hundreds of transactions (as private citizens and public officials) with foreign governments, foreign investors, and foreign corporations around the world. It appears from the Clinton Foundation donor list and the roster of those who have sponsored speeches that there is barely an oligarch, royal family, or foreign investor in trouble with the law that is not represented.

As we saw earlier, four of the Clinton Foundation trustees have been charged or convicted of financial crimes. Is there another foundation anywhere in the world that has faced similar problems? More to the point, why would a former American president choose to associate with such dubious characters?

Hillary's apparent involvement in these transactions is even more troubling. While Bill was a private citizen, Hillary was still a government official. Her tenures as a senator and as secretary of state are marked by an alarming pattern of large money flows: the sources of the funds, the amounts, and the timing were frequently suspect. Many payments occurred as Hillary was grappling with vital national security questions involving everything from uranium to the Keystone XL pipeline.

In fact, the money flow did not slow down when Hillary became America's chief diplomat. On the contrary, it *accelerated*, especially the funds from overseas. And the funds came from a collection of troubling sources: foreign governments, third world oligarchs, and foreign corporations. The biggest paydays came not from countries like Great Britain or Germany, but from countries and industries with cultures where bribery and corruption are common and occur on a massive scale.

In March 2012 Hillary delivered remarks in the grand ballroom of the Mayflower Hotel in downtown Washington, DC. The occasion was a dinner for Transparency International, an international organization that fights corruption. Hillary spoke at length about how "sunlight [is] the best disinfectant" and declared that fighting corruption is an "integral part of national security." Hillary said, "our credibility depends on practicing what we preach."[11]

But as we've seen, the Clintons have failed to live up to their commitments to President Obama, the US Senate, and the American people to simply disclose the names of all Clinton Foundation major contributors. Multimillion-dollar foreign contributions have not been reported. Contributions of shares of stock in foreign companies that had business before the State Department were also not disclosed. Foreign corporations that poured in millions have been hidden from view. Moreover, the cases chronicled in this book are only the ones we know of.

And when it comes to Bill's speeches, the Clintons have often failed to fully disclose who is actually paying for the speeches. Why do the Clintons do this? Why do they put themselves again and again in positions that raise serious questions about their ethical conduct?

Opinions run the gamut. Defenders claim that it is not about the money: Bill and Hillary don't really care that much about it. That's an odd argument. If wealth is not the goal, why charge six-figure speaking fees and pocket the money? Why not charge a minimal fee or donate the proceeds to charity?

Money definitely appears to be a factor. The Clintons are just like many in politics: money carries serious weight. Gather enough weight and you can intimidate most people into not questioning how you got it.

Indeed, as noted above, the Clintons have always been shamelessly transactional. During Bill's tenure as governor of Arkansas, for example, it was Hillary who benefited the family financially through deals with those who wanted something from her husband. Her remarkable success in cattle futures comes to mind. James Blair, who was an outside counsel to Tyson Foods, set up her accounts. In the same period, Tyson was a beneficiary of several state actions.[12]

Most recently, of course, the roles have been reversed. Those seeking help from Hillary became the ones throwing money at Bill. Foreign money has flowed to the Clintons and their foundation from people and entities with intense personal interests in the political choices of the secretary of state. And in several instances that we have described, the evidence suggests that Hillary shifted course to the benefit of those providing the funds.

Moreover, the latest game has been played not at the level of state or even national affairs, but on a global scale. The era of globalization has opened up a bonanza of opportunities for businessmen willing and able to cut resource extraction deals around the world. Many of these deals, as we have seen, are made in developing countries where civilized rules do not always apply and where the players involved are unsavory.

The Clintons are perhaps the most politically sophisticated public figures of their generation. They know how things work in the corridors of power and around the world; they know that foreign governments are trying to influence American foreign policy; and they know that bribery is rampant around the world. They have numerous avenues for making money. Some of those avenues might not be as lucrative as giving a $700,000 speech in Nigeria, but they would be much cleaner.

Even if nothing illegal occurred, one has to wonder about the political judgment involved. Surely the mere appearance of selling American power and influence to foreign interests should be enough to cause a former US president—and a possible future one—to steer well clear of such potentially embarrassing entanglements. "Bribery interferes with trade, investment, and development," Hillary Clinton said at the OECD's fiftieth-anniversary forum in 2011. "It undermines good governance and encourages greater corruption. And of course, it is morally wrong—and far too common."

On that we can all agree.

Acknowledgments

This investigative project required an extraordinary amount of in-depth research that included everything from reviewing Canadian tax records to Ukrainian shipping records. Because of the global reach of this project, it also required tracking down information from sources around the world. Because of the sensitive nature of this project, the researchers asked that their names not be included in the acknowledgments. I am nonetheless grateful for their professionalism, doggedness, and attention to detail.

The Government Accountability Institute has benefited from terrific leadership in our little more than three years of existence. This includes our chairman and CEO Stephen K. Bannon, as well as our board of directors, Owen Smith, Ron Robinson, and Hunter

Lewis. I want to say a special thanks to those who have supported our research over the past couple of years, which has offended both Republicans and Democrats in Washington.

Love and gratitude always to my children, Jack and Hannah. You both mean the world to me.

My family has been enormously supportive as I've walked through this complicated project. Thanks to my wife, Rhonda (to whom this book is dedicated); my mom, Kerstin Schweizer; as well as my family "up north": Maria and Joe, Danny and Adam. Thanks, too, to Ava and Raquel. Welcome to the family!

I've benefited from tremendous professional guidance and camaraderie over the course of my writing career. I appreciate my agents, Glen Hartley and Lyn Chu, for their sage advice and counsel, and was so pleased to be working again with Adam Bellow, a longtime friend, on this project.

As always, the author alone is responsible for the contents of this book.

Notes

CHAPTER 1: THE LINCOLN BEDROOM GOES GLOBAL

1. Solomon, John, and Jeffrey H. Birnbaum, "Clinton Library Got Funds from Abroad," *Washington Post*, December 15, 2007, http://www.washingtonpost.com/wp-dyn/content/article/2007/12/14/AR2007121402124.html.

2. Storace, Patricia, "Q&A: How Bill Clinton Is Changing the World," *Condé Nast Traveler*, August 15, 2007, http://www.cntraveler.com/stories/2007-08-15/q-a-how-bill-clinton-is-changing-the-world.

3. "Bluman v. Federal Election Commission Case Files," *SCOTUSblog*, http://www.scotusblog.com/case-files/cases/bluman-v-federal-election-commission/.

4. Von Oldershausen, Sasha, "Are the Clintons Trying to Duck Property Taxes in New York?" *The*

Real Deal, June 17, 2014, http://therealdeal.com/blog/2014/06/17/are-the-clintons-trying-to-duck-property-tax-payments/.

5. Marquis, Christopher, "Clintons Buy $2.85 Million Washington Home," *New York Times*, December 29, 2000, http://www.nytimes.com/2000/12/30/us/clintons-buy-2.85-million-washington-home.html.

6. Van Natta, Don, Jr., Jo Becker, and Mike Mcintire, "In His Charity and Her Politics, Many Clinton Donors Overlap," *New York Times*, December 19, 2007, http://www.nytimes.com/2007/12/20/us/politics/20clinton.html?pagewanted=all&_r=1&.

7. Ibid.

8. Ibid.

9. Ibid.

10. "Sorting Out the Pardon Mess," *New York Times*, February 22, 2001, http://www.nytimes.com/2001/02/23/opinion/sorting-out-the-pardon-mess.html.

11. "Carter: Rich Pardon 'Disgraceful,'" *CBSNews*, February 21, 2001, http://www.cbsnews.com/news/carter-rich-pardon-disgraceful/.

12. Berke, Richard L., "The Clinton Pardons: The Democrats; This Time, the Clintons Find Their Support Buckling from the Weight of New Woes," *New York Times*, February 23, 2001, http://www.nytimes.com/2001/02/23/us/clinton-pardons-democrats-this-time-clintons-find-their-support-buckling-weight.html.

13. Reid, Tim, "Donors List Raises Fears over Hillary Clinton Role as Secretary of State," *The Times* (London), December 19, 2008, http://www.thetimes. co.uk/tto/news/world/americas/article1998893.ece.

14. Mehta, Pratap Bhanu, "Charity at Home?" *Indian Express*, October 18, 2010, http://archive.indianex-press.com/news/charity-at-home-/699359/.

15. Hitchens, Christopher, "Why Are So Many Oligarchs, Royal Families, and Special-interest Groups Giving Money to the Clinton Foundation?" *Slate*, January 12, 2009, http://www.slate.com/articles/news_and_politics/fighting_words/2009/01/more_than_a_good_feeling.html.

16. Calabresi, Massimo, "A Blip in Hillary Clinton's Senate Lovefest: Bill's Donations," *Time*, January 14, 2009, http://content.time.com/time/nation/article/0,8599,1871526,00.html.

17. US Senate, Committee on Foreign Relations, *Nomination of Hillary R. Clinton to be Secretary of State* (2009), 8 (testimony of Richard Lugar).

18. Ibid., 11.

19. Ibid.

20. Calabresi, "A Blip in Hillary Clinton's Senate Lovefest."

21. US Senate, Committee on Foreign Relations, *Nomination of Hillary R. Clinton to be Secretary of State* (2009), 156 (testimony of Hillary Clinton).

22. Ibid., 286.

23. "Saudis, Indians among Clinton Foundation Donors," *Economic Times, India Times,* December 18, 2008, http://articles.economictimes.indiatimes.com/2008-12-18/news/27709369_1_annual-charitable-conference-income-and-speeches-william-j-clinton-foundation.

24. Allen, Jonathan, and Amie Parnes, *HRC: State Secrets and the Rebirth of Hillary Clinton* (New York: Crown Publishing Group, Random House, 2014), 81.

25. "The Clinton Foundation," *Washington Post,* December 21, 2008, http://www.washingtonpost.com/wp-dyn/content/article/2008/12/20/AR2008122001647.html.

26. Ibid.

27. Ghattas, Kim, *The Secretary: A Journey with Hillary Clinton from Beirut to the Heart of American Power* (New York: Picador, 2013), 40–41.

28. Jack, Andrew, "Charm Offensive Five Years after Leaving Office, Bill Clinton Is Applying His Famous Drive and Charisma to Talk AIDS in Africa," *Financial Times,* August 19, 2006.

29. Wiener, Jon, "Hillary's Big Ethics Problem: Bill," *The Nation,* November 22, 2008, http://www.thenation.com/blog/hillarys-big-ethics-problem-bill.

30. Leigh, David, "WikiLeaks Cables: US Keeps Uzbekistan President Onside to Protect Supply Line," *The Guardian,* December 12, 2010, http://www.

theguardian.com/world/2010/dec/12/wikileaks-us-conflict-over-uzbekistan.

31. US Department of State, Embassy in Tashkent, "Uzbekistan: Rumors of Succession Planning, Government Reshuffling," WikiLeaks, July 31, 2009, http://www.wikileaks.org/plusd/cables/09TAS HKENT1357_a.html.

32. Stump, Scott, "Fashion Week Cancels Show from Dictator's Daughter," Today.com, September 9, 2011, http://www.today.com/id/44452554/ns/today-style/t/fashion-week-cancels-show-dictators-daughter/#. U_ZBSf3DdBM.

CHAPTER 2: THE TRANSFER

1. Becker, Jo, and Don Van Natta Jr., "After Mining Deal, Financier Donated to Clinton," *New York Times*, January 31, 2008, http://www.nytimes.com/2008/01/31/us/politics/31donor.html?pagewanted=all&_r=0.

2. "How to Make Money in Kazakhstan," TheNewswire.ca, October 14, 2011, http://www.metalinvestment-news.com/how-to-make-money-in-kazakhstan/.

3. World Health Organization, "Summary Country Profile For HIV/AIDS Treatment Scale-Up," December 2005, http://www.who.int/hiv/HIVCP_KAZ.pdf. *UNAIDS Sub-Saharan Africa Fact Sheet*,

report, May 25, 2006, http://data.unaids.org/pub/
GlobalReport/2006/200605-fs_subsaharanafrica_en.
pdf.

4. Nichol, Jim, "Kazakhstan: Recent Developments
    and U.S. Interests," Congressional Research Service,
    June 20, 2008, http://assets.opencrs.com/rpts/97-
    1058_20080620.pdf. Foust, Joshua, "The Gilded
    Age of Asia," *Foreign Policy*, April 11, 2013, http://
    www.foreignpolicy.com/articles/2013/04/11/the_
    gilded_cage_of_asia. Watt, Nicholas, "Kazakhstan's
    Autocratic President Tells David Cameron: I
    Would Vote for You," *The Guardian*, July 1, 2013,
    http://www.theguardian.com/world/2013/jul/01/
    kazakhstan-president-david-cameron-vote.

5. Mayr, Walter, "Ex-Stepson Talks in Family Feud:
    Tapping Kazakstan's Natural Resources," *Spiegel*,
    May 19, 2009, http://www.spiegel.de/international/
    world/ex-stepson-talks-in-family-feud-the-long-
    arm-of-kazakhstan-s-president-a-625720-2.html.

6. Love, James, "The Well-Connected Dictator,"
    Huffington Post, May 25, 2011, http://www.huffing-
    tonpost.com/james-love/the-wellconnected-dictato_
    b_67423.html. Kilner, James, "Copper Tycoon Tops
    Kazakhstan's Rich List," *The Telegraph*, May 15,
    2012, http://www.telegraph.co.uk/news/worldnews/
    asia/kazakhstan/9268133/Copper-tycoon-tops-
    Kazakhstans-rich-list.html. Buckley, Neil, "ENRC
    Founders Made Good in Kazakhstan," *Financial*

Times, May 3, 2013, http://www.ft.com/intl/cms/s/0/71a13774-b3e0-11e2-ace9-00144feabdc0.html#axzz351P7vNvu.

7. Hoffman, Andy, "Renaissance Man," *Globe and Mail* (Toronto), June 27, 2008, http://www.theglobe-andmail.com/report-on-business/renaissance-man/article17988489/?page=all. Humphreys, Tommy, "Stop Taking Yourself so Seriously, Says Tycoon Frank Giustra," Mining.com, June 28, 2013, http://www.mining.com/web/stop-taking-yourself-so-seriously-says-tycoon-frank-giustra/.

8. Cernetig, Miro, "Frank Giustra: A Man of Many Hats," *BC Business*, November 5, 2011, http://www.bcbusiness.ca/people/frank-giustra-a-man-of-many-hats. Smith, Elliot Blair, "Clinton Used Giustra's Plane, Opened Doors for Deals (Correct)," Bloomberg.com, February 22, 2008, http://www.bloomberg.com/apps/news?pid=newsarchive&sid=aa2b8Mj3NEWQ.

9. Canada's *Globe and Mail* explained Giustra's approach this way: "A mining promoter will buy a cheap 'shell' company already listed on the stock exchange, gather some friends to help fund the acquisition, and then, some time down the road, load it up with mining assets (remember the shuffle?) and do another share offering. These deals can be very lucrative, especially if you're in the promoter's 'circle of trust.'" Hoffman, Andy, and Sinclair Stewart, "How to (Still) Get Rich

in Mining," *Globe and Mail* (Toronto), globeadvisor. com, May 19, 2007, https://secure.globeadvisor.com/ newscentre/article.html?/servlet/GIS.Servlets.Wire FeedRedirect?cf=sglobeadvisor/config_blank&vg= BigAdVariableGenerator&date=20070519&archive= gam&slug=RCOVER19.

10. Hoffman, "Renaissance Man."

11. Remnick, David, "The Wanderer: Bill Clinton's Quest to Save the World, Reclaim His Legacy—and Elect His Wife," *The New Yorker*, September 18, 2006, http://www.newyorker.com/magazine/2006/09/18/ the-wanderer-3.

12. Becker and Van Natta, "After Mining Deal, Financier Donated to Clinton."

13. Jenkins, Iain, "Fun and Games with Penny Stocks," *New York Times*, March 9, 1996, http://www.nytimes. com/1996/03/09/your-money/09iht-penns.t.html. McNish, Jacquie, *The Big Score: Robert Friedland and the Voisey's Bay Hustle* (Toronto: Doubleday Canada, 1998), ix, 45.

14. "Corporate Info," Diamond Fields International Ltd., http://www.diamondfields.com/s/Management.asp (accessed 2014). Morais, Richard C., "Friends in High Places," *Forbes*, August 10, 1998, http://www. forbes.com/global/1998/0810/0109038a.html.

15. Morais, "Friends in High Places."

16. McNish, *The Big Score*, ix, 40.

17. Morais, "Friends in High Places."

18. McNish, *The Big Score*, ix, 45.

19. Becker and Van Natta, "After Mining Deal, Financier Donated to Clinton."

20. Hoffman, Andy, "Who Sold Key Asset to Uranium One?" *Globe and Mail* (Toronto), May 29, 2009, http://www.theglobeandmail.com/report-on-business/who-sold-key-asset-to-uranium-one/article4274871/.

21. Becker and Van Natta, "After Mining Deal, Financier Donated to Clinton."

22. Clinton, William J., "President's News Conference with President Nursultan Nazarbayev of Kazakhstan," American Presidency Project, February 14, 1994, http://www.presidency.ucsb.edu/ws/?pid=49652.

23. Nichol, "Kazakhstan: Recent Developments and U.S. Interests."

24. US Department of State, "Visits to the U.S. by Foreign Heads of State and Government—1999," http://2001-2009.state.gov/r/pa/ho/15730.htm. "Kazakh President, Clinton to Meet," *American Metal Market*, December 21, 1999. Kazakhstan Goldfields Corp., "Open Letter to President Nazarbayev of Kazakhstan," December 20, 1999, http://www.infomine.com/index/pr/Pa034388.PDF.

25. Sidorov, Dmitry, "An Interview with Sergei Kurzin," *Forbes*, April 20, 2009, http://www.forbes.com/2009/04/17/clinton-sergei-kurzin-opinions-contributors-sidorov.html.

26. "A Russian's Underground Route to the Stock Market," *The Telegraph* (UK), February 15, 2004.

27. Becker and Van Natta, "After Mining Deal, Financier Donated to Clinton."

28. Sidorov, "An Interview with Sergei Kurzin."

29. "Wall Street Journal Publishes Letter from Frank Giustra that Corrects Misinformation," *Reuters*, May 01, 2008, http://webcache.googleusercontent.cohttp:// webcache.googleusercontent.com/search?q=cache: UsTisocqOKUJ:www.reuters.com/article/2008/05/ 01/idUS188740+01-May-2008+PRN20080501 &cd= 1&hl=en&ct=clnk&gl=us.

30. Clinton Foundation, "Statement on Frank Giustra from President Clinton," January 15, 2009, http://www.clintonfoundation.org/main/news-and-media/statements/statement-on-frank-giustra-from-president-clinton.html.

31. Clinton Foundation, "Statement on Frank Giustra from President Clinton."

After "Borat-gate" broke, certain points of fact and interpretation were vigorously disputed by both Frank Giustra and the Clintons. Their objections can be summarized into two categories. First, the agreement struck by Giustra and his partners was with private parties in Kazakhstan and not with the government in general or Kazatomprom in particular. Second, as Giustra and his partners had been working on the transaction for over a year inside Kazakhstan, they did not need President Clinton to complete the deal.

The first objection is misleading in that it uses the answer to one question—did Giustra and his partners pay a private party for the right to mine uranium in Kazakhstan? While the answer is technically yes, this obscures two much more pertinent questions. First, did UrAsia enter into a commercial relationship with the Kazakh government through its state nuclear agency, Kazatomprom? And second, was the deal in its entirety contingent upon Kazakh government approval? The answer to those two questions is an unequivocal yes. What Giustra secured in 2005 were two joint ventures encompassing three uranium mining sites, each of which featured Kazatomprom as a commercial partner by UrAsia's own corporate filings. For at least one of the sites, the Kazakh government transferred the rights a mere five days *after* Clinton's trip. Giustra et al. paid $350 million for the rights to that site and one other (to the Betpak Dala LLP). Without that transfer of rights, Giustra would have had nothing to buy.

The objection is more straightforwardly wrong for three other reasons. First, accounts of the deal given either before or without reference to its controversy treat it as a deal with the Kazakh government—and Kazatomprom in particular—from start to finish.

This is true not only of Giustra et al.'s early 2006 victory lap in Canada's *Financial Post*, but also a mining trade publication's interview with Sergey Kurzin, with whom Giustra had done business in Kazakhstan, off and on, since the mid-1990s. Kurzin recounts that the deal started with a meeting he arranged for himself, Giustra, and other figures crucial to the deal with Mukhtar Dzhakishev, head of Kazatomprom. Second, in late May 2009 Dzhakishev was arrested and brought up on criminal charges related to the UrAsia deal. By this time UrAsia's successor company, Uranium One, had taken over the disputed holdings. Anxious to calm investors, Uranium One's then president Jean Nortier stated in no uncertain terms that both UrAsia's and Uranium One's mining rights enjoyed explicit governmental approval: "UrAsia's acquisition of these assets, as well as Uranium One's subsequent acquisition of UrAsia, were completed in accordance with the requirements of Kazakh law, and both transactions were approved by the Kazakh authorities." Third, UrAsia and Uranium One's *own* corporate filings unequivocally demonstrate that any transfer of subsurface mineral rights in Kazakhstan *must* be approved by Kazkhstan's Ministry of Energy and Mineral Rights (MEMR). Incidentally, MEMR's head in 2005, Vladimir Shkolnik, later became head of Kazatomprom after Dzhakishev was arrested. Not long after, his son-in-law, Vadim Jivov, ascended to the board of Uranium One (he eventually became its president) while Giustra's good friend and Clinton Foundation donor Ian Telfer was chairman of the board. In any case, the key fact revealed by the evidence is not so much Kazatomprom's commercial participation with UrAsia, but the Kazakhstan government's complete authority over the company's acquisition of mining rights and its subsequent operations within the country. There would have been no deal had Kazakh authorities failed to sign off on it.

As to whether President Clinton's participation was necessary to close the deal, consider the words of Gordon Keep, longtime Giustra associate and officer for UrAsia: "we had only six weeks to complete a fourteen-week deal." By the time Clinton joined Giustra in Kazakhstan his friends at Canaccord and GMP Securities had raised $504 million Canadian and put it on the line to capitalize the venture, a figure cited in the Canadian financial press as a first for such an enterprise. Stipulating Giustra's commitment to global charity, it beggars credulity that an investor so experienced and shrewd with $504 million worth of credibility on the line, would have introduced President Clinton, a politician legendary for his ability to strike a deal, into the delicate negotiation's closing moments if his presence was not integral to it. Kazakhstan's dictator, Nursultan Nazarbayev, obviously had the power to kill the venture at whim, nor were Nazarbayev and Kazakhstan lacking for other prospective investors in uranium.

Nazarbayev's eagerness for bribes was well known, including, allegedly, from multibillion-dollar Western companies such as Chevron. What would he have expected from an effective, but comparatively small-time player such as Giustra? Furthermore, as discussed below, Clinton had something very real to offer Nazarbayev: an endorsement for the OSCE chairmanship, an honor that would have opened diplomatic and commercial doors in Europe otherwise closed to him. The Kazakh embassy posted notice of the endorsement online the same day, a fact that speaks for itself.

32. Stewart, Sinclair, and Andy Hoffman, "Uranium One Ensnared in Kazakh Scandal," *Globe and Mail* (Toronto), May 27, 2009, http://www.theglobeandmail.com/globe-investor/uranium-one-ensnared-in-kazakh-scandal/article4211504/.

33. Chapman, David, "Glowing Prospects for 6 Uranium Miners," Moneyshow.com, April 17, 2012, http://www.moneyshow.com/articles.asp?aid=Global-27436. Becker and Van Natta, "After Mining Deal, Financier Donated to Clinton."

34. US Department of State, "Kazakhstan: Business as Usual in the Uranium Mining Sector," WikiLeaks, June 17, 2009, https://www.wikileaks.org/plusd/cables/09ASTANA1033_a.html.

35. Seccombe, Allan, "Kazakh Move Stuns Uranium One," *MiningMx*, May 27, 2009, http://www.

miningmx.com/news/energy/kazakh-move-stuns-uranium-one.htm. See note 51.

36. Becker and Van Natta, "After Mining Deal, Financier Donated to Clinton."

37. Pan, Philip P., "Clinton Adviser Intervened with Uranium Deal, Ex-Kazakh Official Says," *Washington Post*, February 24, 2010, http://www.washingtonpost.com/wp-dyn/content/article/2010/02/24/AR2010022403290.html.

38. In 2008 Dzhakishev was arrested by Kazakh security forces along with three other top Kazatomprom officials. It was part of a broader purge that included the head of the state-owned rail and energy companies. According to a leaked State Department cable, the arrests were "denounced as politically motivated" by nongovernment observers. As with so much in Kazakh politics, the events were imbedded with intrigue. Allegations were made that President Nazarbayev's family actually owned part of Kazatomprom and was profiting from the deals. The arrests were allegedly designed to cover it up. Dzhakishev was also a longtime friend of Nazarbayev's estranged son-in-law Rakhat Aliyev. In exile in Europe, Aliyev called Dzhakishev "a political detainee of Nazarbayev's regime."

US Department of State, "Kazakhstan: Changes and Charges at Kazatomprom," WikiLeaks, June 3, 2009, https://www.wikileaks.org/plusd/cables/

09ASTANA943_a.html. Pan, "Clinton Adviser Intervened to Help with Uranium Deal."

39. Ibid., and videos of Dzhakishev: https://www. youtube.com/channel/UC9Ze93MxqaQKPVHLk KmVpeQ; translation by Dr. David Meyer.

40. Lenzner, Robert, "Clinton Commits No Foul in Kazakhstan Uranium Deal," *Forbes*, January 12, 2009, http://www.forbes.com/2009/01/12/giustra-clinton-kazakhstan-pf-ii-in_rl_0912croesus_inl.html.

41. Bronson, Lisa, "Testimony on Cooperative Threat Reduction Program before the Subcommittee on Emerging Threats and Capabilities," March 10, 2004, http://www.globalsecurity.org/wmd/library/congress/2004_h/040310-bronson.pdf.

42. Pan, "Clinton Adviser Intervened with Uranium Deal."

43. Ibid. Tufts University, "Board Members: Tim Phillips," http://www.tuftsgloballeadership.org/about/boards-and-staff/tim-phillips. "About Us," Beyond Conflict, http://www.beyondconflictint.org/about-us/staff/timothy-phillips/.

44. Embassy of the Republic of Kazakhstan, "Weekly News Bulletin," September 7, 2005, http://prosites-kazakhembus.homestead.com/090705.html.

45. Becker and Van Natta, "After Mining Deal, Financier Donated to Clinton."

46. Nichol, "Kazakhstan: Recent Developments and U.S. Interests."

47. Commission on Security and Cooperation in Europe, "Promises to Keep: Kazakhstan's 2010 OSCE Chairmanship," official transcript, July 22, 2008, http://csce.gov/index.cfm?FuseAction=ContentRecords.ViewDetail&ContentRecord_id=434&Region_id=0&Issue_id=0&ContentType=H,B&ContentRecordType=H&CFID=13299032&CFTOKEN=93551824.

48. Signature Resources Ltd., "Signature Enters into Acquisition Agreement with UrAsia Energy Ltd," September 20, 2005, http://www.infomine.com/index/pr/Pa299684.PDF.

49. Becker and Van Natta, "After Mining Deal, Financier Donated to Clinton."

50. Ibid.

51. Ibid.

52. "Kazakhstan Timeline," Knowledge Ecology International, July 30, 2007, http://keionline.org/content/view/110/1. Kazakhstan News Bulletin, www.kazakhembus.com, 5, no. 52, December 7, 2005, http://prosites-kazakhembus.homestead.com/December_7.pdf.

53. Canadian System of Electronic Disclosures (SEDI), http://www.sedi.ca: "Access Public Filings," "View Summary Reports," "Insider Transaction Detail," "Select 'Insider Family Name,'" "Search 'Ian Telfer,'" "Select 'Date of Transaction,'" "Search 'January 1, 2000-present day,'" "Urasia Energy." Hoffman and Stewart, "How to (Still) Get Rich in Mining."

54. Moriarty, Bob, "Girls and Peak Gold: Wheaton River Jr.," 321gold.com, October 7, 2007, http://www.321gold.com/editorials/moriarty/moriarty103007.html (accessed November 2, 2014).

55. Hoffman, Andy, "Ian Telfer: 'I'm More of an Opportunist than a Visionary,'" *Globe and Mail* (Toronto), May 27, 2011, http://www.theglobeandmail.com/report-on-business/careers/careers-leadership/ian-telfer-im-more-of-an-opportunist-than-a-visionary/article582085/?page=all.

56. Kirby, Jason, "Uranium Blockbuster," *National Post* (Canada), January 31, 2006, http://www.canada.com/story.html?id=c8c388e6-ba0b-4ed3-bc67-21a05ec652c2.=.

57. "Coming Soon! A New Uranium Stock," Stocks, Uranium, Exchange, Symbol, November 7, 2005, http://socialize.morningstar.com/NewSocialize/forums/p/158426/2044148.aspx#2044148 (accessed November 2, 2014). "Uranium Mining and Exploration Post #2119," *Investors Hub*, November 7, 2005, http://investorshub.advfn.com/boards/read_msg.aspx?message_id=8398619 (Accessed November 02, 2014). See also "Uranium Blockbuster: Canaccord Adams-led IPO Financing of Uranium Producer UrAsia Energy Faced Language Barriers, a 14-hour Time Difference and a Drop in the Equity Markets. But the Deal Was Done," *Financial Post* (Canada), January 31, 2006.

58. Uranium One, "Uranium One and UrAsia Energy Announce Combination to Create Emerging Senior Uranium Company," news release, February 12, 2007, Uranium1.com, http://www.uranium1.com/index.php/en/component/docman/doc_download/256-uranium-one-and-urasia-energy-announce-combination-to-create-emerging-senior-uranium-company.

59. Lenzner, Robert, "Clinton Commits No Foul in Kazakhstan Uranium Deal," *Forbes*, January 12, 2009, http://www.forbes.com/2009/01/12/giustra-clinton-kazakhstan-pf-ii-in_rl_0912croesus_inl.html.

60. Becker, Jo, and Don Van Natta, Jr., "Ex-President, Mining Deal and a Donor," *New York Times*, January 30, 2008, http://www.nytimes.com/2008/01/31/us/politics/31donor.html?pagewanted=all&_r=1&.

61. Despite initially denying the meeting, Giustra later recanted and "his aides explain that the manner in which the *Times'* fact-checking questions were asked was misleading and did not prompt them to recall the Chappaqua meeting." Lenzner, "Clinton Commits No Foul in Kazakhstan Uranium Deal." Becker, and Van Natta, "Ex-President, Mining Deal and a Donor."

62. Hamm, Nathan, "Joe Biden's Letter to Nursultan Nazarbayev," *Registannet RSS*, March 23, 2007, http://registan.net/2007/03/23/joe-bidens-letter-to-nursultan-nazarbayev/.

63. Becker and Van Natta, "Ex-President, Mining Deal and a Donor." Cooper, Helene, and Peter Baker, "Clinton Vetting Includes Look at Mr. Clinton," *New York Times*, November 16, 2008, http://www.nytimes.com/2008/11/17/us/politics/17memo.html?pagewanted=all&_r=0.

64. Love, James, "The Well-Connected Dictator," *Huffington Post*, October 6, 2007, http://www.huffingtonpost.com/james-love/the-wellconnected-dictato_b_67423.html. "Featured Attendees," Clinton Global Initiative, http://re.clintonfoundation.org/page.aspx?pid=1263. Official Site of the President of the Republic of Kazakhstan, September 26, 2007, http://www.akorda.kz/en/page/page_president-nursultan-nazarbayev-takes-part-in-the-clinton-global-initiative-forum_1348723422.

65. Smith, "Clinton Used Giustra's Plane, Opened Doors for Deals (Correct)."

66. Uranium One, "Uranium One and UrAsia Energy Announce Combination to Create Emerging Senior Uranium Company."

Although reported by some as a buyout, it was actually a reverse merger. Frank Giustra and any other shareholders didn't get bought out; they actually took control of the new company named Uranium One. Hill, Liezel, "Uranium One Wraps Up UrAsia Acquisition, Eyes London Listing," *Engineering News*, April 23, 2007, http://www.engineeringnews.

co.za/article/uranium-one-wraps-up-urasia-acquisition-eyes-london-listing-2007-04-23.

"Immediately following the completion of the arrangement, Uranium One was owned approximately 60% by the former UrAsia shareholders and approximately 40% by the then-existing Uranium One shareholders." Uranium One Inc., *Annual Information Form 2007*, report, March 31, 2008, http://www.uranium1.com/index.php/en/component/docman/doc_download/69-2008-annual-information-form.

67. As *Platts Nucleonics Week* reports, "For accounting purposes, UrAsia Energy became a subsidiary of what was now called Uranium One, but in fact, it was UrAsia Energy shareholders who took control of the new company, according to documents filed with Canadian securities regulators." Stellfox, David, "Uranium One's Russian Deals Pushes Kazakh Probes to the Background," *Platts Nucleonics Week*, June 18, 2009. As the London Stock Exchange reported, "each UrAsia common share will be exchanged for .45 Uranium One common shares. After the completion of the transaction, it is expected that current Uranium One shareholders will own approximately 40 percent of the combined company and current UrAsia shareholders will own approximately 60 percent." "UrAsia Energy Ltd Plans Merger with SXR Uranium," London Stock Exchange Aggregated Regulatory News Service,

February 17, 2007. "UrAsia Energy Ltd (UUU)," *FE Investegate/UrAsia Energy Ltd Announcements*, February 12, 2007, http://www.investegate.co.uk/article.aspx?id=200702120726400752R.

68. Uranium One, "Uranium One Completes Acquisition of Energy Metals," press release, August 10, 2007, http://www.uranium1.com/index.php/en/component/docman/doc_download/239-uranium-one-completes-acquisition-of-energy-metals.

69. "Vadim Zhivov: 'We Can Be Faced by a Deficit of Uranium,'" Rosatom, December 2, 2010, http://www.rosatom.ru/en/presscentre/interviews/4eafad80432eea76ab83eb539abab8a1. Rosatom Corp., "Russia to Acquire 17% Stake in Canada's Uranium One (Update1)," news release, June 19, 2009, ARMZ Uranium Holding Co., http://www.armz.ru/media/File/facts/ARMZ-U1/Bloomberg.pdf.

70. Wright, Lisa, "Clintons' Canadian Buddy," *Toronto Star*, February 3, 2008, http://www.thestar.com/business/2008/02/03/clintons_canadian_buddy.html.

71. "Contributor Information," Clinton Foundation, https://www.clintonfoundation.org/contributors.

72. Hoffman, "Renaissance Man."

73. Becker and Van Natta, "Ex-President, Mining Deal and a Donor." Hoffman, "Renaissance Man."

74. "Contributor Information," Clinton Foundation, https://www.clintonfoundation.org/contributors?category=%24250%2C001+to+%24500%2C000

(accessed 2014). "Frank Edward Holmes," Investing. businessweek.com, http://investing.businessweek. com/research/stocks/people/person.asp?personId=3 10588&ticker=GROW.

75. Hoffman, "Renaissance Man." "President Clinton and Business Leaders Launch Sustainable Development Initiative in the Developing World," press release, Clinton Foundation, June 21, 2007, https://www. clintonfoundation.org/main/news-and-media/press-releases-and-statements/press-release-president-clinton-and-business-leaders-launch-sustainable-developm.html. "Management," Endeavour Mining Corporation, http://www.endeavourmining.com/s/ Management.asp.

76. "Clinton Foundation Donors," *Wall Street Journal*, December 18, 2008, http://online.wsj.com/public/ resources/documents/st_clintondonor_20081218. html. "Transactions (Page 2)," Haywood Securities Inc., http://www.haywood.com/investmentbanking/ searchtransactions.aspx?view=tombstone&field=year &year=2005# (accessed 2014).

77. "Clinton Foundation Donors," *Wall Street Journal*. "Paul D. Reynolds," Investing.businessweek.com, http://investing.businessweek.com/research/stocks/ people/person.asp?personId=1467569&ticker= CF:CN.

78. "President Clinton and Business Leaders Launch Sustainable Development Initiative in the Developing

World." Hoffman, "Renaissance Man." Kirby, "Uranium Blockbuster."

79. "President Clinton and Business Leaders Launch Sustainable Development Initiative in the Developing World." "Robert Melvin Douglas Cross MBA," Investing.businessweek.com, http://investing.businessweek.com/research/stocks/people/person.asp?personId=8052452&ticker=BNK:CN&previousCapId=35511785&previousTitle=B2GOLD%20CORP.

80. "Global Metals & Mining Biographies," BMO Capital Markets, http://www.bmocm.com/industry-expertise/mining/bio/ (accessed 2014). Uranium One, "Uranium One and UrAsia Energy Announce Combination to Create Emerging Senior Uranium Company."

81. Hoffman, "Renaissance Man." Kirby, "Uranium Blockbuster."

82. Hoffman, "Renaissance Man." "Sergey Vladimirovich Kurzin Ph.D.," Investors.businessweek.com, http://investing.businessweek.com/research/stocks/people/person.asp?personId=13061746&ticker=OSU:CN. Sidorov, "An Interview with Sergei Kurzin."

83. Hoffman, "Renaissance Man." "Board of Directors," Uranium One, http://www.uranium1.com/index.php/en/about-uranium-one/board-of-directors (accessed 2014).

84. Clinton Foundation, "President Clinton and Business Leaders Launch Sustainable Development Initiative in the Developing World."

85. Wright, "Clintons' Canadian Buddy."

86. Todd, Douglas, "Frank Giustra: Rescuing Global Capitalism from Itself," *Vancouver Sun*, September 13, 2008, http://blogs.vancouversun.com/2008/09/13/frank-giustra-rescuing-global-capitalism-from-itself/?__federated=1.

87. Ibid.

CHAPTER 3: HILLARY'S RESET

1. Strobel, Warren, and Jonathan Landay, "Russia's Dispute with Bush Could Strain G8 Talks," *Seattle Times*, June 1, 2007, http://seattletimes.com/html/nationworld/2003730264_putin01.html. Finn, Peter, "Putin Threatens Ukraine on NATO," *Washington Post*, February 13, 2008, http://www.washingtonpost.com/wp-dyn/content/article/2008/02/12/AR2008021201658.html. Goldgeier, James, "The 'Russia Reset' Was Already Dead; Now It's Time for Isolation," *Washington Post*, March 2, 2014. http://www.washingtonpost.com/blogs/monkey-cage/wp/2014/03/02/the-russia-reset-was-already-dead-now-its-time-for-isolation/.

2. Lowry, Rich, "The Russian Reset to Nowhere," *National Review Online*, March 7, 2014, http://www.nationalreview.com/article/372817/russian-reset-nowhere-rich-lowry.

3. Mankoff, Jeffrey, "The Russian Economic Crisis," Council on Foreign Relations, *Special Report* no. 53

(April 2010), http://www.google.com/url?sa=t&rc
t=j&q=&esrc=s&source=web&cd=2&ved=0CC4
QFjAB&url=http%3A%2F%2Fwww.cfr.org%2F
content%2Fpublications%2Fattachments%2FRuss
ian_Economy_CSR53.pdf&ei=ORAGVJmwIsLwgw
TxloLgCA&usg=AFQjCNFhANrjMwQyKcHStW5
PkjpDT1FQzA&sig2=l4jMjHA_DU120z8jlUmzbQ.

4. Gornostayev, Dmitriy, "Clinton 'By Far Not the
Worst' for U.S. Secretary of State," *Novosti Press
Agency*, November 23, 2008, http://themoderate-
voice.com/24713/clinton-by-far-not-the-worst-for-
us-secretary-of-state-novosti-of-russia/.

5. Ibid.

6. Owen, Matthews, "How Obama Bought Russia's
(Expensive) Friendship," *Newsweek*, June 24, 2010.

7. Matthews, Owen, "Putin Backs a Major Thaw in
Russian Foreign Policy," *Newsweek*, June 12, 2010,
http://www.newsweek.com/putin-backs-major-thaw-
russian-foreign-policy-72929.

8. Mankoff, "The Russian Economic Crisis." Åslund,
Anders, and Gary Clyde Hufbauer, "Why It's in
the US Interest to Establish Normal Trade Relations
with Russia," Peterson Institute for International
Economics (2011), http://photos.state.gov/libraries/
russia/231771/PDFs/Peterson-Institute-Paper.pdf.

9. "Atomic Castling: Kremlin Makes First Moves to
Consolidate Nuclear Sector," *Russian Life*, May/June
2006.

10. Weir, Fred, "Russia Plans Big Nuclear Expansion," *Christian Science Monitor*, July 17, 2007.

11. Paxton, Robin. "Russia Looks beyond U.S. to Conquer Uranium Markets," *Reuters*, December 10, 2009, http://www.reuters.com/article/2009/12/10/uranium-russia-idUSGEE5B60HS20091210.

12. Rosatom, "Nuclear Weapons Complex," page published April 19, 2010, http://www.rosatom.ru/en/about/activities/nuclear_weapons/.

13. Simes, Dimitri K., "Russia's Crisis, America's Complicity," *National Interest*, Winter 1998.

14. Grigoriadis, Theocaris, "Nuclear Power Contracts and International Cooperation: Analyzing Innovation and Social Distribution in Russian Foreign Policy," in *Responding to a Resurgent Russia: Russian Policy and Responses from the European Union and the United States*, edited by Vino Aggarnal and Kristi Govella (New York: Springer, 2012), http://link.springer.com/book/10.1007%2F978-1-4419-6667-4.

15. Tran, Mark, "Iran to Gain Nuclear Power as Russia Loads Fuel into Bushehr Reactor," *The Guardian*, August 13, 2010, http://www.theguardian.com%2Fworld%2F2010%2Faug%2F13%2Firan-nuclear-power-plant-russia.

16. "Russia Uranium Plans May Include N. Korea," UPI, March 29, 2007, http://www.upi.com/Business_News/Energy-Resources/2007/03/29/Russia-uranium-plans-may-include-N-Korea/UPI-23571175193174/.

Rosatom, "Russia Will Build a NPP and Research Reactor in Venezuela," press release, October 15, 2010, http://www.rosatom.ru/en/presscentre/high-lights/f71874804452bdaa90e3b265d4d5340b. Jagan, Larry, "Myanmar Drops a Nuclear 'Bombshell,'" *Asia Times*, May 24, 2007, http://www.atimes.com/atimes/Southeast_Asia/IE24Ae02.html. Khlopkov, Anton, and Dmitri Konukhov, "Russia, Myanmar and Nuclear Technologies," *Center for Energy and Security Studies*, June 29, 2011, http://ceness-russia.org/data/doc/MyanmarENG.pdf. World Nuclear Association, "Emerging Nuclear Energy Countries," October 2014, http://www.world-nuclear.org/info/Country-Profiles/Others/Emerging-Nuclear-Energy-Countries/.

17. US Department of State, Embassy in Brussels, "Russia Flexes Muscles on Ukraine Nuclear Fuel Supply," unclassified memo, WikiLeaks, October 15, 2009, https://www.wikileaks.org/plusd/cables/09BRUSSELS1385_a.html.

18. Medetsky, Anatoly, "Rosatom Gets $465M to Buy Uranium Assets," *Moscow Times*, December 23, 2009, http://www.themoscowtimes.com/business/article/rosatom-gets-465m-to-buy-uranium-assets/396701.html.

19. US Department of State, Embassy in Astana, "Kazakhstan: Russian Hand in Kazatomprom Drama?" unclassified memo, WikiLeaks, December 22, 2009,

https://www.wikileaks.org/plusd/cables/09ASTANA 2197_a.html.

20. Humber, Yuriy, and Maria Kolesnikova, "Russia to Acquire 17% Stake in Canada's Uranium Ore," Bloomberg.com, http://www.armz.ru/media/File/facts/ARMZ-U1/Bloomberg.pdf.

21. Barber, D. A., "Hot Rocks: Hidden Cost and Foreign Ownership of 'Clean' Nuclear Fuel Emerging," *Huffington Post*, March 30, 2010.

22. Fahys, Judy, "Uranium Company Deal Nearly Done," *Salt Lake Tribune*, December 13, 2010, http://www.sltrib.com/sltrib/home/50850101-76/uranium-company-utah-deal.html.csp.

23. Medetsky, "Rosatom Gets $465M to Buy Uranium Assets."

24. Dombey, Daniel, and Isabel Gorst, "Putin Vexes US over Iran Nuclear Power," *Financial Times*, March 18, 2010, http://www.ft.com/intl/cms/s/0/dba69714-329b-11df-bf20-00144feabdc0.html#axzz39XlLmgqe.

25. Kosharna, Olga, "Nuclear Cooperation with Ukraine Proceeding According to Russia's Plan," *Zerkalo Nedeli* (Ukraine), October 23, 2010.

26. See Canadian Charities reporting; for each year, follow the "Full List," Section C.3, Qualified Donees Worksheet at http://www.cra-arc.gc.ca/ebci/haip/srch/t3010returnlist-eng.action?b=855883583RR0001&n=Fernwood+Foundation&r=http%3A%2F%2

Fwww.cra-arc.gc.ca%3A80%2Febci%2Fhaip%2Fs
rch%2Fbasicsearchresult-eng.action%3Fk%3DFer
nwood%2BFoundation%26amp%3Bs%3Dregistere
d%26amp%3Bp%3D1%26amp%3Bb%3Dtrue.

27. "Clinton Foundation Donors," *Wall Street Jour-nal Online*, December 18, 2008, http://online.wsj.
com/public/resources/documents/st_clintondonor_
20081218.html.

28. "Qualified Donees—Fernwood Foundation—2009,"
Canada Revenue Agency, http://www.cra-arc.gc.ca/
ebci/haip/srch/t3010form21gifts-eng.action?b=85
5883583RR0001&fpe=2009-03-31&n=Fernwood
+Foundation&r=http%3A%2F%2Fwww.cra-arc.
gc.ca%3A80%2Febci%2Fhaip%2Fsrch%2Ft3010f
orm21-eng.action%3Fb%3D855883583RR0001%2
6amp%3Bfpe%3D2009-03-31%26amp%3Bn%3D
Fernwood%2BFoundation%26amp%3Br%3Dhttp
%253A%252F%252Fwww.cra-arc.gc.ca%253A80
%252Febci%252Fhaip%252Fsrch%252Fbasicsearc
hresult-eng.action%253Fk%253DFernwood%252B
Foundation%2526amp%253Bs%253Dregistered%2
526amp%253Bp%253D1%2526amp%253Bb%253
Dtrue.

29. For the reporting periods of March 31, 2009, to March
31, 2012, the Clinton Giustra Sustainable Growth
Initiative functioned as a pass-through to the Clinton
Foundation. For each of these years, the average ratio
of charitable donations to total expenditures was 0.88,

thus 88 cents of every dollar given to CGSGI went to the Clinton Foundation. The ratio was significantly lower in 2013, but even in that year, 100 percent of monies donated went to the Clinton Foundation, which is true of all years discussed. These figures are obtained by comparing figures from Form T3010's Schedule 2 and Schedule 6 (Lines 5000–5010) for the Clinton Giustra Enterprise Partnership, http://www.cra-arc.gc.ca/ebci/haip/srch/t3010returnlist-eng.action?b=846028819RR0001&n=Clinton+Giustra+Enterprise+Partnership+%28Canada%29&r=http%3A%2F%2Fwww.cra-arc.gc.ca%3A80%2Febci%2Fhaip%2Fsrch%2Fbasicsearchresult-eng.action%3Fk%3DClinton%26amp%3Bs%3Dregistered%26amp%3Bp%3D1%26amp%3Bb%3Dtrue.

30. "Qualified Donees—Fernwood Foundation—2010."

31. "Clinton Foundation Donors."

32. *US Global Investors Funds—Form N-Q*, report, May 25, 2011, http://pdf.secdatabase.com/714/0001003715-11-000272.pdf. "Our Team," U.S. Global Investors, http://www.usfunds.com/about-us/our-team/.

33. "Our Team."

34. See, for example, the Endeavour Financial Corporation Investor Presentation, January 2009, p. 14.

35. See "Arrangement Agreement between SRX Uranium One Inc. and Urasia Energy Ltd.," February 11, 2007.

36. https://www.youtube.com/channel/UC9Ze93MxqaQ KPVHLkKmVpeQ; translation by Dr. David Meyer.

37. "Uranium One Signs Credit Agreement and Provides Operational Update," *Market News Publishing*, July 2, 2008, http://business.highbeam.com/1758/article-1G1-180844352/uranium-one-signs-credit-agreement-and-provides-operational.

38. Terentieva, Alexandra, "Mike Hitchen Online: I On Global Trends," *I On Global Trends*, March 31, 2010, http://www.ionglobaltrends.com/2010/03/mining-russias-insatiable-hunger-for.html#.VFPFEeed6Ex.

39. "Where Eight Renowned Investors Think Commodity Prices Are Going," *Globe and Mail* (Toronto), April 20, 2013, http://www.theglobeandmail.com/report-on-business/industry-news/energy-and-resources/where-eight-renowned-investors-think-commodity-prices-are-going/article11435677/ (accessed 2014). Hoffman, Andy, and Sinclair Stewart, "How to (Still) Get Rich in Mining," *Globe and Mail* (Toronto), May 19, 2007, Globeadvisor.com, https://secure.globeadvisor.com/newscentre/article.html?/servlet/GIS.Servlets.WireFeedRedirect?cf=sglobeadvisor/config_blank&vg=BigAdVariableGenerator&date=20070519&archive=gam&slug=RCOVER19.

40. Uranium One, Inc., "Uranium One to Acquire Two More Kazakh Mines from ARMZ and to Pay Special Dividend to Minority Shareholders of at Least US$1.06 per Share," news release via Canada

Newswire, June 8, 2010; see Canadian System for Electronic Document Analysis and Retrieval (Sedar), Search Public Database.

41. Uranium One, Inc., "Notice of Special Meeting of Shareholders and Management: Information Circular for a Special Meeting of Shareholders to Be Held on August 31, 2010, Relating to, among Other Things, a Related Party Transaction between JSC Atomredmetzoloto Its Affiliates and Uranium One, Inc.," August 3, 2010, p. 40. See SEDI, "Uranium One 2010–2011, Insider Transaction Detail."

42. Bouw, Brenda, "Russia Boosts Stake in Uranium One," *Globe and Mail* (Toronto), June 8, 2010, http://www.theprovince.com/business/Russian+faces+hard+sell+uranium+control/3378184/story.html?__federated=1. "The Global Intelligence Files—Russia 100628," WikiLeaks, May 29, 2013, https://wikileaks.org/gifiles/docs/66/661462_russia-100628-.html.

43. "6.3 Interaction with Uranium One, Inc.," JSC Atomredmetzoloto, 2011 Annual Report, 45.

44. "Russian Uranium Giant ARMZ Now Set to Control 50 percent of US Uranium Output," *Australian Uranium News*, December 6, 2010, http://australianuraniumquicksearch.blogspot.com/2010/12/russian-uranium-giant-armz-now-set-to.html.

45. ARMZ Uranium Holding Co., "ARMZ Uranium Holding Co. Announces Acquisition of 51%

Interest in Uranium One Inc.," news release, June 8, 2010, ARMZ.ru, http://www.armz.ru/eng/press/news/?id=209. Saunders, Doug, "Russian Takeover of Uranium One a Benefit, Execs Say," *Globe and Mail* (Toronto), June 27, 2010, http://www.theglobeandmail.com/globe-investor/russian-takeover-of-uranium-one-a-benefit-execs-say/article1389805/.

46. Finley, Bruce, "Russian Company Seeks Control of Canadian Uranium-mining Firm Operating in Rockies," *Denver Post*, October 20, 2010, http://www.denverpost.com/ci_16382080#ixzz32qCvvALO.

47. "Kremlin Submits Bill to Turn Rosatom into All-encompassing State Nuclear Corporation," Bellona.org, October 4, 2007, http://bellona.org/news/nuclear-issues/nuclear-russia/2007-10-kremlin-submits-bill-to-turn-rosatom-into-all-encompassing-state-nuclear-corporation.

48. US House of Representatives, Committee on Foreign Affairs, "Ros-Lehtinen, Bachus, King, McKeon Send Letter to Geithner Opposing Russian Takeover of U.S. Uranium Processing Facility," October 6, 2010, http://archives.republicans.foreignaffairs.house.gov/news/story/?1618.

49. Fugleberg, Jeremy, "Russia Can't Export Wyoming Uranium, Nuclear Regulators Tell Barrasso," *Casper Star-Tribune Online*, March 29, 2011, http://trib.com/news/state-and-regional/russia-can-t-export-wyoming-uranium-nuclear-regulators-tell-barrasso/

article_5018f8f8-c59a-5e1b-9401-c019cd6a8625.
html.

50. Harvey, Cole J., "The U.S.-Russian Agreement for Peaceful Nuclear Cooperation," NTI: Nuclear Threat Initiative, June 22, 2010, http://www.nti.org/ analysis/articles/us-russian-peaceful-cooperation/.

51. Congressman Ed Markey's Office, "Markey & Fortenberry Introduce Resolution of Disapproval of Proposed Nuclear Deal," news release, Ed Markey Congress Website, May 25, 2010, http://www.markey. senate.gov/news/press-releases/may-25-2010-markey-and-fortenberry-introduce-resolution-of-disapproval-of-proposed-nuclear-deal.

52. Bleizeffer, Dustin, "Company: Uranium Won't Go to Russia, Iran," *Billings* (Montana) *Gazette*, September 28, 2010, http://billingsgazette.com/news/ state-and-regional/wyoming/company-uranium-won-t-go-to-russia-iran/article_3c0424ba-cab2-11df-ba2c-001cc4c002e0.html.

53. "Response to Request for Additional Information," Donna Wichers to Keith McConnell, October 18, 2010, http://pbadupws.nrc.gov/docs/ML1029/ ML102940435.pdf.

54. Fugleberg, Jeremy, "Wyoming Mining Officials Tout Technology, Safety, Exports," *Star-Tribune* (Caspar, Wyoming), January 7, 2011, http://trib.com/news/ state-and-regional/wyoming-mining-officials-tout-technology-safety-exports/article_c55415dd-3aae-5e66-b485-83e9e61a5a11.html.

55. US International Trade Commission, "Uranium from Russia," Investigation No. 731-TA-539-C (Third Review), February 2012, http://www.usitc.gov/publications/701_731/pub4307.pdf.

56. Helmer, John, "Putin Urges US Help for Oligarchs," *Asia Times Online*, March 25, 2010, http://www.atimes.com/atimes/Central_Asia/LC25Ag01.html.

57. "Salida Capital Foundation—Quick View," Canadian Revenue Agency, http://www.cra-arc.gc.ca/ebci/haip/srch/t3010form22quickview-eng.action?r=http%3A%2F%2Fwww.cra-arc.gc.ca%3A80%2Febci%2Fhaip%2Fsrch%2Fbasicsearchresult-eng.action%3Fk%3DSalida%2BCapital%26amp%3Bs%3Dregistered%26amp%3Bp%3D1%26amp%3Bb%3Dtrue&fpe=2012-12-31&b=835572066RR0001&n=Salida%20Capital%20Foundation.

58. "Qualified Donees—Salida Capital Foundation," Canadian Revenue Agency, http://www.cra-arc.gc.ca/ebci/haip/srch/t3010form22gifts-eng.action?b=835572066RR0001&fpe=2011-12-31&n=Salida+Capital+Foundation&r=http%3A%2F%2Fwww.cra-arc.gc.ca%3A80%2Febci%2Fhaip%2Fsrch%2Ft3010form22QuickView-eng.action%3Fb%3D835572066RR0001%26amp%3Bfpe%3D2011-12-31%26amp%3Br%3Dhttp%253A%252F%252Fwww.cra-arc.gc.ca%253A80%252Febci%252Fhaip%252Fsrch%252Fbasicsearchresult-eng.action%253Fk%253DSalida%252BCapital%2526amp%

253Bs%253Dregistered%2526amp%253Bp%253D1
%2526amp%253Bb%253Dtrue.

59. Salida's chief business partner in Ukraine is Robert
Bensh, who served as an adviser to Boyko, who served
as energy minister and later deputy prime minister
under President Viktor Yanukovych. Yanukovych
fled the country for Moscow during the Ukrainian
uprising in 2014, and was granted Russian citizenship
by Vladimir Putin. Salida and Bensh are involved in
at least two energy ventures in the Ukraine including CUB Energy and EastCoal. For quotes on Boyko
see: https://cablegatesearch.wikileaks.org/cable.
php?id=06KYIV4313&q=boyko%20kremlin.

60. Rosatom, "Public Annual Report," news release,
Globalreporting.org, http://static.globalreporting.
org/report-pdfs/2013/358637c2a26b8a36867a5bf7b
e2d1793.pdf.

61. The Salida Capital mentioned in the Rosatom
report is owned under a Ukrainian subsidiary Energomashspetsstal, a heavy machine company that
produces industrial metal castings for the nuclear
industry. The Salida Capital Foundation's approximately $2.9 million in donations to the Clinton
Foundation, starting in 2010 and lasting through
2013, is directly linked to the the Canadian hedge
fund Salida Capital Corp., which does business out of
the second floor of the CIBC building in downtown
Toronto. Its principals at the time were executives

with a history in Canadian mining finance. Salida's founder, Danny Guy, was listed in 2009 as an official partner, along with Sergey Kurzin, of the Clinton-Giustra Sustainable Growth Initiative. In 2011 Rosatom, the Russian state nuclear agency that had acquired a controlling stake in Uranium One, began including a "Salida Capital Corp." in its list of subsidiaries. Other Rosatom documents traced the company in question to Panama City, Panama.

On October 3, 2006, Blumont Capital Corporation, which was registered in Canada, announced a new investment initiative with several other Canadian-based hedge funds. One of those funds was Salida Capital Corporation of Ontario. Blumont's principal, Veronika Hirsch, and Salida's principal, Danny Guy, were both long-standing figures in the world of Canadian mining finance. Both of them were involved in bringing investors to Diamond Fields, the Canadian-based company that explored for diamonds in Arkansas during Bill Clinton's governorship. This is the same Diamond Fields in which Frank Giustra's Yorkton Securities invested.

On October 4, 2006, papers were filed with the Panamanian Division of Corporations for a Salida Capital Corp. On November 2, 2006, this entity was officially registered as a corporation in Panama. The very same day, a company called Blumont Capital was registered in Panama by the same law firm, with the exact same board of directors. In fact, two other firms, both corresponding to Canadian investment entities with long-standing ties to Canadian mining finance were also registered the same day, by the same law firm, with the same board of directors. One of the Panamanian companies was First Leeward Investments. It just so happens that a Leeward Investments Company, headed by the colorful Matthew Brendan Kyne, is registered on the same floor as Salida Capital in Toronto's CIBC building. The other Panamanian firm, New Thornhill Investments, corresponds to the Canadian-based Thornhill Investment Funds, run by the perhaps even more colorful Karleris Sarkans. Sarkans, whose book on international negotiations details his experiences "being held down at knifepoint and gunpoint by Russians," was sued in Massachusetts in 2004 for investment fraud. Specifically, he was accused of investing in the Russian bond markets in 1997, when he had specifically promised an investor that he had liquidated his position in the Russian market. The investor lost well over a million dollars. The action resulted in a default judgment against him.

Curiously, Salida Capital Panama has its own Ukrainian connection. Throughout 2008 Salida Capital Panama was used by the Eastern Ukrainian company Energomashspetsstal (EMSS) to import heavy machinery from China and the Czech Republic.

EMSS makes castings and other large steel structures for mining and nuclear power plants. That same year a notorious Ukrainian oligarch and politician named Andriy Klyuev appropriated Ukrainian state funds to EMSS for "capital improvements." EMSS was at that time 80 percent owned by the Industrial Union of Donbass (IUD). Ukrainian media reports as well as academic papers associate IUD with one of eastern Ukraine's most powerful men, Serhiy Taruta. Taruta's business dealings were on the ropes in January 2010. According to reports, Vladimir Putin arranged considerable financial support for them. It is against this background that Rosatom, Russia's state nuclear agency, as it successfully sought CFIUS approval to purchase a controlling stake in Uranium One, acquired EMSS on or about December 9, 2010. Throughout 2010 Salida Capital Canada's newly created charity, the Salida Capital Foundation, received four separate infusions of money totaling $3.376 million (Canadian). That year, Salida's CEO, Courtenay Wolfe, would join Bill Clinton onstage at the Clinton Global Initiative annual dinner to announce a charitable partnership, and its foundation would give to the Clinton Foundation almost $800,000 of what would become approximately $2.9 million by 2013. According to Canadian government records, that money is over 80 percent of all donations ever given by Salida's own foundation.

' By June 2011 Rosatom's corporate documents listed a "Salida Capital Group, Inc.; Panama City, Panama," whose board contact information matched that of the Salida Capital Corp. registered in Panama in November 2006. When Rosatom published its annual report in 2012, it listed a Salida Capital Corp that it held "outside of the consolidated budget perimeter" through "PJSC Energomashspetsstal" or EMSS.

It's essential to understand that Salida Capital Corp. of Canada began publicly to do business in eastern Ukraine in the spring of 2010. It invested first in a natural gas play that would become a Canadian registered firm called Cub Energy and then in a coal operation in the Donbass region that became known as EastCoal. Both firms are well within the same financial, and therefore in Ukraine, political orbit. In this context, the creation of the Salida Capital Foundation at the end of 2009 and its generous donations to the Clinton Foundation demand the utmost scrutiny.

One final question must be asked: why Panama? Panama is perhaps less known than the Cayman Islands as a vehicle for questionable financial dealings, but its virtues are well known by offshoring practitioners. Canadian law in particular allows for the creation of private investment foundations, which can hold international business company stock, but which function essentially as nonprofit corporations.

Services exist in Canada to facilitate creating corporations in Panama that mirror and work with Canadian private investment foundations. The goal of such arrangements, naturally, is to shield assets from taxation and provide anonymity for the beneficiaries. The same law firm created not only Salida Capital Corp. of Panama, but simultaneously Blumont Capital Panama, whose Canadian counterpart was just beginning a new investment venture with Salida Canada. It also created the other two firms with equally curious Canadian parallels. The firm, as it so happens, specializes in creating just such private investment foundations.

Was a Private Investment Foundation created for Salida Canada and its management and investors, who at some point came to include the Russian government who had business before the very secretary of state to whose charitable foundation Salida's own charity was even then making donations? Since my inquiries to both Salida and Lombardi-Aguilar went unanswered, I cannot say for sure. I can only say the facts speak eloquently for themselves and demand an answer from the only parties who can give an answer.

In 2015 Salida Capital Canada changed its name to Harrington Global.

62. Strickland, Ken, and Andrea Mitchell, "Clinton, Obama 'Memo of Understanding,'" NBC News, December 18, 2008, http://firstread.nbcnews.com/

_news/2008/12/18/4426618-clinton-obama-memo-of-understanding.

63. "Clinton Surpasses $75 Million in Speech Income after Lucrative 2010," CNN Political Ticker RSS, July 11, 2011, http://politicalticker.blogs.cnn.com/2011/07/11/clinton-surpasses-75-million-in-speech-income-after-lucrative-2010/.

64. "William Jefferson Clinton Speeches, 2001–2012," Turner.com, http://i2.cdn.turner.com/cnn/2013/images/05/23/clinton.speeches.2001-2012.pdf.

65. "Former Russian Spy Recalls the Golden Age of Espionage," *The Telegraph* (London), January 2, 2011, http://www.telegraph.co.uk/sponsored/rbth/features/8236120/Former-Russian-spy-recalls-the-golden-age-of-espionage.html and http://en.gazeta.ru/news/2012/03/30/a_4116129.shtml; http://www.telegraph.co.uk/sponsored/rbth/features/8236120/Former-Russian-spy-recalls-the-golden-age-of-espionage.html.

66. Low, Valentine, "My Old Friend the KGB Spy," *Evening Standard* (London), December 30, 2002.

67. Weiss, Michael, "Moscow's Long, Corrupt Money Trail," *Daily Beast*, March 22, 2014, http://www.thedailybeast.com/articles/2014/03/22/moscow-s-long-corrupt-money-trail.html.

68. Renaissance Capital, "Uranium One: Company on Schedule; Market Lags," May 27, 2010, centralasia.rencap.com/download.asp?id=10956.

69. "Burn after Reading: Russian Spies in America," *The Economist*, June 29, 2010, http://www.economist.com/blogs/newsbook/2010/06/russian_spies_america; Smith, Ben, "Clinton Friend Was Spy's Target," *Politico*, June 29, 2010, http://www.politico.com/blogs/bensmith/0610/Clinton_friend_may_have_been_spys_target.html.

70. "Spies Assigned to Gather Intel on U.S. Nuke Strategy for Russia, FBI Says," *NTI*, June 29, 2010, http://www.nti.org/gsn/article/spies-assigned-to-gather-intel-on-us-nuke-strategy-for-russia-fbi-says/.

71. Levy, Clifford J., and Ellen Barry, "Putin Criticizes U.S. for Arrests of Espionage Suspects," *New York Times*, June 29, 2010, http://www.nytimes.com/2010/06/30/world/europe/30lavrov.html.

72. Soltis, Andy, "Soviet-style 'Red' Whine," *New York Post*, June 30, 2010, http://nypost.com/2010/06/30/soviet-style-red-whine/.

73. Baker, Peter, "The Mellowing of William Jefferson Clinton," *New York Times*, May 26, 2009, http://www.nytimes.com/2009/05/31/magazine/31clinton-t.html?pagewanted=all.

74. "Bill Clinton Offers Rare US Praise for Putin," *RIA Novosti*, September 25, 2009, http://en.ria.ru/russia/20130925/183725042.html.

75. Anderson, Derek, "Uranium Agreement Faces New Objections from U.S.," *St. Petersburg* (Russia)

Times, October 12, 2010, http://sptimes.ru/index. php?action_id=2&story_id=32688.

76. "Hearings before the Committee on Armed Services, United States Senate: Briefing by Representatives from the Departments and Agencies Represented on the Committee on Foreign Investment in the United States (CFIUS) to Discuss the National Security Implications of the Acquisition of Peninsular and Oriental Steamship Navigation Company by Dubai Ports World, and Government-owned and-controlled Firm of the United Arab Emirates," February 23, 2006, 6, http://www.gpo.gov/fdsys/pkg/CHRG-109shrg32744/html/CHRG-109shrg32744.htm.

77. "Press Release: Hillary Clinton Promotes Plan for Strong Defense and Good Jobs in Indiana," American Presidency Project, April 12, 2008, http://www.presidency.ucsb.edu/ws/?pid=96587.

78. "Facing CFIUS: Better Safe Than Sorry—Law360," *Law360*, July 5, 2012, http://www.law360.com/articles/355660/facing-cfius-better-safe-than-sorry. McConnell, Will, "Feds Query Another Chinese Mining Deal near TOPGUN," *TheDeal*, May 23, 2012, http://www.thedeal.com/content/regulatory/feds-query-another-chinese-mining-deal-near-topgun.php. "US Bars China Wind Farm Deal on Security Grounds," *Space Daily*, September 28, 2012, http://www.spacedaily.com/reports/US_bars_China_wind_farm_deal_on_security_grounds_999.html.

Drye, Kelley, "CFIUS Rejects Chinese Acquisition in U.S.," news release, April 5, 2011, http://www.kelleydrye.com/publications/client_advisories/0654.

79. "6.3 Interaction with Uranium One, Inc.," JSC Atomredmetzoloto, 2011 Annual Report, 44.

80. Uranium One, "Uranium One Enters into Definitive Agreement with ARMZ for Going Private Transaction for CDN$2.86 per Share in Cash," news release, January 14, 2013, Bloomberg.com, http://www.bloomberg.com/article/2013-01-14/abXujiJ0LYIk.html.

81. Gutterman, Steve, "U.S.-Russian Civilian Nuclear Deal Boosts 'Reset,' " Reuters, January 12, 2011, http://www.reuters.com/article/2011/01/11/us-russia-usa-nuclear-idUSTRE70A5LB20110111.

82. Melbye, Scott (executive vice president—marketing, Uranium One), "Uranium One's Experience in Kazakhstan," Kazatomprom Representative Office Opening, Washington, DC, slideshow presentation, May 2013, http://www.kazatomprom.kz/sites/default/files/6_Scott%20Melbye-Uranium%20One's%20Experience%20in%20Kazakhstan.pdf.

83. Baker, Matt, "Moscow's American Uranium," Politico, October 18, 2013, http://www.politico.com/story/2013/10/moscows-american-uranium-98472.html. "Regarding the Willow Creek, Moore Ranch, Jab & Antelope, Ludeman Projects and Well Logging Equipment," Donna Wichers to Andrew Persinko and Roberto J. Torres, January 29, 2013, http://pbadupws.nrc.gov/docs/ML1304/ML13043A505.pdf.

84. "Russian Nuclear Energy Conquers the World," *Pravda*, January 22, 2013, http://english.pravda.ru/russia/economics/22-01-2013/123551-russia_nuclear_energy-0/.

85. "Rosatom Spares No Expense to Buy Out Canada's Uranium One," *RT*, January 14, 2013, http://rt.com/business/rosatom-100-percent-canadian-uranium-966.

86. Baker, "Moscow's American Uranium."

87. Helms, Kathy, "Navajo Protests Canadian-Russian Uranium Mine at Big Boquillas," *Gallup Independent* (New Mexico), May 21, 2013.

88. Horoshko, Sonja, "The Navajo Nation Nixes Access for Uranium Mining," *Four Corners Free Press* (Colorado), June 1, 2013, http://fourcornersfreepress.com/?p=1527.

CHAPTER 4: INDIAN NUKES

1. Baruah, Amit, "India a Partner in Obama's N-efforts?" *Hindustan Times* (New Delhi), April 6, 2009, http://www.hindustantimes.com/india-news/india-a-partner-in-obama-s-n-efforts/article1-397262.aspx.

2. Nayar, K. P., "Time to Tell a Prophetic Secret," *The Telegraph* (Calcutta), December 24, 2004, http://www.telegraphindia.com/1041224/asp/nation/story_4169260.asp.

3. Sen, Chanakya, "A Review of *Engaging India: Diplomacy, Democracy and the Bomb* by Strobe Talbott," *Kashmir Herald*, December 2004/January 2005, http://www.indiatoday.com/itoday/17051999/books.html.

4. Krepon, Michael, "Looking Back: The 1998 Indian and Pakistani Nuclear Tests," *Arms Control Today*, Arms Control Association, May 2008, http://www.armscontrol.org/act/2008_05/lookingback. Diamond, John, *The CIA and the Culture of Failure: U.S. Intelligence from the End of the Cold War to the Invasion of Iraq* (Stanford, CA: Stanford Security Series, 2008), 268. Richey, Bill, "Early Report 5/15: Indian Nuclear Test: All Eyes on Pakistan's Response," *Foreign Media Reaction Daily Digest* (US Information Agency), May 15, 1998, http://fas.org/news/pakistan/1998/05/980515-usia-fmrr.htm.

5. Sen, Canakya, "Two Villages and an Elephant," *Asia Times* (Hong Kong), December 16, 2004, http://www.brookings.edu/research/articles/2000/06/summer-india-cohen.

6. Clinton, Hillary, "Remarks of First Lady Hillary Rodham Clinton at a Special Event at the UN Social Summit," UN Social Summit, Denmark, Copenhagen, March 6–12, 1995, http://www.un.org/documents/ga/conf166/gov/950307142511.htm.

7. Clinton, Hillary, "Security and Opportunity for the Twenty-first Century," *Foreign Affairs*, November/

December 2007, http://www.foreignaffairs.com/articles/63005/hillary-rodham-clinton/security-and-opportunity-for-the-twenty-first-century.

8. Federation of American Scientists, "Nomination of Hillary R. Clinton to Be Secretary of State," January 13, 2009, http://fas.org/irp/congress/2009_hr/hillary.html.

9. "Clinton's India Connection," *Times of India* (Mumbai), August 24, 2003, http://timesofindia.indiatimes.com/home/stoi/Clintons-India-connection/articleshow/144077.cms.

10. "Sant Singh Chatwal: Rise and Rise of an American Punjabi Hotelier," *Sify Finance*, n.d., http://www.sify.com/finance/sant-singh-chatwal-rise-and-rise-of-an-american-punjabi-hotelier-imagegallery-4-others-mbsqduaghdfsi.html.

11. Port, Bob, and Edward Lewine, "Donor Gives Hillary a Soft $210G," *New York Daily News*, November 3, 2000, http://www.nydailynews.com/archives/news/donor-hillary-soft-210g-article-1.884254.

12. Haniffa, Aziz, "Amar Singh Gave Millions to Clinton Foundation," *Rediff India Abroad*, December 19, 2008, http://www.rediff.com/news/2008/dec/19amar-singh-gave-millions-to-clinton-foundation.htm.

13. Venugopal, Arun, "South Asians Lean to Clinton . . . or Obama," WNYC News, February 4, 2008, http://www.wnyc.org/story/78329-south-asians-lean-to-clinton-or-obama/.

14. Gurley, George, "Vikram Chatwal, Turban Cowboy," *New York Observer*, November 18, 2002, http://observer.com/2002/11/vikram-chatwal-turban-cowboy/#ixzz38gg8TRbI.

15. Nelson, Dean, "Hillary Clinton's Playboy Fundraiser Arrested over Heroin and Cocaine," *The Telegraph* (UK), April 5, 2013, http://www.telegraph.co.uk/news/worldnews/us-politics/9975344/Hillary-Clintons-playboy-fundraiser-arrested-over-heroin-and-cocaine.html.

16. Sherman, William, "Tax Deadbeat Is Livin' Large: Clinton's Buddy Owes City $2.4M," *New York Daily News*, November 24, 2002, http://www.nydailynews.com/archives/news/tax-deadbeat-livin-large-clinton-buddy-owes-city-2-4m-article-1.496489?pgno=2.

17. Ibid.

18. Solomon, John, and Matthew Mosk, "When Controversy Follows Cash," *Washington Post*, September 3, 2007, http://www.washingtonpost.com/wp-dyn/content/article/2007/09/02/AR2007090201436_2.html.

19. Port and Lewine, "Donor Gives Hillary a Soft $210G."

20. "Sant Singh Chatwal: Rise and Rise of an American Punjabi Hotelier."

21. US Department of State, Embassy in New Dehli, "Political Bargaining Continues Prior to Key Vote in Parliament," WikiLeaks, July 17, 2008, https://search.

wikileaks.org/plusd/cables/08NEWDELHI1972_a. html. "Sant Chatwal Says WikiLeaks Allegations Baseless," *Deccan Herald* (India), March 18, 2011, http://www.deccanherald.com/content/146770/F.

22. Chakraborty, Tapas, "Clinton First, Sick Kids Later— Mulayam Woos Dollars as Rahul Visits Death Zone," *The Telegraph—Calcutta*, September 8, 2005, http:// www.telegraphindia.com/1050908/asp/nation/story_ 5212257.asp.

23. Haniffa, "Amar Singh Contributed Millions to Clinton Foundation."

24. "Can Obama Make India an Ally?" *Hindustan Times* (New Delhi), October 30, 2010.

25. "Indian 'Cash for Votes' MP Amar Singh Freed on Bail," BBC News, September 15, 2011, http://www. bbc.co.uk/news/world-south-asia-14925984.

26. Chakraborty, "Clinton First, Sick Kids Later."

27. Aron, Sunita, "Clinton, Romance and All That . . . ," *Hindustan Times* (New Delhi), September 7, 2005.

28. Ibid.

29. "Rural Health Mission Launch Today," *Hindustan Times* (New Delhi), September 6, 2005.

30. "Clinton Visit: Celebs Show Has Just Begun, Says Amar," *Hindustan Times* (New Delhi), September 10, 2005.

31. Dutt, Ela, "The World Cannot Do without Muslims, and Muslims Cannot Do without America:

Singh," *News India-Times* (New York), October 21, 2005.

32. Ibid.

33. Ibid.

34. "Amar Singh Makes Huge Donation to Clinton Foundation," *Times of India* (Mumbai), December 18, 2008, http://timesofindia.indiatimes.com/india/Amar-Singh-makes-huge-donation-to-Clinton-Foundation/articleshow/3864349.cms.

35. Bagchi, Indrani, " . . . But May Slow Down N-deal, Doha Round," *Times of India* (Mumbai), November 9, 2006, http://timesofindia.indiatimes.com/india/-But-may-slow-down-N-deal-Doha-round/articleshow/374508.cms.

36. Haniffa, Aziz, "Indian-American Community Upset with Hillary," *Rediff*, June 30, 2006, http://www.rediff.com/news/2006/jun/30aziz.htm.

37. Mcintire, Mike, "Indian-Americans Test Their Clout on Atom Pact," *New York Times*, June 4, 2006, http://www.nytimes.com/2006/06/05/washington/05indians.html?pagewanted=all&_r=0.

38. Gerstein, Josh, "Clinton Taps Newly Active Indian Donors," *New York Sun*, June 12, 2007, http://www.nysun.com/national/clinton-taps-newly-active-indian-donors/56332/.

39. Srivastava, Siddharth, "India: Wheeling and (Nuclear) Dealing," *Asia Times Online*, July 6, 2006, http://

www.atimes.com/atimes/South_Asia/HG06Df01. html.

40. "India Inc. Gives Millions to Clinton Foundation," *Business Standard News* (India) December 20, 2008, http://www.business-standard.com/article/economy-policy/india-inc-gives-millions-to-clinton-foundation-108122001012_1.html.

41. Prashad, Vijay, "What Did Hillary Clinton Do?" *Counterpunch* (blog), March 10, 2009, http://www.counterpunch.org/2009/03/10/what-did-hillary-clinton-do/.

42. Talbott, Strobe, *Engaging India: Diplomacy, Democracy, and the Bomb* (Washington, DC: Brookings Institution Press, 2006), 231.

43. "Foreign Policy Brain Trusts: Clinton Advisers," Council on Foreign Relations Backgrounder, June 20, 2008, http://www.cfr.org/elections/foreign-policy-brain-trusts-clinton-advisers/p16204.

44. Weiss, Leonard, "India and the NPT," *Strategic Analysis* 34, no. 2 (March 2010): 255–71, doi:10.1080/09700160903537856.

45. Markey, Edward J., and Ellen O. Tauscher, "Don't Loosen Nuclear Rules for India," *New York Times*, August 19, 2008, http://www.nytimes.com/2008/08/20/opinion/20markey.html.

46. Parnes, Aime, "Clinton Allies Distance 'Decisive' Hillary from 'Passive' Obama," *The Hill*, September 10, 2014, http%3A%2F%2Fthehill.com%

2Fhomenews%2Fnews%2F217216-clinton-allies-distance-decisive-hillary-from-passive-obama.

47. Meyer, Bill, "Bill Clinton Made Millions from Foreign Sources," Cleveland.com, January 27, 2009, http://www.cleveland.com/nation/index.ssf/2009/01/bill_clinton_made_millions_fro.html.

48. "Not a Pygmy, but a Giant," *Indiatoday*, March 17, 2003, http://indiatoday.intoday.in/story/india-today-conclave-bill-clinton-lays-down-his-vision-for-india-with-analysis-of-key-concerns/1/206930.html.

49. Zajac, Andrew, "Clinton Donors Wooed, Baggage and All," *The Swamp* (*Chicago Tribune*), June 30, 2008, http://weblogs.baltimoresun.com/news/politics/blog/2008/06/obama_woos_clinton_donors_bagg.html.

50. Zajac, Andrew, "Talks Not Cheap for Clinton," *Chicago Tribune*, April 8, 2008, http://articles.chicagotribune.com/2008-04-08/news/0804070831_1_sen-hillary-clinton-fee-disaster-relief.

51. Haniffa, Aziz, "From the Bottom of My Heart, I Salute You," *India Abroad*, October 10, 2008.

52. Malhotra, Jyoti, "Whoops of Delight Greet Nuclear Deal," BBC News, November 17, 2006, http://news.bbc.co.uk/2/hi/south_asia/6158076.stm.

53. "Democrats Will Not Hinder N-deal Passage: Hillary Clinton," Indo-Asian News Service, September 14, 2008, http://www.hindustantimes.com/world-news/democrats-will-not-hinder-n-deal-passage/

article1-337687.aspx. As the article points out: "Democrats' support is crucial as they control both the House of Representatives and the Senate."

54. Prashad, Vijay, "What Did Hillary Clinton Do?" *CounterPunch: Tells the Facts, Names the Names* (blog), March 10, 2009, http://www.counterpunch. org/2009/03/10/what-did-hillary-clinton-do/. Haniffa, Aziz, " 'I Have Staked a Lot on the Nuclear Deal,' " *Rediff,* September 23, 2008, http://www. rediff.com/news/2008/sep/23inter.htm.

55. Haniffa, Aziz, "US Senate to Vote on N-deal on Wednesday," *Rediff,* October 1, 2008, http://www. rediff.com/news/2008/oct/01ndeal2.htm.

56. Haniffa, Aziz, " 'It's the Greatest Moment in India-US History,' " *Rediff,* October 2, 2008, http://www. rediff.com/news/2008/oct/02ndeal3.htm.

57. "Amar Singh Makes Huge Donation to Clinton Foundation."

58. "Clinton 'Donation' Complaint," *The Telegraph* (Calcutta), December 24, 2008, http://www.tele-graphindia.com/1081224/jsp/nation/story_10294845. jsp.

59. Ibid.

60. "Bill a Friend but No Dollars to Donate," *The Telegraph* (Calcutta), December 19, 2008, http:// www.telegraphindia.com/1081220/jsp/nation/story_ 10277419.jsp.

61. "Indians Gave Millions to Clinton Foundation," *Hindustan Times* (New Delhi), December 20, 2008.

62. "Sant Singh Chatwal: Rise and Rise of an American Punjabi Hotelier."

63. Jacob, Sarah, "I Am Proud of What I Have Done: Chatwal to NDTV," NDTV, February 13, 2010, http://www.ndtv.com/article/india/i-am-proud-of-what-i-have-done-chatwal-to-ndtv-16248.

64. "I Have No Interest in Indian Politics: Chatwal," *Siasat Daily* (Hyderabad, India), March 30, 2011, http://www.siasat.com/english/news/i-have-no-interest-indian-politics-chatwal?page=0%2C1.

65. Jacob, "I Am Proud of What I Have Done."

66. "Amar, Jaya Expelled from SP," *Times of India* (Mumbai), February 2, 2010, http://timesofindia.indiatimes.com/india/Amar-Jaya-expelled-from-SP/articleshow/5527183.cms.

67. Nelson, "Hillary Clinton's Playboy Fundraiser Arrested over Heroin and Cocaine."

68. Clifford, Stephanie, and Russ Buettner, "Clinton Backer Pleads Guilty in a Straw Donor Scheme," *New York Times*, April 17, 2014, http://www.nytimes.com/2014/04/18/nyregion/clinton-backer-pleads-guilty-in-a-straw-donor-scheme.html?_r=0.

69. US Department of Justice, "Hotel Magnate Pleads Guilty to Federal Election Campaign Spending Limits Evasion Scheme and Witness Tampering,"

press release, April 17, 2014, http://www.justice.gov/opa/pr/2014/April/14-crm-400.html.

70. US Attorney's Office, Eastern District of New York, "Hotel Magnate Sant Singh Chatwal Pleads Guilty to Scheme to Evade Federal Election Campaign Contribution Limits, and to Witness Tampering," news release, April 17, 2014, http://www.justice.gov/usao/nye/pr/April14/2014Apr17.php.

71. Colvin, Jill, "Hotel Magnate Pleads Guilty to Campaign Finance Fraud," *New York Observer,* April 17, 2014, http://observer.com/2014/04/hotel-magnate-pleads-guilty-to-campaign-finance-fraud/.

72. "Building the Chatwal Brand," *Leaders Magazine* 33, No. 3 (2010), http://www.leadersmag.com/issues/2010.3_Jul/PDFs/Chatwal.pdf.

CHAPTER 5: THE CLINTON BLUR (I)

1. "Lease Event: A Decade of Difference (Clinton Foundation Event)," Hollywood Bowl, October 15, 2011, http://www.hollywoodbowl.com/tickets/lease-event-decade-of-difference-clinton-foundation-event/2011-10-15.

2. Brown, August, "Live: Bill Clinton's 'Decade of Difference' Party at Hollywood Bowl," *Los Angeles Times,* October 16, 2011, http://latimesblogs.latimes.com/music_blog/2011/10/live-bill-clintons-decade-of-difference-party-at-hollywood-bowl.html.

3. US Securities and Exchange Commission, "SEC Files Settled Enforcement Action against Schering-Plough Corporation for Foreign Corrupt Practices Act Violations," news release, sec.gov, June 9, 2004, http://www.sec.gov/litigation/litreleases/lr18740.htm.

4. Matthews, Christopher M., "Clinton Defends FCPA, as U.S. Chamber Lobbies for Changes to Law," *Wall Street Journal*, March 23, 2012.

5. McLean, Bethany, "The Power of Philanthropy," *Fortune*, September 7, 2006, http://archive.fortune.com/magazines/fortune/fortune_archive/2006/09/18/8386185/index.htm.

6. Rauch, Jonathan, "This Is Not Charity," *The Atlantic*, October 1, 2007, http://www.theatlantic.com/magazine/archive/2007/10/-this-is-not-charity/306197/5/.

7. Takiff, Michael, *A Complicated Man: The Life of Bill Clinton as Told by Those Who Know Him* (New Haven, CT: Yale University Press, 2010), 403.

8. Kanter, Rosabeth Moss, "Bill Clinton and How to Use Convening Power," *Harvard Business Review*, September 19, 2011, http://blogs.hbr.org/2011/09/bill-clinton-and-how-to-use-co/.

9. Foer, Franklin, "Ira Magaziner," *Slate*, January 11, 1998.

10. Magaziner, Ira, Tushar Khadloya, and Samuel Magaram, "The Clinton Foundation: Global

Operations," *Brown Journal of World Affairs* 15, no. 2 (January 31, 2009): 11–21, http://brown. edu/initiatives/journal-world-affairs/14.2/clinton-foundation-global-operations.

11. "Leadership Team," Clinton Foundation, June 2014, https://www.clintonfoundation.org/about/leadership-team.

12. Ibid.

13. BBB Charity Review, "Bill, Hillary and Chelsea Clinton Foundation," November 2013.

14. "Charity Navigator Profile—Bill Hillary & Chelsea Clinton Foundation," Charity Navigator, http://www.charitynavigator.org/index.cfm?bay=search. profile&ein=311580204#.VFP4OFYkHG4.

15. US Securities and Exchange Commission, "SEC Charges InfoGROUP's Former CEO, CFOs, and Audit Committee Chair with Fraud," news release, March 15, 2010, http://www.sec.gov/litigation/litreleases/2010/lr21451.htm. Hubbard, Russell, "Deal Doesn't End Legal Wrangling for Infogroup, Gupta," Omaha.com, February 19, 2014, http://www.omaha.com/money/deal-doesn-t-end-legal-wrangling-for-infogroup-gupta/article_b168e1e9-5398-54c0-bca4-0144e7399998.html?mode=story.

16. US Securities and Exchange Commission, "SEC Charges InfoGROUP's Former CEO." Hubbard, "Deal Doesn't End Legal Wrangling for Infogroup, Gupta."

17. US Attorney's Office, "Hotel Magnate Sant Singh Chatwal Pleads Guilty to Scheme to Evade Federal Election Campaign Contribution Limits, and to Witness Tampering," news release, April 17, 2014, http://www.justice.gov/usao/nye/pr/April14/2014Apr17.php.

18. Cassin, Richard L., "Dahdaleh Prosecution Collapses, Key Witnesses from Akin Gump Refuse to Testify," FCPA Blog, December 10, 2013, http://www.fcpablog.com/blog/tag/victor-dahdaleh#.

19. Armstrong, David, and Alan Katz, "Billionaire Found in Middle of Bribery Case Avoids U.S. Probe," Bloomberg.com, August 14, 2014, http://www.bloomberg.com/news/2014-08-14/billionaire-found-in-middle-of-bribery-case-avoids-u-s-probe.html.

20. Harper, Tom, "Victor Dahdaleh Corruption Case: Billionaire's Fraud Trial Collapses after Key SFO Witnesses Refuse to Give Evidence," *The Independent* (UK), December 10, 2013, http://www.independent.co.uk/news/business/news/victor-dahdaleh-corruption-case-billionaires-fraud-trial-collapses-after-key-sfo-witnesses-refuse-to-give-evidence-8995972.html.

21. Armstrong and Katz, "Billionaire Found in Middle of Bribery Case Avoids U.S. Probe."

22. "Officials, Senior Power Company Executives Face Fraud Charges," DominicanToday.com, February

13, 2013, http://www.dominicantoday.com/dr/local/2013/2/13/46697/Officials-senior-power-company-executives-face-fraud-charges.

23. Lowe, Alison, "Company Seeking BEC Contract Dismisses Fraud Case against CEO," *Nassau* (Bahamas) *Guardian*, February 25, 2014, http://www.thenassauguardian.com/bahamas-business/40-bahamas-business/45422-company-seeking-bec-contract-dismisses-fraud-case-against-ceo.

24. Moriarty, James F. (US ambassador to Bangladesh), "WikiLeaks—Ambassador Urges Prime Minister's Adviser to Accelerate Energy Sector Development," July 29, 2009, https://wikileaks.org/cable/2009/07/09DHAKA741.html.

25. "Lease Event: A Decade of Difference (Clinton Foundation Event)."

26. McLean, "The Power of Philanthropy."

27. *Meeting with Indian Generic Drug Industry*, Proceedings of World Community Advisory Board, India, Mumbai, January 2005, http://www.itpcglobal.org/atomic-documents/11057/11059/WorldCAB2.pdf.

28. Quoted in Takiff, *A Complicated Man*, 408.

29. Kapstein, Ethan B., and Josh Busby, "Making Markets for Merit Goods: The Political Economy of Antiretrovirals," Center for Global Development, Working Paper 179 (August 2009), 24.

30. Khadloya, Tushar, and Samuel Magaram, "The Clinton Foundation: Global Operations: An Interview with Tushar Khadloya and Samuel Magaram," *Brown Journal of World Affairs*, January 31 and February 7, 2009.

31. "HIV/AIDS," MSF USA, http://www.doctorswithoutborders.org/our-work/medical-issues/hivaids.

32. Takiff, *A Complicated Man*, 407.

33. Dugger, Celia W., "Clinton Makes Up for Lost Time in Battling AIDS," *New York Times*, August 29, 2006, http://www.nytimes.com/2006/08/29/health/29clinton.html?pagewanted=all&_r=1&.

34. Jack, Andrew, "Charm Offensive Five Years after Leaving Office . . . ," *Financial Times*, August 19, 2006.

35. US Department of State, Embassy in Maseru (Lesotho), "Former President Clinton Visits Lesotho to Promote Pediatric Treatment Of HIV/AIDS And Launch New Clinic," WikiLeaks, July 25, 2005, https://wikileaks.org/cable/2005/07/05MASERU371.html.

36. McLean, "The Power of Philanthropy."

37. "Clinton Global Citizen Awards, 2009 Annual Meeting," Clinton Foundation, https://www.clintonfoundation.org/clinton-global-initiative/meetings/annual-meetings/2009/clinton-global-citizen-awards. Goldstein, Dana, "Bill Clinton's Rwanda Guilt," *Daily Beast*, September 23, 2012, http://

www.thedailybeast.com/articles/2010/09/23/cgi-bill-clintons-rwanda-guilt.html. French, Howard W., "Kagame's Hidden War in the Congo," *New York Review of Books*, September 24, 2009, http://www.nybooks.com/articles/archives/2009/sep/24/kagames-hidden-war-in-the-congo/.

38. See for example, Kagame, Paul, "President Kagame's Remarks at the Clinton Health Access Initiative (CHAI) Joint Partnership on Nutrition," paulkagame.com, August 5, 2013, http://www.paulkagame.com/index.php/speeches/1162-president-kagames-remarks-at-the-clinton-health-access-initiative-chai-joint-partnership-on-nutrition.

39. Kempner, Jonathan L., "Welcome," *Mortgage Banking*, September 2006.

40. Dowd, Maureen, "The Vodka Chronicles," *New York Times*, April 6, 2008, http://www.nytimes.com/2008/04/06/opinion/06dowd.html?hp.

41. Baker, Peter. "His Changing World," review of *Giving* by Bill Clinton, *Washington Post*, September 9, 2007. http://www.washingtonpost.com/wp-dyn/content/article/2007/09/06/AR2007090602053.html.

CHAPTER 6: THE CLINTON BLUR (II)

1. Helderman, Rosalind S., "For Hillary Clinton and Boeing, a Beneficial Relationship," *Washington Post*,

April 13, 2014, http://www.washingtonpost.com/politics/for-hillary-clinton-and-boeing-a-beneficial-relationship/2014/04/13/21fe84ec-bc09-11e3-96ae-f2c36d2b1245_story.html.

2. Dwoskin, Elizabeth, "Hillary Clinton's Business Legacy at the State Department," *Bloomberg Businessweek*, January 10, 2013, http://www.businessweek.com/articles/2013-01-10/hillary-clintons-business-legacy-at-the-state-department.

3. US Department of State, USAID, "Partnering with Power Africa," http://www.usaid.gov/powerafrica/partner-power-africa.

4. Helman, Christopher, "Obama's 'Power Africa' Plan Greases Billions in Deals for General Electric," *Forbes*, July 1, 2013, http://www.forbes.com/sites/christopherhelman/2013/07/01/with-power-africa-plan-obama-to-grease-billions-in-deals-for-g-e/.

5. Kolbert, Elizabeth, "Election Staffs Resemble Candidates," *New York Times*, January 4, 1992, http://www.nytimes.com/1992/01/05/us/election-staffs-resemble-candidates.html?pagewanted=all&src=pm. Long, Ray, and James Kimberly, "Governor Asked Lobby Firm to Help Pick Board," *Chicago Tribune*, July 15, 2004, http://articles.chicagotribune.com/2004-07-15/news/0407150257_1_new-members-rod-blagojevich-new-board. "Hecate Energy Leadership Team," HecateEnergy, http://hecateenergy.com/who-we-are/.

6. Allen, Jonathan, and Amie Parnes, *HRC: State Secrets and the Rebirth of Hillary Clinton* (New York: Crown Publishing Group, Random House, 2014), 128.

7. Ibid., 9.

8. Ibid., 128.

9. *Diplomacy in a Time of Scarcity* (Washington, DC: American Academy of Diplomacy, 2012), http://www.academyofdiplomacy.org/publications/Diplomacy_in_a_Time_of_Scarcity.pdf.

10. Confessore, Nicholas, and Amy Chozick, "Unease at Clinton Foundation over Finances and Ambitions," *New York Times*, August 13, 2013, http://www.nytimes.com/2013/08/14/us/politics/unease-at-clinton-foundation-over-finances-and-ambitions.html?pagewanted=all&_r=0.

11. Hernandez, Raymond, "Weiner's Wife Didn't Disclose Consulting Work She Did While Serving in State Dept.," *New York Times*, May 16, 2013, http://www.nytimes.com/2013/05/17/nyregion/weiners-wife-huma-abedin-failed-to-disclose-consulting-work-done-while-a-state-dept-aide.html.

12. US Department of Commerce, Office of the Assistant General Counsel for Administration, "Ethics Rules–Balancing Responsibilities to the Government and Personal Interests," February 1, 2013, 4, http://www.commerce.gov/sites/default/files/documents/2013/february/sge_summary_of_ethics_rules-2013-e.pdf.

13. Ibid., 6.

14. "Top Govt. Aides Shouldn't Also Serve as Outside Consultants," editorial, *Boston Globe*, July 29, 2013, http://www.bostonglobe.com/opinion/editorials/2013/07/28/top-aides-like-huma-abedin-shouldn-serve-outside-consultants/B9zQtY7mNv0U4Lxgqw XxuL/story.html.

15. Allen and Parnes, *HRC*.

16. McKelvey, Tara, "Hillary's Power Grab," *Daily Beast*, January 14, 2011, http://www.thedailybeast.com/articles/2011/01/14/hillary-clintons-power-grab-for-usaid.html.Rieff, David, "If Disaster Aid Is Key to the War on Terrorism, Then Why Won't Obama Appoint Someone to Coordinate Disaster Aid?" *New Republic*, September 17, 2010, http://www.newrepublic.com/blog/foreign-policy/77740/if-disaster-aid-key-the-war-terrorism-then-why-wont-obama-appoint-someone-hillary-clinton-david-rieff.

17. Kimes, Mina, and Michael Smith, "Laureate, a For-profit Education Firm, Finds International Success (with a Clinton's Help)," *Washington Post*, January 18, 2014, http://www.washingtonpost.com/business/laureate-a-for-profit-education-firm-finds-international-success-with-a-clintons-help/2014/01/16/13f8adde-7ca6-11e3-9556-4a4bf7bcbd84_story.html.

18. "Laureate Vai Abrir um Novo Campus No Sul," *ProfessorNews* (Brazil), October 20, 2011, http://

www.professornews.com.br/index.php/pos-gradua-
cao/stricto-sensu/1027-laureate-vai-abrir-um-novo-
campus-no-sul.

19. Kimes and Smith, "Laureate, a For-profit Education
    Firm, Finds International Success."

20. Laureate International Universities, "President Bill
    Clinton Inspires Leadership Commitment among
    Students during Visits to Laureate International
    Universities Member Institutions in Mexico and
    Honduras," news release, May 5, 2012, http://www.
    laureate.net/NewsRoom/PressReleases/2012/05/
    PresidentBillClintoninspiresleadershipcommitmenta
    mongstudentsduringvisitstoLIUmemberinstitutions.

21. Kimes and Smith, "Laureate, a For-profit Education
    Firm, Finds International Success."

22. Bill Clinton stated, "Last year I had the opportunity to
    visit Laureate's universities in Spain, Brazil, and Peru
    to speak to students, faculty, and the communities
    that they serve." Dorgan, Julie, "Laureate Education
    Inc.," Docstoc.com, April 3, 2012, http://www.
    docstoc.com/docs/117852713/13/Laureate-Education-
    Inc.

23. National Hispanic University, "Henry Cisneros,
    Former Secretary of HUD, Delivers NHU Comm-
    encement Address," news release, PR Newswire,
    May 15, 2013, http://www.prnewswire.com/news-
    releases/henry-cisneros-former-secretary-of-hud-
    delivers-nhu-commencement-address-207594091.

html. Rodriguez, Joe, "San Jose's National Hispanic University Will Close by 2015," *San Jose Mercury News*, March 19, 2014, http://www.mercurynews.com/ci_25379797/san-joses-national-hispanic-university-will-no-longer.

24. Melo, Fabiola, "Comisión de diputados detecta siete universidades con irregularidades," *La Tercera* (Santiago, Chile), June 19, 2012, http://www.latercera.com/noticia/educacion/2012/06/657-467415-9-comision-de-diputados-detecta-siete-universidades-con-irregularidades.shtml.

25. "El reporte de Laureate que explica como extrae ganancias de sus universidades en Chile," el monstrador.pais, April 10, 2014, http://www.elmostrador.cl/pais/2014/04/10/el-reporte-de-laureate-que-explica-como-extrae-ganancias-de-sus-universidades-en-chile/. And http://webcache.googleusercontent.com/search?q=cache:ULzk8tbeAgMJ:sec.edgar-online.com/laureate-education-inc/10-k-annual-report/2006/03/16/section2.aspx+&cd=1&hl=en&ct=clnk&gl=us&client=firefox-a.

26. "Youth Leaders in Turkey to Benefit from Expansion of IYF's YouthActionNet® Program," news release, International Youth Foundation, https://web.archive.org/web/20110113131729/http://www.iyfnet.org/news/1432 (accessed 2014).

27. Laureate International Universities, "Laureate Education and International Youth Foundation Announce YouthActionNet® Program Commitment at

the Clinton Global Initiative Annual Meeting," news release, September 21, 2010, http://www.laureate.net/ NewsRoom/PressReleases/2010/09/International YouthFoundation.

28. Otero, Maria, "Remarks to the International Youth Foundation's 20th Anniversary Reception," speech, International Youth Foundation's 20th Anniversary Reception, Washington, DC, October 7, 2010, http:// www.state.gov/j/149203.htm.

29. "USAID Awards International Youth Foundation with 'Alliance of the Year' for 2006," news release, USAID, *The Free Library*, February 21, 2007, http:// www.thefreelibrary.com/USAID+Awards+Internat ional+Youth+Foundation+With+%27Alliance+of+ the . . .-a0159607696.

30. "International Youth Foundation 990 Tax Forms," Foundation Center, http://990finder.foundationcen-ter.org/990results.aspx?990_type=&fn=&st=&zp= &ei=382935397&fy=&action=Find (accessed 2014).

31. Inter-American Development Bank, "Conference Tackles Youth Unemployment in Latin America," June 24, 2011, http://www.iadb.org/en/news/ann-ouncements/2011-06-24/conference-on-youth-employment-mif,9438.html.

CHAPTER 7: PODIUM ECONOMICS

1. Mcintire, Mike, "Clintons Made $109 Million in Last 8 Years," *New York Times*, April 4, 2008, http://www.

nytimes.com/2008/04/05/us/politics/05clintons. html?pagewanted=print&_r=0. Sullivan, Sean. "Hillary Clinton on 'Dead Broke' Comment: 'I Regret It,' " *Washington Post*, July 29, 2014, http://www.washingtonpost.com/blogs/post-politics/wp/2014/07/29/ hillary-clinton-on-dead-broke-comment-i-regret-it/.

2. "The Keystone XL Pipeline Timeline," *Wall Street Journal*, April 24, 2014, http://blogs.wsj.com/washwire/2014/04/24/the-keystone-xl-pipeline-timeline/. Priaro, Mike, "A 'Canada-first' Canadian Energy Strategy," Mining.com, October 26, 2012, http:// www.mining.com/web/a-canada-first-canadian-energy-strategy/.

3. US Department of State, "Application of Transcanada Keystone Pipeline," May 4, 2012, http:// keystonepipeline-xl.state.gov/documents/organization/189504.pdf.

4. Louvel, Yann, "Dodgy Deal: Keystone XL Pipeline," Banktrack.org, March 5, 2014, http://www.banktrack.org/manage/ajax/ems_dodgydeals/createPDF/ keystone_xl_pipeline.

5. Volcovici, Valerie, "Opponents Seek to Debunk U.S. Keystone Claims; Joint Green Report," *Financial Post* (Canada), August 30, 2013.

6. Baker, Peter, and Helene Cooper, "Clinton Is Said to Accept Secretary of State Position," *New York Times*, November 21, 2008, http://www.nytimes.com/2008/11/22/us/politics/22obama.html.

7. "Hillary Clinton 2008 Personal Financial Disclosure," OpenSecrets.org, January 5, 2009, http://pfds.opensecrets.org/N00000019_2008_Nom.pdf.

8. "Hillary Clinton 2009 Personal Financial Disclosure," OpenSecrets.org, June 24, 2010, http://pfds.opensecrets.org/N00000019_2009.pdf.

9. "Hillary Clinton 2010 Personal Financial Disclosure," OpenSecrets.org. July 11, 2011, http://pfds.opensecrets.org/N00000019_2010.pdf.

10. Shecter, Barbara, "How TD Bank Is Linking Up with Bill Clinton to Win over the U.S. Market," *Financial Post* (Canada), July 23, 2014, http://business.financialpost.com/2014/07/23/how-td-bank-is-linking-up-with-bill-clinton-to-win-over-the-u-s-market/?__federated=1.

11. "Centre to Honour Frank McKenna; Former U.S. President Bill Clinton Will Be on Hand in Antigonish for Launch," *News and Transcript* (New Brunswick), April 8, 2011. "Executive Biographies: Frank McKenna," TD Bank Financial Group, 2014, http://www.td.com/about-tdbfg/corporate-information/executive-profiles/mckenna.jsp.

12. Harder, Amy, "U.S. Oil Giants Poised to Gain on Keystone Pipeline," *National Journal*, August 4, 2011, http://www.nationaljournal.com/energy/u-s-oil-giants-poised-to-gain-on-keystone-pipeline-20110804. "Board of Directors," Canadian Natural, 2014, http://www.cnrl.com/about-cnq/board-of-directors.

13. Pasternak, Sean B., "Goolsbee Says U.S. Opponents of TransCanada's Keystone Pipeline Are Naive," Bloomberg.com, November 8, 2011, http://www. bloomberg.com/news/2011-11-28/goolsbee-says-those-in-u-s-opposing-keystone-xl-are-na-ve-.html.

14. Eilperin, Juliet, and Steven Mufson, "Keystone Pipeline Lobbyist Works All the Angles with Former Colleagues," *Washington Post*, September 22, 2011, http://www.washingtonpost.com/national/health-science/transcanada-pipeline-lobbyist-works-all-the-angles-with-former-colleagues/2011/09/16/gIQAYq3BnK_story.html.

15. Alberts, Sheldon, "State Department Denies Bias on Keystone Pipeline," *Calgary Herald*, October 4, 2011, D1 sec.

16. De Souza, Mike, "Alberta Hired Ex-Clinton Aide to 'Blunt' Keystone Criticism," *Toronto Star*, August 14, 2014, A2 sec.

17. Kroll, Andy, "Exclusive: State Dept. Hid Contractor's Ties to Keystone XL Pipeline Company," *Mother Jones*, March 21, 2013, http://www.motherjones.com/politics/2013/03/keystone-xl-contractor-ties-transcanada-state-department.

18. "Hillary Clinton 2011 Personal Financial Disclosure," OpenSecrets.org, June 29, 2012, http://pfds.opensecrets.org/N00000019_2011.pdf.

19. McCarthy, Shawn, "State Department E-mails Trigger Allegations of Bias in Keystone Review,"

Globe and Mail (Toronto), September 22, 2011, http://
www.theglobeandmail.com/globe-investor/state-
department-e-mails-trigger-allegations-of-bias-in-
keystone-review/article595214/.

20. US House of Representatives, Energy and Commerce
Committee, "Keystone XL: #TimeToBuild," http://
energycommerce.house.gov/content/keystone-xl
(accessed January 2015).

21. VanderKlippe, Nathan, "How a Pipeline Was
Defeated: Actors, Activists and One Key Conversation," *Globe and Mail* (Toronto), November 11, 2011,
http://www.theglobeandmail.com/globe-investor/
how-a-pipeline-was-defeated-actors-activists-and-
one-key-conversation/article4200493/.

22. Sheppard, Kate, "Clinton Tips Hand in Favor of
TransCanada's Massive Pipeline?" *Mother Jones*,
October 20, 2010, http://www.motherjones.com/blue-
marble/2010/10/clinton-tips-hand-favor-transcana-
das-massive-pipeline.

23. VanderKlippe, "How a Pipeline Was Defeated."

24. McCarthy, Shawn, "U.S. Values Canada as Energy
Supplier," *Globe Advisor*, May 11, 2012, https://
secure.globeadvisor.com/servlet/ArticleNews/print/
gam/20120511/RBSTATEENERGYMCCARTHY
ATL. US House of Representatives, Energy and
Commerce Committee, "Keystone XL: #TimeTo
Build."

25. Dixon, Darius, and Dan Berman, "Bill Clinton on Keystone XL Pipeline: 'Embrace' It," *Politico*, February 29, 2012, http://www.politico.com/news/stories/0212/73445.html.

26. Goodman, Lee-Anne, "Bill Clinton Goes to Bat for Keystone XL Even as His Wife Decides Its Fate," *Canadian Press*, February 29, 2012, http://www.stalbertgazette.com/article/GB/20120229/CP02/302299787/-1/SAG08/bill-clinton-puts-in-good-word-for-keystone-xl-wife-to-decide-its&template=cpArt.

27. "TD Bank (TD) to Start Selling Shares of Keystone XL Pipeline after Obama Speech Hints the Project May Not Be Approved," *The Free Library*, June 28, 2013, http://www.thefreelibrary.com/TD+Bank+(TD)+To+Start+Selling+Shares+Of+Keystone+XL+Pipeline+After . . .-a0335294529.

28. Ibid.

29. "Clinton: I've Traveled Around Canada Avoiding Answering Questions About the Keystone Pipeline," online video clip, Rising ICYMI, *Youtube*, January 21, 2015, https://www.youtube.com/watch?v=ui3qagfMIJI

30. Shecter, Barbara, "How TD Bank is linking up with Bill Clinton to win over the U.S. market," *Financial Post*, July 23, 2014, http://business.financialpost.com/2014/07/23/how-td-bank-is-linking-up-with-bill-clinton-to-win-over-the-u-s-market/.

31. Jackson, David, "Bill Clinton Made $13.4M in 2011 Speech Fees," *USA Today*, July 5, 2012, http://content. usatoday.com/communities/theoval/post/2012/07/ bill-clinton-made-134m-in-2011-speech-fees/1#.U_ suCP3DdBM.

32. Spirgel, Larry, "Form 20-F for the Fiscal Year Ended December 31, 2009," report, September 29, 2010, http://www.sec.gov/Archives/edgar/data/717826/ 000119312510219206/filename1.htm.

33. Ibid.

34. US Department of State, Embassy in Stockholm, "Swedish-Iranian Economic Relations: Business as Usual, Resistance to Financial Sanctions," WikiLeaks, December 15, 2009, http://www.wikileaks.org/plusd/ cables/09STOCKHOLM778_a.html.

35. US Department of State, "2010 Human Rights Report: Belarus," report, April 8, 2011, http://www. state.gov/j/drl/rls/hrrpt/2010/eur/154414.htm.

36. Elgin, Ben, "House Bill May Ban U.S. Surveillance Gear Sales," Bloomberg.com, December 9, 2011, http:// www.bloomberg.com/news/2011-12-09/house-bill- would-ban-surveillance-gear-sales-by-american- firms.html.

37. "Escalating Sanctions on Iran," *Frontline*, PBS, June 3, 2011, http://www.pbs.org/wgbh/pages/frontline/ tehranbureau/2011/06/-qa-w-patrick.html.

38. US Department of State, Bureau of Public Affairs, "New Sanctions on Iran," news release, November

21, 2011, http://www.state.gov/r/pa/prs/ps/2011/11/177609.htm.

39. "House Bill May Ban U.S. Surveillance Gear Sales," Bloomberg.com, December 9, 2011, http://www.bloomberg.com/news/2011-12-09/house-bill-would-ban-surveillance-gear-sales-by-american-firms.html. President of the United States, Executive Order no. 13590, 3 C.F.R. (2011).

40. Puzzanghera, Jim, "U.S. puts sanctions on telecom firms in Syria, Iran, Los Angeles Times, April 25, 2012, http://articles.latimes.com/2012/apr/23/business/la-fi-obama-tech-sanctions-20120424; Stecklow, Steve, "Exclusive: Ericsson helps Iran telecoms, letter reveals long-term deal," *Reuters*, November 20, 2012, http://www.reuters.com/article/2012/11/20/us-iran-ericsson-idUSBRE8AJ0IY20121120.

41. Chrisafis, Angelique, "Tunisia: Gang Violence Mars Celebration of Popular Uprising," *The Guardian*, January 15, 2011, http://www.theguardian.com/world/2011/jan/15/tunisia-protests-zine-al-abidine-ben-ali. Batty, David, "Egypt Bomb Kills New Year Churchgoers," *The Guardian*, January 1, 2011, http://www.theguardian.com/world/2011/jan/01/egypt-bomb-kills-new-year-churchgoers.

42. Finn, Tom, "Yemeni Protesters Shot Dead at Sana'a University," *The Guardian*, February 23, 2011, http://www.theguardian.com/world/2011/feb/23/yemen-protesters-shot-dead-university. Black, Ian,

"Arrests and Deaths as Egypt Protest Spreads across Middle East," *The Guardian,* February 14, 2011, http://www.theguardian.com/world/2011/feb/14/middle-east-iran-bahrain-yemen.

43. "US Sanctions Foreign Firms Trading with Iran," *BBC News,* May 24, 2011, http://www.bbc.co.uk/news/world-middle-east-13528637. US Department of State, "Seven Companies Sanctioned under the Amended Iran Sanctions Act," May 2011, http://www.state.gov/r/pa/prs/ps/2011/05/164132.htm.

44. "US Hits Iranian Shipping with Sanctions," *Agence France-Presse,* June 20, 2011, http://www.mojahedin.org/newsen/13104/US-hits-Iranian-shipping-with-sanctions.

45. Ibid.

46. US Department of State, Embassy in Abu Dhabi, "Codel to Lowey with UAE Foreign Minister on Iran," WikiLeaks, February 22, 2010, http://www.wikileaks.org/plusd/cables/10ABUDHABI97_a.html.

47. "Abu Dhabi Global Environmental Data Initiative (AGEDI)," BlueCarbonPortal.org, http://bluecarbonportal.org/?dt_portfolio=abu-dhabi-global-environmental-data-initiative-agedi (accessed January 2015). "Hillary Clinton 2011 Personal Financial Disclosure," OpenSecrets.org, June 29, 2012, http://pfds.opensecrets.org/N00000019_2011.pdf.

48. Smith, Mark, "On UAE National Day, We Honor Dubai's Eye-Popping Milestones," *Condé Nast*

Traveler, December 2, 2011, http://www.cntraveler.com/stories/2011-12-02/uae-national-day.

49. "Global Eye on Earth Summit Launched in Abu Dhabi," *International Diplomat*, http://thediplomat-magazine.com/events-gallery/global-eye-on-earth-summit-launched-in-abu-dhabi/.

50. "UAE Foreign Minister Meets with US Secretary of State," UAEinteract, December 15, 2011, http://www.uaeinteract.com/docs/UAE_Foreign_Minister_meets_with_US_Secretary_of_State/47685.htm. Aside: Tracing the funding for the speeches can be difficult. Based on the Clinton's personal financial disclosure forms, apart from this speech, there were no speeches sponsored by companies officially owned by the royal family.

51. *Judicial Watch v. U.S. Department of State*, Case No. F-2011-03401, Doc No. C05459127 (2014), 419.

52. "E-Commerce Association Welcomed," *People's Daily* (China), June 22, 2000, http://english.peopledaily.com.cn/english/200006/22/eng20000622_43679.html.

53. *Judicial Watch v. U.S. Department of State*, 213.

54. Cendrowski, Scott, "China's Baddest Billionaire Builder," *Fortune*, July 7, 2014, http://fortune.com/2014/07/07/yah-jiehe-china/.

55. Zhang Yiwen, "Yan Jiehe Talks about Enterprise Development," *China Daily*, September 6, 2012, http://cbl.chinadaily.com.cn/2012-09/06/content_15738486.htm.

56. "Clinton Corruption Bombshells," *Judicial Watch*, August 1,2014, http://www.judicialwatch.org/press-room/weekly-updates/clinton-corruption-bomb-shells/.

57. *Judicial Watch v. U.S. Department of State.*

58. Powell, Catherine, "Dean Harold Koh: A Great Nomination for State Department Legal Advisor," *Huffington Post*, April 10, 2009, http://www.huff-ingtonpost.com/catherine-powell/dean-harold-koh-a-great-n_b_185816.html.

CHAPTER 8: WARLORD ECONOMICS

1. Democratic Republic of the Congo, "Relief, Security, and Democracy Promotion Act of 2006," Pub.L. 109–456 (2006), https://www.govtrack.us/congress/bills/109/s2125/text.

2. "Clinton Global Initiative Announces BD's Commitment to Biamba Marie Mutombo Hospital," PR Newswire, October 29, 2014.

3. "Clinton: US Committed to Good Governance in Congo," Voice of America, August 11, 2009, http://www.voanews.com/content/a-13-2009-08-10-voa38-68820817/364539.html. "Hillary Clinton Will Take UN Plane to Epicenter of African Conflict," CNN Wire, August 10, 2009, http://politicalticker.blogs.cnn.com/2009/08/10/hillary-clinton-will-take-u-n-plane-to-epicenter-of-african-conflict/.

4. Dizolele, Mvemba Phezo, "Hope But No Change," *Foreign Policy*, July 16, 2012, http://foreignpolicy. com/2012/07/16/hope-but-no-change/.

5. Dizoelel, Mvemba Phezo, "Hope but No Change," ForeignPolicy.com, July 16, 2012, http://www. foreignpolicy.com/articles/2012/07/16/hope_but_no_ change.

6. "Hillary: I'm in, and I'm in to Win," online video clip, PoliticsTV.com, *Youtube*, January 20, 2007, https://www.youtube.com/watch?v=xvyRN9ka5Fw.

7. "Lundin Group Commits 100 million to Clinton Giustra Sustainable Growth Initiative," press rele- ase, Clinton Foundation, July 6, 2007, https://www. clintonfoundation.org/main/news-and-media/press- releases-and-statements/press-release-lundin- group-commits-100-million-to-clinton-giustra- sustainable-gr.html.

8. Clarke, Duncan, *Africa: Crude Continent—The Struggle for Africa's Oil Prize* (London: Profile Books, 2010).

9. Goldstein, Ritt, "Sudanese Blood Spills into Asia," Asiatimes.com, June 25, 2010, http://www.atimes. com/atimes/Global_Economy/LF25Dj01.html.

10. "Business Family Pledges 100 Million Dollars to Clinton Charity," Deutsche Presse-Agentur, July 10, 2007.

11. "Rising Star: Africa Oil Corp," *Energy Intelligence Finance*, February 27, 2013.

12. Jorde, Sigurd, "The Pension Funds Profit from Gold Rush in Eritrea," *Framtiden* (Norway), October 16, 2012, http://www.framtiden.no/english/fund/the-pension-fund-profits-from-gold-rush-in-eritrea.html.

13. "Canada: Kinross Gold to Acquire 100% of Red Back Mining for US $7.1 Billion," *Tendersinfo*, August 5, 2010.

14. Grant, Dale, "Canadians Cry 'Havoc,' and Let Slip the Dogs of War," *Toronto Star*, March 9, 1999, http://articles.philly.com/1997-05-11/news/25564930_1_shaba-lubumbashi-president-mobutu-sese-seko. "Mining Concern Agrees to Pay Rebels for Right to Mine in Zaire," *Business Day* (Johannesburg, South Africa), May 13, 1997. McGeough, Paul, "Jets Follow Promise of Glittering Mineral Wealth in the East," *Sydney Morning Herald* (Australia), May 13, 1997.

15. Quoted in Maykuth, Andrew, "Outside Mining Firms Find Zaire an Untapped Vein; Deals Are Being Made with the Rebels, Who Need the Cash; the Rival Companies Are Themselves Also Coming into Conflict," *Philadelphia Inquirer*, May 11, 1997.

16. Abadie, Delphine, Alain Deneault, and William Sacher, "This Is Not an Ethnic Conflict—Vested Interests and Complex Networks behind the DRC Fighting," *Le Monde Diplomatique*, December 1, 2008.

17. Abadie, Delphine, "Canada and the Geopolitics of Mining Interests: A Case Study of the Democratic Republic of Congo," *Review of African Political Economy* 38, no. 128 (June 2011), and Donville, Christopher, "Friedland Seeks Congo Funding After Gobi Exit: Corporate Canada," September 13, 2012, http://www.bloomberg.com/news/2012-09-13/friedland-seeks-congo-funding-after-gobi-exit-corporate-canada.html.

18. Rosen, Armin, "The Warlord and the Basketball Star: A Story of Congo's Corrupt Gold Trade," *The Atlantic*, March 1, 2012.

19. UN Security Council Working Group on Children and Armed Conflict, "Statement by Chairman of Security Council Working Group on Children and Armed Conflict," March 18, 2011, http://www.un.org/press/en/2011/sc10202.doc.htm.

20. Gordon, Greg, and Will Connors, "Clinton Fundraiser Faces Legal Problems in Nigeria," Ocnus.net, April 6, 2008, http://www.ocnus.net/artman2/publish/Africa_8/Texas_Oil_Man_The_Kase_Lawal_Fugitive_Scandal.shtml.

21. CAMAC Group, "Pacific Asia Petroleum & CAMAC Complete Oilfield Transaction," news release, April 7, 2010, www.camac.com/pacific-asia-petroleum-camac-complete-transaction-regarding-the-oyo-oilfield/.

22. Rosen, "The Warlord and the Basketball Star."

23. Cause, DC-11-04005, 134th Judicial District, Dallas County, Texas. Jones, Pete, "Obama-appointed U.S. Trade Advisor Linked to Illegal Deal in Congolese Gold," *The Guardian*, February 5, 2011, http://www.theguardian.com/world/2012/feb/05/us-adviser-linked-illegal-drc-gold.

24. For a full detailed account of this story, see the UN report at http://reliefweb.int/sites/reliefweb.int/files/resources/N1155632.pdf.

25. Cause, DC-11-04005, 134th Judicial District, Dallas County, Texas.

26. "Mohammed Al Amoudi: Ethiopia's Richest Man Spots Opportunities at Home," *Ventures Africa*, April/May 2013.

27. Allen, Terry J., "Global Land Grab," *In These Times*, August 22, 2011, http://inthesetimes.com/article/11784/global_land_grab.

28. Davison, William, "Ethiopia: Saudi Billionaire Signs $600 Million Ethiopian Steel-Plant Deal," Nazret.com, October 5, 2012, http://nazret.com/blog/index.php/2012/10/05/ethiopia-billionaire-mohammed-al-amoudi-signs-600-million-steel-plant-deal. "The Ethiopian Billionaire: Sheikh Mohammed Al Amoudi," *Ventures*, July 20, 2012, http://www.ventures-africa.com/2012/07/the-ethiopian-billionaire-sheikh-mohammed-al-amoudi/.

29. "Ethiopia—Al Amoudi Donates $20 million to Clinton Foundation," Nazret.com, May 14, 2007, http://

nazret.com/blog/index.php/2007/05/14/midroc_
donates_20_million_to_foundation

30. "Midroc's Friends in Washington," *Indian Ocean Newsletter* no. 889, January 29, 2000. All three senators were connected to the lobbying firm Verner Lipfert Bernard McPherson and Hand, which was a paid adviser to Midroc.

31. Letter written by Ethiopian Americans for Justice, February 10, 2009. Kifle, Elias, "Ethiopian Groups Concerned about Al Amoudi Donation," *Ethiopian Review*, February 10, 2009, http://www.ethiopianreview.com/index/8520.

32. Letter written by Ethiopian Americans for Justice, February 10, 2009. Kifle, "Ethiopian Groups Concerned About Al Amoudi Donation."

33. Bekele, Getahune, "Al Amoudi: The Black Billionaire Survives Health Scare," *Ethiopian News & Opinions*, August 29, 2012, http://ecadforum.com/2012/08/29/al-amoudi-the-black-billionaire/. Wax, Emily, "Ethiopian Leader Meles Zenawi Dies at 57," *Washington Post*, August 21, 2012, http://www.washingtonpost.com/local/obituaries/meles-zenawi-ethiopian-leader-dies-abroad/2012/08/21/f637bf62-e7b2-11e1-936a-b801f1abab19_story.html.

34. "Al Amoudi Says 'I Lost My Right Hand' over Death of PM Meles Zenawi," Ethiomedia, August 30, 2012, http://ethiomedia.com/2012_report/4590.html.

35. Davison, William, "Ethiopia's Foreign Land Leases Fail to Deliver Food for Export," *Business Report*,

November 26, 2013, http://www.iol.co.za/business/international/ethiopia-s-foreign-land-leases-fail-to-deliver-food-for-export-1.1612220.

36. "The Ethiopian Billionaire: Sheikh Mohammed Al Amoudi." Davison, William, "Ethiopia: Saudi Billionaire Signs $600 Million Ethiopian Steel-Plant Deal," Nazret.com, October 5, 2012, http://nazret.com/blog/index.php/2012/10/05/ethiopia-billionaire-mohammed-al-amoudi-signs-600-million-steel-plant-deal.

37. "How Politicians Gave Away $100 Bn of Land," Novafrica Developments, *The African Report* no. 42 (July 15, 2012).

38. Loewenberg, Samuel, "Aid Agencies Accused of Ignoring Rights Abuses in Ethiopia," *The Lancet* 382, issue 9896 (September 2013), http://www.thelancet.com/journals/lancet/article/PIIS0140-6736%2813%2961920-0/abstract.

39. Rosen, Armin, "The Zenawi Paradox: An Ethiopian Leader's Good and Terrible Legacy," *The Atlantic*, July 20, 2012, http://www.theatlantic.com/international/archive/2012/07/the-zenawi-paradox-an-ethiopian-leaders-good-and-terrible-legacy/260099/.

40. "Obituary: Meles Zenawi," *The Telegraph* (UK), August 22, 2012, http://www.telegraph.co.uk/news/obituaries/politics-obituaries/9491934/Meles-Zenawi.html.

41. Hillenbrand, Barry, "An Abrupt End of an Era," *The Herald*, September 1, 2012, http://eandeherald.com/2012/09/01/news-of-ethiopia-11/.

42. "Ethiopia—PM Meles Participation in Pittsburgh Summit Confirmed," WikiLeaks, http://www.wikileaks.org/plusd/cables/09ADDISABABA2084_a.html.

43. US State Department, Embassy in Addis Ababa, "Under Secretary Otero's Meeting with Ethiopian Prime Minister Meles Zenawi—January 31, 2010," report, WikiLeaks, February 2, 2010, https://cablegatesearch.wikileaks.org/cable.php?id=10ADDISABABA163.

44. Lyman, Princeton N., and Stephen B. Wittels, "No Good Deed Goes Unpunished: The Unintended Consequences of Washington's HIV/AIDS Programs," *Foreign Affairs*, July/August 2010, http://www.foreignaffairs.com/articles/66464/princeton-n-lyman-and-stephen-b-wittels/no-good-deed-goes-unpunished.

45. US State Department, Embassy in Addis Ababa, "PM Welcomes New Charge with Substance," WikiLeaks, January 21, 2010, http://wikileaks.org/cable/2010/01/10ADDISABABA82.html.

46. US Office of the Federal Register, "FY 2012 Fiscal Transparency Report," https://www.federalregister.gov/articles/2013/03/04/2013-04914/2012-fiscal-transparency-report.

47. US State Department, "Ethiopia: Report on Fiscal Transparency," WikiLeaks, April 21, 2009, http://

www.wikileaks.org/plusd/cables/10ADDISABA
BA83_a.html.

48. US Office of the Federal Register, vol. 76, issue 191,
61134.

49. Dashen Bank, 17th Annual Report for the Year
Ending June 30, 2013, November 14, 2013. See the
Notes to the Financial Statements for the Year Ended
30 June 2013 available at dashenbanksc.com.

50. "Success Story: U.S. Firms Partner with Ethiopia's
Almeda Tetils in Long-Term Apparel Deal," USAID:
East Africa.

51. "Prospective Presidents and Their Networks," *Indian
Ocean Newsletter*, Africanintelligence.com, no. 1226,
November 17, 2007, http://www.africaintelligence.
com/ION/politics-power/2007/11/17/prospective-
presidents-and-their-networks,34997823-EVE.

52. "Obama's Team Not Yet Finalized," *Indian Ocean
Newsletter*, no. 1258 (March 21, 2009), http://www.
africaintelligence.com/ION/politics-power/2009/03/
21/obama-s-team-not-yet-finalised,57923115-ART.

53. Wilson, Joseph C., "The Real Hillary I Know—and
the Unreal Obama," *Huffington Post*, May 25, 2011,
http://www.huffingtonpost.com/joe-wilson/the-real-
hillary-i-know-a_b_77878.html. US Senate, Select
Committee on Intelligence, "Report on the U.S. Intelligence Community's Prewar Intelligence Assessment
on Iraq," July 7, 2004, http://www.nytimes.com/
packages/html/politics/20040709iraqreport2.pdf.

54. "Joseph Wilson and Valerie Plame Wilson," Physicians for Social Responsibility, Los Angeles, April 23, 2007, http://www.psr-la.org/joseph-wilson-and-valerie-plame-wilson/. "Valerie Plame Wilson: The Housewife CIA Spy Who Was 'Fair Game' for Bush," *The Telegraph* (UK), February 15, 2011, http://www.telegraph.co.uk/culture/film/8318075/Valerie-Plame-Wilson-the-housewife-CIA-spy-who-was-fair-game-for-Bush.html.

55. Moffat-Chaney, Casey, "Ambassador Joe Wilson Stumps for Hillary in Portland," BlueOregon.com, April 29, 2008, http://www.blueoregon.com/2008/04/ambassador-joe/. Emig, Aeriel, "The Plame Affair," Alibi.com 17, no. 30, July 2008, http://alibi.com/news/24023/The-Plame-Affair.html. Kornblut, Anne E., "Stern Constitutions Needed for Globe-trotting with Bill Clinton," *Washington Post*, August 6, 2008, http://www.washingtonpost.com/wp-dyn/content/article/2008/08/05/AR2008080503544.html.

56. "Obama's Team Not Yet Finalized."

57. "Joseph C. Wilson," profile, *Huffington Post*, http://www.huffingtonpost.com/joe-wilson/.

58. "Jarch Capital, Strategy," http://www.jarchcapital.com/strategy.php.

59. "Former Wall Street Banker Philippe Heilberg Gambles on a Warlord's Continuing Control of 400,000 Hectares of Land in South Sudan," *Sudan Watch*, January 10, 2009, http://sudanwatch.blogspot.com/2009/01/former-wall-street-banker-philippe.

html. "Ambassador Joe Wilson Begins Working with Jarch Capital," *Sudan Tribune*, January 19, 2007, http://www.sudantribune.com/spip.php?article1 9833.

60. Silverstein, Ken, "Jarch Capital's Sudanese Gambit," *Harper's*, November 20, 2007, http://harpers.org/blog/2007/11/jarch-capitals-sudanese-gambit/.

61. "Southern Sudan: Oil Investor Banking on Succession?" *Ratio* Magazine, June 3, 2009, http://www.ratio-magazine.com/20090603665/Southern-Sudan/Southern-Sudan-Oil-Investor-Banking-on-Secession.html.

62. Blas, Javier, and William Wallis, "Buyer Sees Profit in Warlord's Land," *Financial Times*, January 10, 2009, http://www.ft.com/intl/cms/s/0/2ddacbdc-deb9-11dd-9464-000077b07658.html#axzz3OdxxHjf7.

63. "Southern Sudan: Oil Investor Banking on Succession?"

64. "New SPLA General, Tanginya, Becomes Advisor to US Company Jarch," *Sudan Tribune*, October 23, 2010, http://www.sudantribune.com/spip.php?page=imprimable&id_article=36702.

65. Ibid.

66. Ibid.

67. "South Sudan VP Confirms Apology for Bor Massacre," *Sudan Tribune*, April 3, 2012, http://www.sudantribune.com/spip.php?article42124.

68. "Profile: South Sudan Army Defector Peter Gadet," BBC.com, July 11, 2014, http://www.bbc.com/news/world-africa-25447527.

69. See Hillary Clinton's Personal Financial Disclosures, 2011–2012, available at opensecrets.org.

70. Ragaza, Angela, "Using Star Power to Repair Nigeria's Image," *New York Times*, July 10, 2008, http://www.nytimes.com/2008/07/10/business/worldbusiness/10nigeria.html?_r=0.

71. Abedowale, Segun, "THISDAY Awards Cheques to Nigerian Teachers Bounce," *Eagle Online*, April 4, 2013, http://theeagleonline.com.ng/tag/thisday-awards/.

72. US State Department, "Country Reports on Human Rights Practices for 2012," http://www.state.gov/j/drl/rls/hrrpt/2012humanrightsreport/index.htm?year=2012&dlid=204153#wrapper.

73. Gambrill, Jon, "Newspaper Strike Hits Flamboyant Nigerian Publisher," *AP The Big Story*, May 10, 2013, http://bigstory.ap.org/article/newspaper-strike-hits-flamboyant-nigeria-publisher. Ward, Alex, "Nigerian President 'Spent $1 Million of Aid Money Meant for Poverty-stricken Country on Star-studded Festival Featuring Beyoncé and Jay-Z,'" *Daily Mail* (UK), February 23, 2013, http://www.dailymail.co.uk/news/article-2283453/Nigerian-president-spent-1million-aid-money-meant-poverty-stricken-country-star-studded-festival-featuring-Beyonc-Jay-Z.html.

74. Olson, Elizabeth, "Swiss Freeze a Dictator's Giant Cache," *New York Times*, January 29, 2000, http://www.nytimes.com/2000/01/26/news/26iht-swiss.2.t_3.html.

75. Okonta, Ike, and Oronto Douglas, *Where Vultures Feast: Shell, Human Rights, and Oil* (New York: Verso, 2003), 38. Rupert, James, "Corruption Flourished in Abacha's Regime," *Washington Post*, June 9, 1998, http://www.washingtonpost.com/wp-srv/inatl/longterm/nigeria/stories/corrupt060998.htm. Adegbamigbe, Ademola, "Nigeria: The Crude Pirate," *The News* (Lagos), July 28, 2000, http://allafrica.com/stories/200007280213.html. Salami, Semiu, "Nigeria's Oil Mafia," *The News* (Lagos), January 4, 1999, http://allafrica.com/stories/199901040007.html.

76. Silverstein, Ken, "Clinton Foundation Donors and Hillary's Confirmation," *Harper's*, January 21, 2009, http://harpers.org/blog/2009/01/clinton-foundation-donors-and-hillarys-confirmation/.

77. US Justice Department, "U.S. Forfeits Over $480 Million Stolen by Former Nigerian Dictator in Largest Forfeiture Ever Obtained Through a Kleptocracy Action," August 7, 2014, http://www.justice.gov/opa/pr/us-forfeits-over-480-million-stolen-former-nigerian-dictator-largest-forfeiture-ever-obtained.

78. Urevich, Robin, "Chasing the Ghosts of a Corrupt Regime," *Frontline*, PBS, January 8, 2010, http://www.pbs.org/frontlineworld/stories/bribe/2010/01/

nigeria-chasing-the-ghosts-of-a-corrupt-regime. html.

79. Rupert, "Corruption Flourished in Abacha's Regime."

80. Solomon, John, "Billionaire Clinton Pal Finally Gets Waiver from U.S. No-fly List," Center for Public Integrity, May 21, 2010, http://www.publicintegrity. org/2010/05/21/2669/billionaire-clinton-pal-finally-gets-waiver-us-no-fly-list.

81. Apple, R. W., "Clinton in Africa: The Policy; U.S. Stance Toward Nigeria and Its Ruler Seems to Shift," *New York Times*, March 28, 1998, http:// www.nytimes.com/1998/03/28/world/clinton-africa-policy-us-stance-toward-nigeria-its-ruler-seems-shift.html.

82. "Nigeria: Chronology of the Struggle for Stability and Democracy," AllAfrica, August 24, 2000, http:// allafrica.com/stories/200008240352.html.

83. Urevich, "Chasing the Ghosts of a Corrupt Regime."

84. Silverstein, "Clinton Foundation Donors and Hillary's Confirmation."

85. "Eko Atlantic City," www.africa-ventures.com, http:// edition.cnn.com/WORLD/africa/africanawards/pdf/2013/tolu-ogunlesi/tolu-ogunlesi-eko-atlantic-story. pdf.

86. Esposito, Richard, Rhonda Schwartz, and Brian Ross, "No-Fly Terror List Includes Big Financial

Backer of Clinton," *ABC News,* February 17, 2010, http://abcnews.go.com/Blotter/no-fly-terror-list-includes-big-donor-clinton-initiative/story?id=9791786.

87. St. Lucia Prime Minster's Office, "Prime Minister's Address in Honour of the Honourable William Jefferson Clinton," January 18, 2003.

88. Emshwiller, John R., "Bill Clinton's Complicated World," *Wall Street Journal,* December 20, 2008, http://online.wsj.com/articles/SB122973023139522863.

89. Urevich, "Chasing the Ghosts of a Corrupt Regime."

90. "Nigeria: N27 Billion Halliburton Scam IBB, Abdulsalami, Diya, 77 Others Indicted," AllAfrica, April 14, 2010, http://allafrica.com/stories/201004150046.html. Silverstein, Ken, "Clinton Donor Figures in New Halliburton Bribe Document," *Harper's,* April 13, 2010, http://harpers.org/blog/2010/04/clinton-donor-figures-in-new-halliburton-bribe-document/. "Halliburton Settles Nigeria Bribery Claims for $35 Million," CNN, December 21, 2010, http://www.cnn.com/2010/WORLD/africa/12/21/nigeria.halliburton/.

91. "Ambassador Gilbert Chagoury 2005 Pride of Heritage Honoree," Lebanese American Foundation, Inc., http://www.houseoflebanon.com/what_we_do/previous_recipients/chagouri_2005.html.

92. Lagos (Nigeria) State Government, "Eko Atlantic

City Gets Global Recognition, Wins CGI Award," September 25, 2009, http://www.lagosstate.gov.ng/news2.php?k=158.

93. Ammann, Daniel, *The King of Oil: The Secret Lives of Marc Rich* (New York, St. Martin's, 2009), 100.

CHAPTER 9: RAINFOREST RICHES

1. "President Bill Clinton and Philanthropists Frank Giustra and Carlos Slim Launch Fondo Acceso SAS, a USD $20 Million Fund for Small and Medium-sized Enterprises (SMEs) in Colombia," press release, Clinton Foundation, June 9, 2010, https://www.clintonfoundation.org/main/news-and-media/press-releases-and-statements/press-release-president-bill-clinton-and-philanthropists-frank-giustra-and-carlo.html.

2. Clinton, Hillary Rodham, *Hard Choices* (New York: Simon & Schuster, 2014), 253.

3. Uribe Velez, Alvaro, *No Lost Causes* (New York: Celebra, 2012), 179.

4. "Hillary Clinton Voices Ongoing US Support for Columbia," *BBC News*, June 10, 2010, http://www.bbc.com/news/10282709.

5. "U.S. Senators Seek Changes to Plan Colombia: US-Colombia," *Latin American Herald Tribune* (Caracas), EFE News Service (Madrid), January 27,

2010, http://www.laht.com/article.asp?ArticleId=351 189&CategoryId=12393.

6. Romero, Simon, "Colombia Extradites 14 Paramilitary Leaders," *New York Times*, May 14, 2008, http://.www.nytimes.com/2008/05/14/world/americas/14 colombia.html?pagewanted=print&_r=0.

7. Brody, Daniel, "Uribe meets with Bill Clinton," Colombiareports, June 10, 2010. Begg, Kristen, "Clinton to Meet Uribe, Santos, and Mockus," Colombiareports, June 8, 2010, http://colombiareports.co/clinton-to-meet-with-uribe-santos-and-mockus/.

8. "Clintons Stand Up for Colombia," *Investor's Business Daily*, June 14, 2010, http://news.investors.com/ibd-editorials/061110-537128-clintons-stand-up-for-colombia.htm?ntt=free.

9. "Prima Colombia Hardwood Inc. Completes Acquisition of REM Forest Products Inc, and Closing of $5,500,000, Financing" *Canada Newswire, Digital Journal*, September 22, 2010, http://www.newswire.ca/en/story/612439/prima-colombia-hardwood-inc-completes-acquisition-of-rem-forest-products-inc-and-closing-of-5-500-000-financing.

10. "Prima Colombia Hardwood Inc. Completes Acquisition of Rem Forest Products Inc. and Closing of $5,500,000 Financing," *Newswire*, September 22, 2010, http://www.newswire.ca/en/story/612439/prima-colombia-hardwood-inc-completes-acqui-

sition-of-rem-forest-products-inc-and-closing-of-5-500-000-financing.

11. Jimenez, Carlos, "Frank Giustra," *ElPais.com.co*, January 20, 2012, http://www.elpais.com.co/elpais/opinion/columna/carlos-jimenez/frank-giustra. .

12. Pacific Rubiales Energy, "Pacific Rubiales Energy Awarded Six Blocks in the '2010 ANH Round' Bidding Process," press release, June 23, 2010, http://www.pacificrubiales.com/2010/153-23062010.

13. Quoted in Forero, Juan, "Venezuelan Oilmen Pushed Out by Hugo Chavez Find Opportunities in Colombia," *Washington Post*, September 12, 2011, http://www.washingtonpost.com/world/americas/venezuelan-oilmen-find-opportunities-in-colombia/2011/09/12/gIQAiOcjTK_story.html.

14. Pacific Rubiales Energy, "Where Talent and Knowledge Meet Opportunity," investor presentation, December 2010, http://www.pacificrubiales.com/archivos/investor/CEOs_Investors_presentation_Canaccord_Conference_Dec_2010.pdf.

15. Humphreys, Tommy, "Los Minerales Hermanos: How Two Friends Made a Fortune in Colombia and Expect to Do It Again," CEO.ca, April 2, 2013, http://ceo.ca/2013/04/02/colombia-giustra-iacono/.

16. Clinton Foundation, "Press Release: Projects of the Clinton Giustra Sustainable Growth Initiative," March 1, 2008, https://www.clintonfoundation.org/main/

news-and-media/press-releases-and-statements/
press-release-projects-of-the-clinton-giustra-sus-
tainable-growth-initiative.html.

17. Pacific Rubiales Energy, "Petro Rubiales Energy
and Underwriters Contributing $4.4 Million to
Clinton Giustra Sustainable Growth Initiative," press
release, July 24, 2007, http://www.pacificrubiales.
com/2007/35-24072007.

18. "El primer día de la Acción Humanitaria y Laboral
a Puerto Gaitán es una aclaración, de que la USO
no ha firmado ningun acuerdo con," USOPAZ, October 11, 2011, http://www.pasc.ca/en/action/updates-
conflict-canadian-oil-company-pacific-rubiales#
sdendnote8sym.

19. Petroamerica Oil Corp., "Petroamerica Receives Key
Colombian Approval," press release, June 21, 2010,
http://www.petroamericaoilcorp.com/main/index.
php?id=newsroom_read&news=33.

20. Humphreys, Tommy, and Tekoa da Silva, "Energy
Heavyweights Engineering a Turnaround?" CEO.
CA, Augusst 20, 2012, http://ceo.ca/2012/08/20/pta/.

21. Estimates from Petroamerica executive Robert Gill-
crest were that the land it could now drill on boasted
between "[t]wo to twenty million barrels maximum"
of oil.

22. US Department of State, Embassy in Bogotá,
"Colombia: Energy Sector to Expand with Exim

Financing," WikiLeaks, November 18, 2009, https://cablegatesearch.wikileaks.org/cable.php?id=09BOGOTA3415&q=clint.

23. The secretary of state has the power to review, approve, deny, or delay ExIm financing to any country, entity, or person, http://www.exim.gov/about/whoweare/charterbylaws/upload/Updated_2012_EXIM_Charter_August_2012_Final.pdf.

24. "EXMAR, IFC Sign Floating Liquefaction Unit Financing Deal," LNG World News, December 6, 2012, http://www.lngworldnews.com/exmar-ifc-sign-floating-liquefaction-unit-financing-deal-belgium/.

25. Endeavour Mining, "Endeavour's Growth Plan," October 2010, http://www.endeavourmining.com/i/pdf/Presentations/Investor-20101001.pdf.

26. "Merchant Banking, Endeavour Financial Corporation," BMO Global Resource Conference, February 2009, http://www.endeavourmining.com/i/flashpaper/EDV_Investor_Presentation_BMO_Feb_09.swf.

27. Baja Mining, quarterly report, first quarter 2011, http://www.bajamining.com/content/pdfs/financials/BAJ_Q12011_MDA.pdf.

28. US Export-Import Bank, "Semi-Annual Report to Congress, April 1–September 30, 2013," 30, 31, http://www.exim.gov/oig/upload/OIG_Report_FA13_508.pdf.

29. Humphreys, "Los Minerales Hermanos."

30. Isaacson, Adam, "Colombia: Don't Call It a Model," Washington Office of Latin America, July 13, 2010, http://www.wola.org/publications/colombia_dont_ call_it_a_model.

31. Good, Chris, "Republicans Support Obama's Trade Agenda. Do Democrats?" *The Atlantic*, September 17, 2011, http://www.theatlantic.com/politics/archive/ 2011/09/republicans-support-obamas-trade-agenda- do-democrats/245248/. "Carnation Revolution: A Long-awaited Pact Comes into Force," *The Economist*, May 19, 2012, http://www.economist.com/node/ 21555592.

32. According to Maria Consuelo Araujo, "President Alvaro Uribe said the country can not continue living preferences. On TLC there is concern because some American analysts believe that the current Congress would not give its approval to the agreement." Araujo, "Uribe, tras prórroga de ayuda comercial," *El Pais* (Bogotá), September 1, 2014, http://translate.google. com/translate?hl=en&sl=es&u=http://historico. elpais.com.co/paisonline/notas/Noviembre142006/ aptdea.html&prev=/search%3Fq%3D%2522hillary %2BClinton%2522%2Band%2B%2522uribe%252 2%26biw%3D1216%26bih%3D706%26tbs%3Dcd r:1,cd_min:1/1/2004,cd_max:12/31/2006.

33. Smith, Elliot Blair, "Clinton Used Giustra's Plane, Opened Doors for Deals," Bloomberg.com, February 22, 2008, http://www.bloomberg.com/apps/news?pi d=newsarchive&sid=aa2b8Mj3NEWQ.

34. Stein, Sam, "Bill Clinton's Ties to Colombia Trade Deal Stronger than Even Penn's," *Huffington Post*, May 25, 2011, http://www.huffingtonpost.com/2008/04/08/bill-clintons-ties-to-col_n_95651.html.

35. Emshwiller, John, and Jose De Cordoba, "Bill Clinton's Complex Charities," *Wall Street Journal*, February 14, 2008, http://online.wsj.com/articles/SB120296323202367961.

36. Ibid.

37. "Plan Colombia—the Sequel," *The Economist* August 21, 2003, http://www.economist.com/node/2009304. Carter, Zach, "Trade Deals Face Growing House Opposition amid Continued Violence in Colombia," video, *Huffington Post*, August 11, 2011, http://www.huffingtonpost.com/2011/08/11/house-opposition-to-trade_n_924418.html.

38. Fenwarth, Andres Espinosa, "Opinion—Colombia atenta a posicion de Hillary Clinton sobre TLC," *Noticias Financieras*, November 14, 2007.

39. "Colombia to Honor Clinton for His Efforts to Help Country's Image," *Arkansas Online*, May 24, 2007, http://www.arkansasonline.com/news/2007/may/24/colombia-honor-clinton-his-efforts-help-countrys-i/?print.

40. Isikoff, Michael, and Mark Hosenball, "It's So Nice to Be Here," *Newsweek*, April 21, 2008, http://www.newsweek.com/its-so-nice-be-here-85467.

41. Ibid.

42. Davis, Susan, "Clinton Aide Met on Trade Deal; Penn Held Talks on Colombia Pact Opposed by Senator," *Wall Street Journal*, April 4, 2008. Kirchgaessner, Stephanie, "Colombia Sacks PR Firm Led by Clinton Strategist," *Financial Times*, April 7, 2008, http://www.ft.com/cms/s/0/d2be41d8-043a-11dd-b28b-000077b07658.html#axzz3Dmm4umKz.

43. Kirchgaessner, "Colombia Sacks PR Firm Led by Clinton Strategist."

44. Javers, Eamon, "HRC Colombia ties don't stop with Penn," April 7, 2008, http://www.politico.com/news/stories/0408/9433.html.

45. "Clinton Reiterates Opposition to Colombia Trade Pact," *Los Angeles Times*, April 9, 2008, http://articles.latimes.com/2008/apr/09/nation/na-penn9.

46. "Uribe Criticizes Obama over Free Trade Pact," *Colombia Reports*, April 3, 2008, http://colombiareports.co/uribe-criticizes-obama-over-free-trade-pact/.

47. "Colombia Business Forecast Report," *Business Monitor International*, 2nd Quarter 2008 Report.

48. "U.S. Secretary of State Willing to Work with Colombia on Trade Deal—Official," BBC Monitoring Americas, February 26, 2009.

49. Muscara, Aprille, "U.S.: Spate of Trade Deals Move toward Passage," *Global Information Network*, January 28, 2011, http://www.ipsnews.net/2011/01/us-spate-of-trade-deals-move-toward-passage/.

50. "Secretary Clinton's Remarks to the Press at the

Release of the 2010 Human Rights Reports," Humanrights.gov, April 8, 2011.

51. US Department of State, "2010 Colombia Human Rights Report," http://www.state.gov/documents/organization/160452.pdf.

52. Dougherty, Jill, "Hillary Clinton Tells U.S. Businesses 'We Need to Up Our Game,' Abroad," CNN.com, July 12, 2011, http://www.cnn.com/2011/US/07/12/clinton.business.abroad/.

53. AFL-CIO, "Colombia," http://www.aflcio.org/Issues/Trade/Colombia/Colombia.

54. Jimenez, Carlos, "Frank Giustra," *ElPais.com.co*, January 20, 2012, http://www.elpais.com.co/elpais/opinion/columna/carlos-jimenez/frank-giustra.

55. Press Office of Senator Jorge Enrique Robledo (Colombia), "Rather than Just Leaving Zamora ANH," September 13, 2011, moir.org.co/Mas-que-justa-la-salida-de-Zamora.html.

56. "Letter from Senator Jorge Enrique Robledo, Bogotá, August 23, 2011, to Ronald Pantin, President of Pacific Rubiales Energy, Bogotá," http://www.pasc.ca/fr/node/3390.

57. "Canadian Billionaire Frank Giustra May Not Harvest Timber in Choco," August 24, 2012, http://vox-populi.com.co/billonario-canadiense-frank-giustra-no-podra-extraer-madera-en-el-choco/.

CHAPTER 10: DISASTER CAPITALISM CLINTON-STYLE

1. Haberman, Maggie, "50 Politicos to Watch: Cheryl Mills," *Politico*, July 19, 2013, http://www.politico.com/story/2013/07/50-politicos-to-watch-cheryl-mills-94182.html.

2. US Government Accountability Office, "Haiti Reconstruction U.S. Efforts Have Begun, Expanded Oversight Still to Be Implemented," report, May 2011, http://www.gao.gov/assets/320/318629.pdf.

3. "Bill Clinton's New Plan to Fix Haiti," *Esquire*, August 7, 2010, http://www.esquire.com/blogs/politics/bill-clinton-haiti-news-070810.

4. US Department of State, "Fast Fact on U.S. Government's Work in Haiti: Interim Haiti Recovery Commission," fact sheet, January 8, 2011, http://www.state.gov/p/wha/rls/fs/2011/154141.htm; http://www.gao.gov/assets/320/318629.pdf.

5. US Government Accountability Office, "Haiti Reconstruction U.S. Efforts Have Begun."

6. US Government Accountability Office, "Haiti Reconstruction: USAID Infrastructure Projects Have Had Mixed Results," June 2013, http://www.gao.gov/assets/660/655278.pdf.

7. World Bank, "Indonesia: A Reconstruction Chapter Ends Eight Years after the Tsunami," December 26, 2012, http://www.worldbank.org/en/news/feature/

2012/12/26/indonesia-reconstruction-chapter-ends-eight-years-after-the-tsunami.

8. US Government Accountability Office, "Haiti Reconstruction: U.S. Efforts Have Begun."

9. Sontag, Deborah, "Rebuilding in Haiti Lags after Billions in Post-Quake Aid," *New York Times*, December 23, 2012, http://www.nytimes.com/2012/12/24/world/americas/in-aiding-quake-battered-haiti-lofty-hopes-and-hard-truths.html?pagewanted=all&_r=0.

10. Herz, Ansel, and Kim Ives, "WikiLeaks Haiti: The Post-Quake 'Gold Rush' for Reconstruction Contracts," *The Nation*, June 15, 2011, http://www.thenation.com/article/161469/wikileaks-haiti-post-quake-gold-rush-reconstruction-contracts.

11. Clary, Mike, "Broward Rivals Battle for Work in Post-quake Haiti," *Sun Sentinel* (Florida), July 14, 2010, http://articles.sun-sentinel.com/2010-07-14/news/fl-haiti-recovery-rivals-20100714_1_ashbritt-post-earthquake-haiti-debris.

12. Echeverria, Lily, "Contractors Bet on Work in Helping Haiti Recover," *The Ledger* (Lakeland, FL), May 26, 2010, http://www.theledger.com/article/20100526/NEWS/5265081.

13. Iuspa-Abbott, Paola, "Developer Takes Fact-finding Mission to Haiti," *Daily Business Review*, March 4, 2010, http://www.dailybusinessreview.com/id=1202466755176/Developer-takes-factfinding-mission-to-Haiti?slreturn=20141003155631.

14. O'Grady, Mary Anastasia, "Clinton for Haiti Czar?" *Wall Street Journal*, January 24, 2010, http://www.wsj.com/articles/SB100014240527487045097045750190704357201 54.

15. Herz and Ives, "WikiLeaks Haiti."

16. Boyer, Peter J., "General Clark's Battles," *New Yorker*, November 17, 2003, http://www.newyorker.com/magazine/2003/11/17/general-clarks-battles.

17. Haberman, Maggie, "Wes Clark Also 'Ready for Hillary' Clinton," *Politico*, June 23, 2013, http://www.politico.com/story/2013/06/wes-clark-ready-for-hillary-clinton-93194.html.

18. US Department of State, Embassy in Port-au-Prince, "Earthquake Sitrep as of 1800," Wikileaks, February 1, 2010, https://wikileaks.org/cable/2010/02/10PORTAUPRINCE110.html.

19. Viglucci, Andres, "Low Cost Cabins Offered for Post-Haiti Earthquake Housing," *Miami Herald*, February 25, 2010. Brinkmann, Paul, "Claudio Osorio Target in $220M Swiss Probe," *South Florida Business Journal*, January 27, 2011, http://www.bizjournals.com/southflorida/news/2011/01/27/claudio-osorio-target-of-swiss-probe.html?page=all.

20. US Overseas Private Investment Corporation, "Non-confidential Information Summary for the Public," InnoVida Holdings LLC, n.d., http://www.opic.gov/sites/default/files/docs/innovida_haiti_smef.pdf.

21. Gray, Kevin, "Claudio Osorio Arrested on Fraud Charges over Innovida Haiti Housing Scam," video,

Huffington Post, December 7, 2012, http://www.huffingtonpost.com/2012/12/07/claudio-osorio-fraud-charges-jeb-bush-innovida_n_2262717.html.

22. Chiarella, Tom, "While Most of the World Has Stopped Paying Attention to Haiti, Bill Clinton Is the De Facto Leader of the Effort to Rebuild the Country," *Esquire,* July 19, 2010, http://www.esquire.com/features/impossible/bill-clinton-haiti-relief-0810-7.

23. Charles, Jacqueline, "Bill Clinton to take on key Haiti reconstruction role," *Miami Herald,* March 30, 2010, http://sbrewsterw.typepad.com/thebrewstereport/2010/03/the-miami-herald-bill-clinton-to-take-on-key-haiti-reconstruction-role.html.

24. Pierre-Pierre, Garry, "Our Man in Haiti: Bill Clinton," *America's Quarterly,* Fall 2009, http://www.americasquarterly.org/garry-pierre-pierre-haiti.

25. Hujer, Marc, "A Stubborn Savior: Is Bill Clinton Haiti's Hope for Salvation?" *Spiegel,* January 10, 2012, http://www.spiegel.de/international/world/a-stubborn-savior-is-bill-clinton-haiti-s-hope-for-salvation-a-807377.html.

26. Archibold, Randal C., "Haiti's Prime Minister Quits after 4 Months," *New York Times,* February 25, 2012, http://www.nytimes.com/2012/02/25/world/americas/garry-conille-resigns-as-haitis-prime-minister.html.

27. "Haiti Economy: Bill Clinton's Role in Economic

Policy Increases," *Economist Intelligence Unit (EIU) Newswire,* November 15, 2011, http://country.eiu.com/article.aspx?articleid=978596082&Country=Haiti&topic=Economy&subtopic=Current+policy&subsubtopic=Economic+policy:+Bill+Clinton%27s+role+in+economic+policy+increases.

28. Johnston, Jake, "Outsourcing Haiti," *Boston Review,* January 16, 2014, http://www.bostonreview.net/world/jake-johnston-haiti-earthquake-aid-caracol.

29. Ibid.

30. Valbrun, Marjorie, "Haitian Firms Few and Far between on Reconstruction Rosters," Center for Public Integrity, January 11, 2012, http://www.publicintegrity.org/2012/01/11/7846/haitian-firms-few-and-far-between-reconstruction-rosters.

31. Uttley, Jimmy, "An Eventful Time for Haiti: Did Anyone Notice?" *Haiti Observateur,* May 27, 2009.

32. Marcus, Ruth, "Reelection Team Repeatedly Asked President's Aid," *Washington Post,* September 22, 1997, http://www.washingtonpost.com/wp-srv/politics/special/campfin/stories/cf092297.htm.

33. Byron, Christopher, "Pols' Haiti Hook-up," *New York Post,* March 2, 2005, http://www.haitipolicy.org/content/2882.htm?PHPSESSID=.

34. O'Grady, Mary Anastasia, "Democrats for Despotism," *Wall Street Journal,* October 27, 2008, http://online.wsj.com/articles/SB122506507943370505.

35. Ibid.

36. Heinrich, Erik, "Haiti's Mobile Redemption," *Fortune,* August 15, 2013, http://fortune.com/2013/08/15/haitis-mobile-redemption/.

37. Ibid.

38. Jackson, Steven, "Digicel Operating Profit Hits Record US$1B," *The Gleaner* (Jamaica), June 6, 2012, http://jamaica-gleaner.com/gleaner/20120606/business/business5.html.

39. Bramhill, Nick, "Bill Clinton Praises Ireland for Being First to Help with His Global AIDS Initiative," *IrishCentral,* October 10, 2013, http://www.irish-central.com/news/bill-clinton-praises-ireland-for-being-first-to-help-with-his-global-aids-initiative-227204991-237782151.html.

40. "Find a Goal for Jamaica to Embrace, Says Bill Clinton," *Jamaica Observer,* October 27, 2010, http://m.jamaicaobserver.com/mobile/business/Find-a-goal-for-Jamaica-to-embrace-says-Bill-Clinton_8091662.

41. Humphreys, Joe, "Bill Clinton Visit Cements Close Working Relationship with Denis O'Brien," *Irish Times,* October 10, 2013, https://www.irishtimes.com/search/search-7.1213540?article=true&q=&tag_person=Mr%20O%20Brien&tag_company=Conrad%20Hotel&tag_organisation=Un.

42. Clinton, Bill, "The Case for Optimism," *Time,*

October 1, 2012, http://content.time.com/time/magazine/article/0,9171,2125031,00.html.

43. Browne, Vincent, "O'Brien's Record Should Disbar Him from Having a Disproportionate Hold on Media," *Dennis O'Brien News*, August 14, 2013, http://www.denisobriennews.com/?p=25; Tribunal of Inquiry (Ireland), "Report of the Tribunal of Inquiry into Payments to Politicians and Related Matters," part II, vols. 1 and 2, *The Guardian* March 2011, http://www.theguardian.com/world/2011/mar/22/irish-minister-accused-collusion-telecoms; http://www.moriarty-tribunal.ie/asp/detail.asp?objectid=310&Mode=0&RecordID=545.

44. See VCSmining.com and Evens Sanon and Danica Coto, "Haiti Awards Gold, Copper Mining Permits," *Associated Press*, December 21, 2012.

45. Pulitzer Center on Crisis Reporting, "Haiti's 'Gold Rush' Promises El Dorado—but for Whom?" June 27, 2012, http://pulitzercenter.org/reporting/haiti-lakwev-gold-rush-north-america-mining-company-corruption.

46. Regan, Jane, "Haitian Senate Calls for Halt to Mining Activities," *Inter Press Service*, February 24, 2013.

47. Reitman, Janet, "Beyond Relief: How the World Failed Haiti," *Rolling Stone*, August 4, 2011, http://www.rollingstone.com/politics/news/how-the-world-failed-haiti-20110804?page=7.

48. Ibid.

49. Ibid.

50. US Agency for International Development, Office of Inspector General, "Audit of USAID's Efforts to Provide Shelter in Haiti," April 19, 2011, https://oig.usaid.gov/sites/default/files/audit-reports/1-521-11-003-p.pdf.

51. Macdonald, Isabel, and Isabeau Doucet, "The Shelters that Clinton Built," *The Nation*, August 1–8, 2011, http://www.thenation.com/article/161908/shelters-clinton-built.

52. Doucet, Isabeau, and Isabel MacDonald, "Shelters in Leogare Inspected by Clinton Foundation," *The Gazette* (Montreal), August 27, 2011.

53. Sontag, Deborah, "Rebuilding in Haiti Lags after Billions in Post-Quake Aid," *New York Times*, December 23, 2012, http://www.nytimes.com/2012/12/24/world/americas/in-aiding-quake-battered-haiti-lofty-hopes-and-hard-truths.html?pagewanted=all&_r=0.

54. Regan, Jane, "Haiti: Housing Exposition Exposes Waste, Cynicism," *The WorldPost*, December 3, 2012, http://www.huffingtonpost.com/jane-regan/haiti-housing-exposition-_b_1911898.html. "Haiti: Housing Exposition Exposes Waste, Cynicism," *Global Information Network*, October 2, 2012, http://www.ipsnews.net/2012/10/haiti-housing-exposition-exposes-waste-cynicism/.

55. "Haiti's Two-Million-Dollar Ghost Town," Inter Press Service News Agency, October 2, 2012, http://www.ipsnews.net/2012/10/haitis-two-million-dollar-ghost-town/.

56. "Haiti: Housing Exposition Exposes Waste, Cynicism," *Global Information Network*, October 2, 2012.

57. Watkins, Tate, "A $300 Million Development Project—and Haiti's Future—Depend on America's Open Markets," *Quartz*, May 8, 2013, http://qz.com/79015/a-300-million-development-project-and-haitis-future-depend-on-americas-open-markets/.

58. Charles, Jacqueline, "Haitian Garment Industry Uplifted by Korean Investment," Cleveland.com, April 10, 2011, http://www.cleveland.com/business/index.ssf/2011/04/haitian_garment_industry_uplif.html.

59. Sontag, Deborah, "Earthquake Relief Where Haiti Wasn't Broken," *New York Times*, July 5, 2012, http://www.nytimes.com/2012/07/06/world/americas/earthquake-relief-where-haiti-wasnt-broken.html?pagewanted=all.

60. US General Accountability Office, "Report to Congressional Requesters, Haiti Reconstruction: USAID Infrastructure Projects Have Mixed Results and Face Sustainability Challenges," June 2013, 8, 10.

61. Sontag, "Earthquake Relief Where Haiti Wasn't Broken."

62. Johnston, Jake, "Outsourcing Haiti," *Boston Review*, January 16, 2014, http://www.bostonreview.net/world/jake-johnston-haiti-earthquake-aid-caracol.

63. Watkins, "A $300 Million Development Project."

64. Louis, Newton, and Andre Michel, "Haiti—Justice: Me Newton and Me Michel Initiate an Action against Former President Clinton," *Haiti Libre*, April 17, 2014, http://www.haitilibre.com/en/news-10960-haiti-justice-me-newton-and-me-michel-initiate-an-action-against-former-president-clinton.html. O'Grady, Mary A., "Bill, Hillary and the Haiti Debacle," *Wall Street Journal*, May 18, 2014, http://online.wsj.com/articles/SB10001424052702304547704579564651201202122.

CHAPTER 11: QUID PRO QUO?

1. Clinton, Hillary, "International Anti-Corruption Day," US Department of State, December 9, 2009, http://www.state.gov/secretary/20092013clinton/rm/2009a/12/133339.htm.

2. "Secretary of State Hillary Rodham Clinton to Receive Transparency International-USA's Integrity Award," US Department of State, Office of the Spokesman, March 21, 2012, http://www.state.gov/r/pa/prs/ps/2012/03/186148.htm.

3. OECD Working Group on Bribery, "Annual Report 2013," December 4, 2013, http://www.oecd.org/daf/anti-bribery/AntiBriberyAnnRep2012.pdf, 6.

4. *United States v. Abbey* 560 F.3d 513, 518–19 (6th Cir. 2009). Henning, Peter J., and Lee Radek, *The Prosecution and Defense of Public Corruption: The Law and Legal Strategies* (New York: Oxford University Press, 2011), 114.

5. Metcalf, Tom, "Ireland's Would-Be Carlos Slim Sells Mobiles to Masses," Bloomberg.com, November 12, 2013, http://www.bloomberg.com/news/2013-11-13/ireland-s-would-be-carlos-slim-sells-mobiles-to-masses.html. Clinton Foundation, "Contributor Information," https://www.clintonfoundation.org/contributors?category=%241%2C000%2C001+to+%245%2C000%2C000.

6. Lenzner, Terry F., "A Second Presidential Scandal," in *The Investigator: Fifty Years of Uncovering the Truth* (New York: Penguin Group, 2013), 290–314.

7. US Senate, Governmental Affairs Committee, *Majority Report: Executive Summary*, March 5, 1998, http://www.washingtonpost.com/wp-srv/politics/special/campfin/stories/execsumm030698.htm.

8. Ibid.

9. Ibid.

10. Fournier, Ron, "White House Database: Hotel Link to Lincoln Bedroom," *Lubbock Avalanche-Journal,* January 1, 1997, http://lubbockonline.com/news/013197/white.htm.

11. Clinton, Hillary, "Remarks at the Transparency International-USA's Annual Integrity Award Dinner," speech, Transparency International Integrity Award Dinner, Mayflower Hotel, Washington DC, March 22, 2012, http://m.state.gov/md186703.htm. Geman, Ben, "Clinton: SEC Oil, Mining Regs Will Have 'Profound' Effect," *The Hill,* March 23, 2012, http://thehill.com/policy/energy-environment/217885-clinton-says-sec-oil-transparency-regs-will-have-profound-effect.

12. Gerth, Jeff, "Top Arkansas Lawyer Helped Hillary Clinton Turn Big Profit," *New York Times,* March 17, 1994, http://www.nytimes.com/1994/03/18/us/top-arkansas-lawyer-helped-hillary-clinton-turn-big-profit.html.

About the Author

PETER SCHWEIZER is the author of *Extortion, Throw Them All Out, Architects of Ruin,* and other books that have revealed political wrongdoing and led to congressional resignations and new ethics laws. He is a research fellow at the Hoover Institution and the founder and director of the Government Accountability Institute, a team of investigative researchers and journalists committed to investigating and exposing crony capitalism, misuse of taxpayer monies, and other governmental corruption or malfeasance.

THE NEW LUXURY IN READING

We hope you enjoyed reading
our new, comfortable print size and found it
an experience you would like to repeat.

Well — you're in luck!

HarperLuxe offers the finest in fiction and
nonfiction books in this same larger print size and
paperback format. Light and easy to read, HarperLuxe
paperbacks are for book lovers who want to see
what they are reading without the strain.

For a full listing of titles and
new releases to come, please visit our website:

www.HarperLuxe.com